LEE'S LOST DISPATCH

and Other Civil War Controversies

PHILIP LEIGH

WESTHOLME

Yardley

Westholme Publishing, LLC
904 Edgewood Road
Yardley, Pennsylvania 19067
Visit our Web site at www.westholmepublishing.com

First Printing April 2015
10 9 8 7 6 5 4 3 2 1
ISBN: 978-1-59416-226-8
Also available as an eBook.

Printed in the United States of America

To Gary Sorensen

CONTENTS

AUTHOR'S NOTE

More Americans were killed in the Civil War than in any other, despite the fact that our country's population was only about a tenth of the present 312 million. If Civil War casualty ratios were applied to our current population, the number of deaths would total over six million, compared to about four hundred thousand in World War II. Partly because of the enormous number of casualties and partly because it was fought in our own land, the Civil War is one of the great mythological themes of American history. Thus, it will probably continue to be a rich source of historical writing and literature for decades to come. But viewpoints about it shift unpredictably from one perspective to another and then get stuck in a rut. Thereafter, they follow Newton's law of inertia until acted upon by a fresh impulse. Consider, for example, how Michael Shaara's Pulitzer Prize-winning *The Killer Angels* altered opinions about major Gettysburg personalities. Shaara demonstrated that new directions might emerge by inspecting unexamined assumptions, which is one of the aims of this book.[1]

Lee's Lost Dispatch and Other Civil War Controversies revisits eleven episodes of the Civil War era—some lesser known than others—that, upon reexamination, may challenge our received understanding of the course of that conflict. It is hoped that this small volume will promote discussion and debate among those who enjoy Civil War history and contemplating alternatives to conventional conclusions and analyses.

THE BIGGEST CONFEDERATE ERROR?

While imprisoned two years at Fort Monroe, Virginia, after the end of the Civil War, former Confederate president Jefferson Davis admitted that the Confederacy should have replaced King Cotton Diplomacy for a nearly opposite policy. Failure to do so was perhaps the Confederacy's biggest error.

For months Davis was held in virtual isolation except for the occasional company of a US Army physician. Lieutenant Colonel John Craven, MD, kept a record of their conversations, summarizing many in various writings, including the 1866 book *Prison Life of Jefferson Davis*. Although King Cotton Diplomacy sought to restrict cotton exports as a means of motivating diplomatic recognition for the Confederacy from European nations, Craven reports that Davis realized it would have been better to export as much cotton as possible at the start of the war so that the staple could be safely warehoused overseas and sold as needed for foreign exchange. Historian Burton Hendrick states, "With the metal obtained from [cotton sales] deposited in London and Paris banks, the Confederacy would construct a stronger financial foundation than that of the Federal Government. Mr. Davis would quickly become a richer President than Mr. Lincoln."[1]

Hendrick summarizes Craven's notes and recollections with Davis on the matter:

"South Carolina placed Mr. Memminger in the Treasury," Craven quotes [Davis] as saying, "and while [I respect] the man, the utter failure of Confederate finance was the failure of the cause. Had Mr. Memminger acted favorably on the proposition of depositing . . . cotton in Europe and holding it there for two years as a basis for [our] currency, [it] might have maintained itself at par until the . . . [end]; and that in itself would have insured victory."

"More than three million bales of cotton rested unused in the South at the time of secession; if these had been rushed to Europe before the blockade . . . [was effective], said . . . [Davis,] they would have ultimately brought in a billion dollars in gold. "Such a sum," Craven quotes Davis as saying, "would have more than sufficed for all the needs of the Confederacy during the war."[2]

KING COTTON

Although ultimately flawed, King Cotton Diplomacy appeared to be logically sound at the start of the war. Great Britain was the world's leading economy, and cotton textile manufacturing was the country's largest industry. Nearly a quarter of its people were economically dependent upon the sector. In 1860, nearly 90 percent of Britain's cotton imports came from the United States, all of which was grown in the South. According to historian Frank Owsley, "all [British leaders] believed alike . . . that the cutting-off of cotton supply in the South would destroy England's chief industry . . . and bring ruin and revolution on the land." Faced with revolution at home, it was logical to conclude that few British and French leaders could resist recognizing the Confederacy in an effort to obtain more cotton. French leaders were particularly sensitive to such concerns since the country counted among its citizens some who were old enough to remember the Reign of Terror following the French Revolution.[3]

However, the strategy failed for two reasons.

First, the European economies were buoyed by demands in America for armaments to fight the Civil War. That the South was dependent upon overseas sources for most of its weapons is widely appreciated. However, even the North relied upon imports to a considerable extent. For example, until autumn 1862, over half of the shoulder arms used by Union soldiers were European imports. Consequently, the decline of the cotton textile sector in Europe that was induced by the shortage of raw materials was more than favorably offset by growing demand for arms exports.

Second, about a year after the war started, the Confederacy realized it was necessary to sell cotton in order to purchase the supplies required to continue fighting. Thus, the European cotton shortage peaked early in 1863, steadily improving thereafter.[4]

JUDAH'S WISDOM

On March 4, 1861, the same day President Abraham Lincoln made his first inaugural address, President Davis held his first cabinet meeting. During the session, Confederate attorney general Judah Benjamin stated that if war came, he was convinced it was going to be a long and bloody one. Therefore, he recommended that large quantities of cotton immediately be shipped to Europe, where the government could sell it for specie. Any unsold bales could be inventoried and sold as needed in the future to raise hard currency. Secretary of State Robert Toombs and Vice President Alexander Stephens supported the suggestion. Although Davis agreed that any resultant war was likely to be long and bloody, Treasury Secretary Christopher Memminger ridiculed Benjamin's idea. It was contrary to prevailing King Cotton dogma. He also did not believe the central government had the constitutional authority to become a cotton trader.[5]

According to Owsley, about four million cotton bales were available in the South in 1861, and at least half could have been exported because the federal blockade was practically nonexistent during the first year of the war. By comparison, the European textile mills required about 3.8 million bales of cotton feedstock annually, with Great Britain alone needing about 2.6 million bales. Thus, if the Confederacy were able to ship two million bales to Europe and sell an average of five hundred thousand bales yearly, that would have supplied less than 15 percent of the normal annual (1860) demand.[6]

It is not likely that such a meager increase in the actual wartime supply could have prevented a significant rise in cotton prices. Thus, the Confederates should have realized a disproportionately large amount of proceeds from limited tonnage sales. As historically recorded, cotton prices during the war averaged over seventy cents per pound in the commercial markets. If Benjamin's proposal had caused them to average sixty cents per pound, Owsley's estimate of two million 500-pound bales would be valued at about $600 million in specie. Since US greenbacks traded as low as forty cents per dollar of specie, the $600 million specie value of Confederate cotton abroad would have been as much as $1.5 billion.[7]

Judah Benjamin, attorney general of the Confederacy. (*Library of Congress*)

Interestingly, if Benjamin's suggestion had been attempted, it's likely that the politically powerful cotton growers would have welcomed it because Southern farmers needed credit as early as autumn 1861. They had massive inventories that King Cotton Diplomacy encouraged them to embargo out of patriotism. Although officially voluntary, the embargo was airtight. For example, during the prewar four-month period from September 1, 1860, to January 31, 1861, the top five Southern ports received 1.5 million cotton bales from the hinterlands. In the corresponding period a year later, they received less than ten thousand bales, a decline of over 99 percent. Ultimately, much of the cotton would be wastefully burned to keep it out of Union hands when the Yankee army increasingly occupied Confederate territory as the war progressed.[8]

Instead of burning cotton, the growers would have gladly preferred to sell it to the Confederate government, thereby obtaining the financial resources to continue operating at normal capacities. Such a scheme was considered in autumn 1861. The plan called on the government to purchase cotton with newly issued Confederate bonds or notes. The action would relieve planters of the burden of unsold inventory and provide the government with a fungible asset that could be shipped to Europe and sold for foreign exchange credits as needed.[9]

The federal blockade was largely ineffective during this period. Contrary to popular belief, fast blockade runners of special designs, including low silhouettes, were unnecessary until the second year of the war. During fall and winter 1861–1862, ordinary deep-water vessels could easily enter most Southern ports without a significant risk of being stopped by blockading patrols. Author Hendrick explains:

The disappearance of English vessels from the South in the fall and winter of 1861–1862 is . . . easily explained. They were not scared away by the federal blockade. . . . Foreign carriers abandoned southern ports for the best of commercial reasons—there were no cargoes to be obtained. Blockade running in 1862 and afterward became one of the most profitable industries. . . . It would have been similarly profitable in [1861], and vessels would have swarmed into southern ports, had not . . . [the embargo] been concentrated on preventing exports.[10]

OTHER ADVOCATES

President Davis was not the only Confederate leader to eventually realize that cotton was a badly misused asset. Vice President Alexander Stephens realized it sooner. In a November 1862 speech in Crawfordville, Georgia, he summarized his earlier opposition to King Cotton Diplomacy in favor of his own Rube Goldberg variation of a plan to get cotton to Europe, where it could be sold for specie.[11]

He proposed that the government issue cotton growers fifty dollars in new bonds yielding 8 percent annually for each five-hundred-pound cotton bale. He calculated that such a plan could have acquired four million bales at a cost of $200 million. The cotton was to be pledged to European shipbuilders who agreed to provide deep-water ironclad ships at a cost of $2 million each. He reasoned that perhaps five ships would have been delivered by January 1862 to convoy the cotton to Europe, with additional ironclads arriving regularly thereafter. Even if his plan was started belatedly in November 1862, he envisioned that the warships acquired would wreck the federal blockade.[12]

While his dream seems unrealistic, in fairness to Stephens it should be noted that Great Britain and France built their first deep-water ironclads shortly before the American Civil War began. Furthermore, during an October 1862 audience with Napoleon III, the Confederate minister to Paris urged the emperor to dispose of Lincoln's blockading fleet with the French deep-water ironclads, *Gloire, Couronne,* and *Normandie.* The emperor replied that he would rather see the Confederacy build its own navy and that the rebels ought to have some ships like the three mentioned. He agreed that a few such ships could destroy Union commerce and open the Southern ports. Essentially, he was implying that the Confederacy should place orders for new deep-water ironclads with French ship-builders. However, Napoleon also wanted to avoid war with the United States. Therefore, if such orders were placed, they should specify that the buyer was a neutral country like Italy. Eventually Napoleon declined to let the Confederacy act on his own suggestion, but there was at least a straw of validity for Stephens to grasp at, at the time.[13]

Less whimsically, Stephens told his Crawfordville audience that the South should continue growing cotton, although it was also important to plant crops that could yield provender for the army as well as civilians. He correctly perceived that certain British interests would benefit if the South stopped growing cotton. Specifically, cotton could be grown in some of the British possessions, such as India. Although the costs would initially be higher than in a peacetime Confederacy, Great Britain's colonial possessions would be political-ly more secure sources. Thus, he argued, a Southern embargo could not force Britain into diplomatic recognition. Finally, after a time, sources such as India might learn how to produce cotton at costs comparable to those of the Southern states.[14]

Similarly, in his 1874 *Narrative of Military Operations*, General Joseph E. Johnston asserts the Confederacy's misuse of cotton was the chief cause of the rebel defeat. Like Benjamin and Stephens, the former Confederate general concludes that cotton should not have been embargoed but instead sent to Europe, where it would have been a tradable asset. He attributes the failure to adopt such an ini-tiative to "the government." Like historian Hendrick, he concludes that such a plan was "practicable" if executed during the first year of the war. Cotton owners "were ready to accept any terms the govern-ment might fix. . . . The blockade . . . [was] . . . not at all effective until the end of" the winter of 1861–1862. Johnston claims that an army of half a million men could have been promptly armed and still leave the Confederate Treasury "much richer than that of the United States."[15]

Johnston's assertion that a half-million-man army could have been promptly equipped is unrealistic. It is unlikely that all of the European nations combined could have shipped five hundred thou-sand shoulder arms within a few months. Similarly, it would have been difficult to ship the 1861 cotton inventory across the Atlantic that quickly. However, Johnston's conclusion that the Confederate

Treasury would have been wealthier than that of the United States has merit. It depends on the number of cotton bales that could have been sold during the first year of the war. Federal spending in fiscal year 1861 totaled about $80 million, revenues were $50 million, and the gross public debt was about $90 million. On the eve of the Civil War, the nation's total supply of specie in circulation, including the Southern states, was about $250 million. By comparison, if the South had sold four million bales at thirty cents per pound on the London market, it would have generated proceeds of $600 million in specie. Even if it were only half that amount, the total would still exceed the value of all specie in circulation prior to the war throughout the United States.[16]

In his book, Johnston also argues that massive cotton exporting early in the war would have strengthened Confederate currency, thereby minimizing the desertion that plagued the army during the last year of the war. Since judicious cotton sales on the London market would have enabled the Treasury to accumulate specie reserves, the Confederate dollar could have held its value much better. Johnston explained that the typical soldier sent most of his monthly pay home. So long as the buying power of Rebel currency enabled their families to avoid starvation, soldiers held fast to their military duty. However, during the last ten to twelve months of the war, Confederate currency was almost worthless. At that time a soldier's monthly pay "would scarcely buy [a single] meal for his family." Increasingly, the soldiers "were compelled to choose between their military service and the strongest obligation men know—their duties to their wives and children."[17]

At the start of 1862, the market rate for Confederate currency was $1.20 for each $1.00 of specie. A year later it was $3.25 in Rebel paper currency for each $1.00 of specie. By the start of 1864, one dollar of specie could buy $20 of Confederate currency, and by the beginning of 1865, the rate was $60 of Rebel money for each dollar of specie. A week before Appomattox, the rate was 70:1.[18]

MEMMINGER'S EXCUSE

Although Craven explained that Jefferson Davis was not reproaching Memminger, the former Treasury secretary was deeply stung by the criticism of his dismissal of Benjamin's suggestion. He felt compelled to defend himself, but did a poor job of it.

First, he asserted that the Confederacy could not have purchased the idle cotton lying about the Southern states early in the war because in the early months there were no printing presses available to create such financial instruments. But certainly there must have been some way of temporarily meeting that difficulty.

Second, he argued that the 1860–1861 crop had already been gathered and shipped. This excuse may be valid as it applies to the crop warehoused and distributed by the end of January 1861, but it ignores the normal-sized crop that was harvested in fall 1861.[19]

Third, he reasoned that shipping four million bales would require four thousand ships, which was more than were available. But if four million bales were shipped, it need not have been done in one massive operation. If each ship made ten voyages, it would have required only four hundred. Similarly, if only two million bales were shipped, then only two hundred vessels would be needed. But even if only half a million bales reached Europe, an average market value of sixty cents a pound could have provided the Confederacy $150 million. Finally, Memminger assumes that each ship could hold only a thousand bales, but some could carry more than twice that amount.[20]

COTTON AS INTERNATIONAL CREDIT

By fall 1862, the Confederacy's conventional international credits were exhausted. Something had to be done immediately to enable the government to continue purchasing the necessities of war abroad because only limited supplies could be manufactured in the Rebel states. By spring 1862, the Confederate government owned over four hundred thousand cotton bales. They were withheld from export primarily by the voluntary embargo, because the federal blockade was still largely ineffective. Six months later, the government faced the problem of how to get the inventory to Europe or to trade it for international exchange credits while it was still physically located in the Confederacy because of growing effectiveness of the blockade.[21]

Again, Judah Benjamin was the first to offer a solution. In January 1862, he wrote to the agent for a foreign bank who lived in New Orleans with a proposal. He asked if the bank would deposit $1 million specie value at its European branch into the account of the Confederate government, assuming a to-be-negotiated amount of cotton were deposited with the New Orleans branch conditioned upon the cotton remaining in the Confederacy until the blockade was lifted. Union forces captured New Orleans before the proposal matured, but Benjamin had planted a seed that would flower later.

Navy Secretary Stephen Mallory took the first successful steps toward creating additional foreign exchange credits in fall 1862. He was able to purchase ships and supplies by issuing "cotton bonds" that were convertible at the option of the holder into a specific number of bales at a below-market price. The catch, of course, was that the cotton was located inside the Confederacy. Mallory's government was obligated to deliver the cotton to any port controlled by the Confederacy, and it was the bondholder's responsibility to get the cotton through the blockade. Since the bondholders were permitted to exchange their bonds for cotton at a price that was typically only one-fourth of the market price, the potential profit to such holders was sufficiently large to offset the costs, and risks, of running the blockade.[22]

Confederate cotton bonds soon proved to be a popular concept in Europe. The Confederacy's British agent recommended that they be sold in a series of small offerings. He reasoned that the initial ones would be popular enough to drive them to a market price above par, thereby enabling each ensuing series to be sold at increasingly higher prices. It was sound advice, but when the Paris banking house of Erlanger et Compiegne, whose connections to European royalty rivaled those of Rothschild, learned of the financial innovation, they perceived big opportunities for investment banking profit.

Erlanger proposed to underwrite $25 million of cotton bonds, denominated in British pounds or French francs. The bonds were to be convertible into cotton at a price of twelve cents per pound when the market price was about forty-eight cents. Thus, a buyer of a £1,000 bond could convert it into eighty 500-pound bales worth about £4,000 on the date the bonds were issued. If the price of cotton continued to rise, the underlying bond's conversion value would climb in parallel, because the bondholder could still convert it into eighty 500-pound bales. In 1864, cotton reached a high price of almost $1.90 a pound, which implies that each £1,000 bond had a conversion value of nearly £16,000.[23]

But Erlanger drove a hard bargain, which caused the Confederacy to reduce the size of the offering from $25 million to $15 million. Erlanger insisted on the right to purchase the bonds at a substantial discount requiring it to pay only 77 percent of face value.

Additionally, Erlanger was to be paid its customary fees and commissions. Owing to its discounted purchase price, Erlanger was able to offer the bonds to public subscribers at an appealing price of only 90 percent of the face value. That attracted such influential buyers as William Gladstone and Lord Robert Cecil, who both later became British prime ministers.[24]

Since the issue was appealingly priced, the $15 million offering was initially oversubscribed with orders for $80 million.

Unfortunately, initial buyers were required to deposit only 15 percent of the purchase price, with the balance not due until the settlement date of April 24, 1863. Meanwhile, Union diplomats in Europe scrambled for ways to discredit the loan. About a week before the settlement date, stories appeared in London newspapers describing how years earlier, Jefferson Davis had publicly defended Mississippi's default on a bond issue mostly held by Europeans when he was a US senator from that state.

Erlanger panicked and threatened to cancel the offering unless the Confederacy agreed to stabilize the price by using some of the deposited funds to buy bonds on the open market. Ultimately about $6 million of the $15 million issue was used in this manner.[25]

Historian John Schwab concluded that a major portion of the bonds repurchased on the open market to support the price were actually bonds owned by Erlanger et Compiegne. Essentially, Erlanger was profiting from an arbitrage by purchasing the bonds from the Davis government at 77 percent of face value and then requiring the Confederacy to buy them back at market prices approximating 90 percent of face value.[26]

Since the cotton was located in the Rebel states, Confederate authorities were only obligated to deliver the bales to a point within "ten miles of a navigable river or railhead" where the new owner—meaning the bondholder—had to arrange transport to the final destination. Consequently, Erlanger and its British investment-banking partner organized a blockade-running company innocuously named the European Trading Company. One of its ships made 73 round trips between Mobile, Alabama, and Havana, Cuba, before the end of the war.[27]

The biggest use of proceeds the Confederacy received from the Erlanger bonds was to pay off a debt to the British purchasing agency of Isaac, Campbell & Company that bought war supplies for the Confederate government. The agency also took $2 million (at face value) of the bonds as partial settlement. However, when it was later learned that Isaac, Campbell had paid less than it had represented for all items it sold to the Confederacy, the commercial relationship soured. At the least, the action was a violation of trust. At worst, it was fraud. Agents are supposed to earn their fees from disclosed commissions, not hidden mark-ups from the prices paid for merchandise. When the market value of the bonds plummeted after the fall of Vicksburg, Mississippi, and the Rebel defeat at Gettysburg, Isaac, Campbell asked that the Davis government redeem its bond holdings at face value. Richmond declined.[28]

But the Erlanger experience had a good effect as well. It convinced the Davis government that cotton could be an even more valuable foreign exchange medium once transferred out of the Rebel states. Consequently, the Confederacy established blockade-running regulations to get cotton out and war supplies in. In January 1863, it purchased four ships to operate as government-owned blockade runners. By September the ships had run the blockade forty-four times without a capture. Additionally, cotton-for-credit transactions in Europe were centralized under C. J. McRae in Britain. The government started aggressively acquiring cotton throughout the South via outright purchases and taxes-in-kind on cotton growers. The change worked wonders. In July 1864, McRae used some of the available financial credits to order fourteen more steamers for blockade running.[29]

CONCLUSION

In truth, King Cotton was no puppet monarch. It was the most abundant medium of international exchange available in North America. It could have been a primary support for the Confederacy as the foundation of a sound financial system.

But the Rebels misplayed their hand. Instead of initially embargoing cotton, they should have shipped as much as possible to Europe, where it could have been warehoused and sold as required. If such a policy had been vigorously pursued from the start, Jefferson Davis's government would likely have had more sound money than Abraham Lincoln's. Confederate currency would have better held its value. A stronger Confederate dollar might have enabled the typical soldier's monthly pay to adequately support his family at home, thereby sharply reducing the desertions that plagued the Rebel forces during the last year of the war. Given such benefits, the Confederacy may have been able to exhaust Yankee resolve to continue fighting.

2

THE BIGGEST
FEDERAL ERROR?

One morning in September 1942, Colonel Leslie Groves was walking in an empty hallway of the House of Representatives office building when he met General Brehon Somervell, who almost immediately transformed the colonel into "the angriest officer in the United States Army."

"About that duty overseas," said the general, "you can tell them no."

"Why?"

"The secretary of war has selected you for a very important assignment, and the president has approved the selection."

"Where?"

"Washington."

"I don't want to stay in Washington."

"If you do the job right, it will win the war."

"Oh," sighed Groves. "*That* thing."

As the army's deputy chief of construction, the colonel was aware but skeptical of a vague superbomb project. He wanted nothing to do with it. Like most officers, he was eager for combat duty overseas.[1]

Nonetheless, he followed orders to lead the project and was promoted to brigadier general in order to increase his authority. In less than three years, he led the previously floundering Manhattan

Project to create uranium and plutonium bombs and reach a production rate of about one bomb per month at the end of the war. Within a day of the hallway meeting, Groves had taken steps to secure 80 percent of the radioactive ores needed to produce the bombs that forced Japan's surrender. Within a week of the meeting, he activated plans for the Oak Ridge refining plant, a project that would transform a Tennessee forest into a city of eighty-five thousand before war's end and consume one-seventh of the entire country's electricity. Due to a copper shortage caused by demands for brass ammunition cartridges, Groves borrowed almost fourteen thousand tons of silver from the US Treasury for electrical wiring. A second plant for plutonium—which did not exist in nature when he took charge—was built in Washington State. It was a year and a half after Grove's promotion before scientists produced even a few grams of the element for experimentation. Before the war was over, the Manhattan Project employed more than three hundred thousand workers.[2]

The project was a convincing demonstration of the efficacy that government, academic, and industry cooperation can provide for weapons development and production. It enabled the United States to avoid invading the Japanese homeland in order to end World War II. The army chief of staff, General George Marshall, speculated that such an invasion might cause five hundred thousand to one million US casualties "if conventional weapons only were used."[3]

If the Union had similarly backed a project to produce breech-loading and repeating rifles at the start of the Civil War, it might have won the war in less than two years instead of the four required. According to the memoirs of Confederate Brigadier General Porter Alexander, who famously directed the Rebel bombardment prior to Pickett's Charge at Gettysburg, "There is reason to believe that had the Federal infantry been armed from the first with even the breechloaders available in 1861 [the war's first year] the war would have been terminated in a year." The story of why it wasn't is frustrating and fascinating.[4]

In the hands of an experienced soldier, the standard issue Springfield and Enfield rifles used by Union and Confederate infantry could fire at best about three rounds per minute, and likely only two in the heat of combat. That's because they were loaded through the muzzle one round at a time using paper cartridges and a ramrod. First the powder end of the cartridge was torn open, typically with the teeth, and then poured down the barrel. Next the bullet end of the cartridge containing the projectile (known as a Minié ball) was seated against the powder, with the ramrod pushed from the muzzle. The final step was to position a percussion cap on a nipple that had a hole through it to the breech. Pulling the trigger caused a hammer to crush the cap, thereby injecting a flame from the cap to the powder inside the barrel, which exploded to propel the Minié ball. After firing, the entire sequence had to be repeated before a muzzleloader could shoot a second time. For speed, soldiers typically stood up to reload, thereby transforming themselves into bigger targets than if they remained kneeling or lying down.[5]

Despite the numerical dominance of muzzleloaders, breechloaders and repeaters were far superior weapons because they could shoot faster. Although breechloaders were loaded one shell at a time, their cartridges remained intact, obviating the need to load powder and bullet sequentially. While some required a separate percussion cap like the muzzleloaders, others with brass or copper cartridges did not. As a result, instead of firing only two to three bullets per minute, a soldier with a single-shot breechloader, such as the Sharps carbine, could fire eight to ten per minute. The firing rate of repeaters was even higher. For example, the Spencer used a magazine of seven cartridges. Each live round was loaded—and each spent round ejected—with a quick lever action. Although all seven could be fired in ten seconds, the barrel became overheated at such a pace. However, a Spencer-equipped soldier had no difficulty shooting fourteen times per minute.[6]

Table 1 (overleaf) estimates the number and type of shoulder arms procured by the Union and Confederate armies. As a category, shoulder arms includes rifles and carbines. The latter are shorter versions of the rifle used by cavalry for easier handling. Although the Union acquired far more weapons, the Confederates reused many by capturing them on battlefields. Nearly all of the shoulder arms procured by Rebel soldiers were muzzleloaders, as were nearly 90 percent of those for the Union troops. Confederates could only purchase breechloaders via imports, whereas they could rarely buy repeaters at all since the weapons were manufactured in the Northern states. Most of the single-shot breechloaders, and nearly all the repeaters, used by Rebels were captured on the battlefield. For example, during the siege of Atlanta in summer 1864, the Rebel Army of Tennessee had about fifty thousand shoulder arms of all types, but only 58 were Spencer repeaters, which was then the most common repeater.[7]

Table 1. Shoulder Arms Procurement (in thousands of units)

	CONFEDERATE	UNION
Muzzle-Loaders:		
Smooth Bore	183	510
Rifled	425	2,850
Sub Total	608	3,360
Breech Loaders:		
Non-Repeater	4	303
Repeaters	0	100
Sub Total	4	403
Total	612	3,763

Source: Paddy Griffth, *Battle Tactics of the Civil War* (New Haven, CT: Yale University Press, 1989), 80.

As breechloaders and repeaters were gradually adopted in the Union army, their superiority became obvious to nearly everyone. On March 1, 1865, Secretary of War Edwin Stanton directed that breechloaders be issued to all Union soldiers. If Confederate General Robert E. Lee had not surrendered less than a month and a half later, there's little doubt that the Confederate army would have had no hope of resisting the bigger Union one once the federals were equipped with such weapons. When an admittedly inexperienced South Carolina regiment attacked federal cavalry armed with breechloaders at Cold Harbor in June 1864, "The regiment went to pieces in an abject rout and threatened to overwhelm the rest of [our Confederate] brigade. [The witness had] never seen any body of troops in such a condition of utter demoralization." Midway through the war, at Gettysburg in July 1863, the entire Union Army of the Potomac cavalry corps had breechloaders. That is why Major General John Buford's division was able to hold off a superior Rebel force for most of the morning of the battle's first day. Later, Union cavalry Brigadier General James Wilson, in speaking of repeaters (as opposed to breechloaders in general), said, "There is no doubt that the Spencer carbine is the best fire-arm yet put into the hands of the soldier. . . . Our best officers estimate one man armed with it [is] equivalent to three with any other arm."[8]

Given the obvious superiority of breechloaders and repeaters, the uninitiated reader may incorrectly assume that they were not invented until the war was well under way. In truth, single-shot breech-loading rifles and carbines were invented years earlier. One was even patented in 1856 by Ambrose Burnside when he was temporarily a civilian. He later rejoined the army to become a major general and is unfortunately best remembered for commanding

Two unidentified Union soldiers with Spencer repeating carbines. (*Library of Congress*)

the Union army when it was decisively beaten at the Battle of Fredericksburg. Two future Confederate leaders who served as US secretaries of war during the 1850s, Jefferson Davis and John Floyd, evaluated some breechloaders with good results. While Davis felt the weapons should be restricted to cavalry, in 1860 Floyd concluded more generally, "as certainly as the percussion cap has superseded the flint . . . so surely will the breech-loading gun drive out [the muzzleloader.]"As for repeaters, the Henry and the Spencer were each patented in 1860, the year before the war began. The Colt revolving rifle was designed five years earlier on patents borrowed from the company's revolving pistols.[9]

The most popular Civil War single-shot breechloader was the Sharps, which was patented thirteen years before the war began. It was most commonly used as a carbine by Yankee cavalry because the shorter barrel facilitated reloading by mounted troops. It was reliable and capable of being produced in the greatest volume. After an 1853 fight between US dragoons and Indians, Captain Richard Ewell, who later became a high-ranking Confederate general, said the Sharps was "superior to any firearm yet supplied to the dragoons." As early as 1850, an army ordnance board had highly praised the gun. On the eve of the Civil War, in January 1861, another dragoon captain with years of experience using the firearm informed the

US Army Ordnance Department that the weapon was "exceedingly efficient." During the 1850s settlement of Kansas, abolitionists led by clergyman Henry Ward Beecher sent crates of Sharps guns, euphemistically called "Beecher's Bibles," to free-state settlers for use against settlers favoring Kansas's admission to the Union as a slave state.[10]

Although Sharps carbines began to be widely deployed among Union cavalry by the midpoint to the war, there were also early advocates for a long-form rifle of the weapon. Two months after the war began, Hiram Berdan formed two regiments of elite sharpshooters, which were a part of the Army of the Potomac. After Berdan selected the best marksmen, his next task was to choose a shoulder arm. He was disappointed that the ordnance chief, Brigadier General James Ripley, insisted that the rifles be muzzleloaders instead of breechloaders similar to the ones some of Berdan's men owned when they arrived. His encampment quickly became popular among Washington-area sightseers. In September 1861, President Lincoln visited with a group of generals and other officials. Among the group was Assistant War Secretary Tom Scott, who was hostile to Berdan's breechloader request. He asked Berdan to demonstrate his marksmanship on a dummy target in the shape of a man labeled "Jeff Davis." Berdan hit the dummy in the right eye at six hundred yards. Lincoln laughed at Scott and told Colonel Berdan, "come down tomorrow and I will give you the order for the breechloaders."[11]

Lincoln's promise was not enough. The sixty-seven-year-old ordnance chief considered all breechloaders "new fangled gimcracks" and refused to order them. Ripley had been in the army forty-seven years after graduating from West Point. In 1832, he commanded one of the forts in Charleston harbor that might have been required to suppress a rebellion if South Carolina failed to repeal its nullification of the "Federal Tariff of Abominations." For thirteen years, from 1841 to 1854, he was superintendent of the nation's weapons manufacturing armory at Springfield, Massachusetts, where he earned a reputation as a strict disciplinarian, if not a tyrant. Rebellious workers hanged him in effigy three times. He even fired workers who subscribed to a newspaper criticizing him. When the Civil War broke out, he was in Japan on a mission that was supposed to continue on to Europe, but he got the first ship home, where he replaced an even older officer as chief of army ordnance.[12]

For the next two-and-a-half years, Lincoln was open-minded about new weapons and frequently visited the ordnance chief. But Ripley failed to budge from his goal to maximize production of proven instruments because Union armies were too big to be supplied by domestic manufactures alone. Until fall 1862, more than half of the arms issued to federal soldiers were imports. Consequently, he felt the infantry should be armed with muzzleloaders such as the Springfield, which was designed at the Massachusetts armory during his tenure there. He also felt that repeaters and even single-shot breechloaders would encourage soldiers to waste ammunition. His only concession to more modern weapons was that cavalry should be given breech-loading carbines. It was an obvious exception because troops could not readily reload a muzzleloader while mounted. This was convincingly demonstrated during a cavalry clash at Mine Creek, Kansas, when the numerically superior Confederates with muzzleloaders were routed because they could not reload like the breechloader-equipped enemy.

As a result of Ripley's foot-dragging, none of Berdan's soldiers were issued Sharps rifles by December despite Lincoln's September promise. Ripley didn't even put any Sharps on order until February 1862. It took another couple of months for the first deliveries to arrive.[13]

Ripley's avoidance of repeaters is especially frustrating for four reasons. First, both the Spencer and the Henry were not only invented prior to the war but were even issued prewar patents. Their availability was a matter of scaling production, not invention. Second, the first Spencer order was placed in June 1861, only two months after the war began in April. Third, even the initial military test results of samples early in the war were favorable. Fourth, once the weapons were put into field use, the combat results were immediately convincing.

At the outbreak of the war, Christopher Spencer was a twenty-seven-year-old Connecticut inventor who in March of the previous year had patented a repeating rifle containing a seven-round magazine. A lifelong inventor, at age thirteen he converted his grandfather's musket into a carbine. At fifteen he built a steam engine. Before he was thirty, he was driving to work in a self-designed steam automobile. At age eighty-seven, he became absorbed in aviation. For seventeen years, he lived near Mark Twain in Hartford, and the author may have modeled his chief character in *A Connecticut Yankee in King Arthur's Court* after Spencer. Like Twain's fictional character, Spencer worked three years at the Hartford Colt works before hiring on at a silk factory owned by three brothers named Cheney. While employed at the silk factory, he invented the repeater on his own time.[14]

Because Navy Secretary Gideon Wells was a Hartford man and friend of the Cheney family, he arranged for the navy to test the Spencer two months after the war began. The chief of naval ordnance, Commander John Dahlgren, tested five hundred rounds with only one misfire. Dahlgren was impressed enough to order seven hundred rifles in June 1861.[15]

A couple of months later, the Spencer was tested by Alexander Dyer of the army ordnance corps. He fired it eighty times and simulated combat conditions by burying it in sand and saltwater for twenty-four hours. Afterward the gun was loaded and fired without first being cleaned. In November, Spencer demonstrated the weapon for General in Chief George McClellan, who kept his headquarters with the Army of the Potomac. McClellan ordered the ordnance chief for that army to evaluate the rifle and prepare a report. The testing officer was favorably impressed. McClellan also asked a board of three other officers, including Alfred Pleasanton, who would later command the same army's cavalry corps, to provide a separate report. Pleasanton and his colleagues also gave the Spencer a thumbs-up.[16]

None of the favorable army evaluations resulted in orders, but they did compel General Ripley to describe his objections. In December he opined that both the Spencer and the Henry were too heavy when fully loaded. He also falsely concluded that neither was superior to existing single-shot breechloaders. In sum, he did not "consider it advisable to entertain or accept either [the Spencer or Henry] propositions."

The Cheney brothers appealed to a few powerful New Englanders who may have been admitted as shareholders into the Spencer Repeating Rifle Company. Among them were Navy Secretary Welles, Republican leader and future presidential candidate James G. Blaine, and Warren Fisher, a Boston financier. Fisher wrote directly to Secretary of War Simon Cameron, who had a reputation for graft. Whatever—if any—backroom deal applied, Ripley ordered ten thousand Spencers the day after Christmas 1861.[17]

But there were more delays. After a congressional investigation, the questionable Cameron was removed as war secretary. His replacement, Edwin Stanton, reserved the right to review all contracts, while the Cheneys had to admit they could not meet the March 1862 delivery date for the first five hundred because they had only set up a factory in January. As a result, the order was reduced to seven thousand five hundred units, with initial deliveries to begin in June 1862. Left to its own resources, the Spencer company could not even make the June deliveries.[18]

Major General William S. Rosecrans. (*Library of Congress*)

By the time Spencers began to be deployed with combat troops in meaningful numbers, the evidence was overwhelmingly in their favor. Major General William S. Rosecrans, who commanded the Union Army of the Cumberland in Tennessee for about twelve months in 1862–1863, was a strong proponent of repeating rifles. During one nine-month period, he wrote nineteen letters to the secretary of war and other officials requesting breech-loading and repeating rifles for his soldiers. One of his brigade commanders, John T. Wilder, was in full accord. After a frustrating assignment to hunt down Confederate cavalry raider Brigadier General John Hunt Morgan, Wilder was given permission to mount his infantry brigade but was not given any breechloaders. On his own initiative, he wrote to the Henry manufacturer, asking if it would sell repeaters to his troops, which the soldiers would pay for themselves. He was told there was a waiting list. During the wait, Christopher Spencer visited the Army of the Cumberland, where Wilder tested the Spencer. Rosecrans was able to get Ripley to send Wilder's soldiers Spencers in spring 1863.[19]

While Grant held Vicksburg in a death grip in June 1863, Rosecrans launched an offensive against Lieutenant General Braxton Bragg's Confederate Army of Tennessee. He wanted to prevent Bragg from sending troops to fight against Grant and also to maneuver the Rebels out of central Tennessee. Wilder's brigade was part of the plan. They rode quickly ahead of the army to capture and hold a mountain pass called Hoover's Gap until a Union infantry corps could be brought up to solidify the position. Wilder's men did the job on June 25, suffering a total of 62 casualties while inflicting 146. Owing to the Spencer's firing rate, the opposing Confederate commander thought he was outnumbered five to one. Thereafter, Wilder's unit was informally known as the Lightning Brigade.[20]

Wilder even more convincingly demonstrated the Spencer's superiority at the Battle of Chickamauga, September 18–20, 1863. Bragg attempted to launch a surprise attack across bridges along Chickamauga Creek in northern Georgia just south of Chattanooga, Tennessee. In preliminary action on the eighteenth, the Lightning Brigade was guarding Alexander's Bridge. According to historian Glenn Tucker: "The preliminary affair at Alexander's bridge, where Wilder with only part of a single brigade and with but four [cannons] of his battery was able to hold off a division with artillery for nearly five hours, was an important milestone in the progress of the war. It confirmed the value in combat of the Spencer repeating rifle."[21]

Shortly before noon on the last day of the battle, a confusing order prompted a mistaken movement by a defending division that left a gap in the Union line. A massed Confederate column promptly charged through the gap. Almost as quickly as wind shifts battle smoke, nearly the entire right (south) wing of the federal army became a disorganized mob. The fleeing soldiers sought cover in Chattanooga or the intact left wing commanded by Major General George Thomas, who is credited with saving the entire army, earning him the nickname "Rock of Chickamauga." One by one, most of the Union brigades in the south half of the field were routed. But, sustained by confidence in their weapons, Wilder's was one of the few that stood firm. It even put the Rebel attack off balance with counterattacks of its own. Historian Tucker concluded, "Probably, Wilder's attacks . . . had given Thomas the needed margin of time to draw a new defense line." One of Wilder's men described the Spencer's effect on the attacking Rebels: "the head of the column, as it was pushed on by those behind, appeared to melt away or sink into the earth, for, though continually moving, it got no nearer."[22]

Author Robert Bruce says that by July 1864, "a feeling spread through the Union army that Spencer rifles could end the war in a hurry." The rifles were universally coveted. Major General Benjamin Butler promised to give the requested arms to only the most deserving troops and as prizes for gallantry. When Washington, DC, was threatened by a small force under Rebel Lieutenant General Jubal Early in July 1864, the ordnance chief who had replaced Ripley the previous September asked what he could do to help. One colonel answered by requesting that a Massachusetts regiment be issued Spencers. A Rebel prisoner commented to his Spencer-equipped captors, "It's no use for us to fight you'ens with that kind of gun." The British War Office took note and set up a committee to evaluate breechloaders. Based upon the American experience, the committee recommended that the entire British army be equipped with breechloaders.[23]

The versatility of the repeater's ammunition was also an advantage. Historian Richard McMurry relates an incident that occurred when repeater-equipped federal cavalry crossed the last river barrier protecting Atlanta in early July 1864:

> The men who made that crossing were armed with repeating rifles that fired metallic, waterproof cartridges. To avoid Rebel bullets as they waded the river, they stooped down in the water, stood up to fire, and then ducked again beneath the surface. The defending Confederates, accustomed only to singe-shot weapons and bullets that came wrapped with powder in paper tubes, were amazed by the "guns that could be loaded and fired under water." Some of the Secessionists simply ceased shooting and remained to surrender, eager to see the novel weapons used by their enemies.[24]

Although the Spencer was a marked advance in shoulder arms, it was the Henry that evolved into the iconic Winchester '73, to become known as the rifle that "won the west." Benjamin Henry worked for the New Haven Arms Company, owned by Oliver Winchester. When Henry joined it, the company manufactured an unpopular repeater that used poorly designed cartridges. He improved the design to use superior copper rim-fire cartridges. Unlike the Spencer, which had a magazine of seven loads in the butt stock, the Henry's magazine extended underneath the barrel and held sixteen loads. Since few of the rifles and required cartridges had yet been manufactured, Ordnance Chief Ripley ignored the Henry for over a year. Although it had been tested by the navy and the ordnance chief of the Army of the Potomac with favorable results, Ripley refused to place any orders. The first Henrys used in combat

Men of the color guard of the Seventh Illinois Infantry pose with their flag and their Henry rifles. (*Library of Congress*)

were purchased individually on the open market in spring and summer 1862.[25]

Hundreds were sent to Kentucky, where the publisher of the *Louisville Journal* was given one as a gift. He responded by editorializing that one soldier armed with a Henry was equivalent to fifteen using muzzleloaders. After Confederate armies invaded the state in summer 1862, some of the Kentucky Henrys ended up in Rebel hands. These captured repeaters were less valuable to the Confederates because they used specialized ammunition that could not be produced in the South. Nonetheless, in one episode, a besieged Ohio regiment surrendered to a numerically superior Rebel force that included one company armed with the repeaters. By January 1863, knowledge of the Henry's combat value began to spread beyond Kentucky. For example, a number of privately owned Henrys were used during the Battle of Chickamauga. Although federal orders were small, about ten thousand were sold privately to adroit state authorities by the end of the war. As 1864 began, Winchester could sell on the public market all the Henrys he could make, but he could not make very many because he depended on subcontractors and was in a rights dispute with Benjamin Henry. Only one thousand three hundred units were produced in 1862, and only two thousand five hundred in 1863.[26]

Nonetheless, during the 1864 Atlanta Campaign, half the soldiers in one Illinois regiment owned the rifles, purchased at their own expense. They helped prevent the Union rear from being overrun at the Battle of Atlanta. Late that year, at the slaughter of Confederates during the Battle of Franklin, one company of the 65th Illinois Regiment armed with Henrys put forth such a rain of bullets that one participant thought it a wonder "that any of [the attacking Rebels] escaped death or capture."[27]

Oliver Winchester received his first federal government order for Henrys toward the end of Ripley's tenure as ordnance chief in September 1863. The order came from Colonel Lafayette Baker, who organized Lincoln's Secret Service and wanted the arms for a four-company ranger unit he was forming in the second half of 1863 to support his detective force. Although Ripley pared the order to 250 rifles, Ripley's successor increased it by eight hundred.[28]

CONCLUSION

There is no doubt that single-shot breechloaders and repeaters such as the Spencer and Henry were far superior weapons to the standard muzzleloaders like the Springfield and Enfield. In fall 1864, then Ordnance Chief Alexander Dyer concluded that all soldiers should have breechloaders. It is also undeniable that such superior shoulder arms were a virtual Union monopoly. Repeater manufacturing was an absolute Yankee monopoly, and the Northern states had much of the world's production capacity for the best single-shot breechloaders. Although Prussia had a breechloader, it tried to keep it secret, and it was not as good as the Sharps. Finally, based on the combat record, it's unlikely that Confederate armies could remain in the field for more than a few months after the majority of Union soldiers possessed such weapons. The central dispute is whether the Union could have deployed them more rapidly.[29]

Critics often blame Ripley for the slow adoption of breechloaders and repeaters, partly because Lincoln evidently blamed him, since the general was replaced a month after the president test fired a Spencer in August 1863. Although Ripley was undeniably reluctant, his defenders argue three points. First, he agreed that breechloaders were the right choice for cavalry; his opposition was limited to their use by infantry. Second, Ripley supporters contend he was correct to focus on getting as many rifles into the hands of infantry as possible. Even if they were muzzleloaders, they were as good as anything the Confederates had. Third, private producers did not expand production capacity fast enough to materially speed up deployment.[30]

Taken in isolation, those are reasonable arguments, but from the larger perspective of overall Union leadership, they are not satisfying. The fault is as much with Lincoln as with Ripley. In short, Lincoln neglected to implement a Civil War equivalent to World War II's Manhattan Project. Nobody was given supreme authority to mobilize the nation's development and production capability, although the superiority of the applicable weapons was obvious from the beginning. A progressive ordnance chief might have attempted to assume such authority, or at least advocate for it. However, when Lincoln finally replaced Ripley in September 1863 with Brigadier General George Ramsay, the president yielded to objections from War Secretary Stanton, who wanted his own man to run the ordnance department, leaving Ramsay little more than a figurehead. Consequently, Ramsay resigned after a year, accomplishing far less than he had hoped.[31]

Lincoln could have selected qualified new-weapons enthusiasts such as Alexander Dyer or John Dahlgren to fulfill a role similar to that of General Groves in World War II's Manhattan Project. (In fact, Dyer was made ordnance chief after Ramsay, but that was late in the war.) Both men had given early thumbs up to tests on repeaters, although Dyer later had a dissatisfying experience with a hastily assembled Henry presented for tests. Dyer was in his mid-forties when the war started, and Dahlgren was in his early fifties, compared to Ripley, who was sixty-seven.[32]

Regardless of who might have been designated as a federal Civil War weapons production czar, his challenge would have been far less difficult than the one Groves faced. Unlike the nuclear bomb prior to World War II, repeating rifles were not mere theoretical concepts in 1861. The Spencer and Henry were not only prior inventions, but both were already patented. They were made from common materials, whereas the Hiroshima and Nagasaki bombs relied on isotopes that had never before been seen with the unaided eye. Furthermore, the Sharps and other single-shot breechloaders were in commercial production years before the Civil War started. If Lincoln had replaced Ripley with a Groves-like character in the first half of 1862 (as Ripley's foot-dragging warranted), much could have been accomplished by the next summer. Gettysburg could have ended the war.

While private manufacturers had difficulty reaching volume production, it is important to understand that they got no help from the federal government. Even though Republicans were notorious advocates of public works spending and subsidies for private business sectors, there was no federal investment in the industry. Instead the relationship between the ordnance department and manufacturers was often adversarial, with penalties and cancellations for late deliveries. Inventors like Spencer and Henry received no material assistance or even advice about how to scale production. Similarly, the government failed to arbitrate the rights dispute between Winchester and Henry that restricted production of their repeater to pathetically low volumes. In contrast, fifty years later, upon entering World War I, the federal government promptly required cross licensing and ready access to all radio and aviation patents because of the important roles such new technologies could play in the fighting.[33]

While Lincoln is most culpable, other Union leaders cannot escape critical scrutiny. War Secretaries Cameron and Stanton are obvious examples. However, the successive army generals in chief might have been more assertive, although they admittedly had no official authority over the ordnance department. As noted, McClellan had a good opinion of repeaters as early as autumn 1861, but his position was probably not secure enough to risk creating bureaucratic enemies like Ripley. McClellan's successor, Major General Henry Halleck, was typically passive.

The last Civil War general in chief was Lieutenant General Ulysses Grant, who enjoyed enough popular acclaim to promote breechloaders and repeaters. Although he advanced the career of repeater proponent and cavalry Brigadier General James Wilson, Grant's opinion of Wilson probably had little to do with the latter's affinity for repeaters. For the most part, Grant did not seem interested in breechloaders and repeaters. For example, in November 1863, he banished General Rosecrans to Missouri to await orders that never came. Since Rosecrans was the highest-ranking advocate of such weapons in the field, he could have been a more effective proponent if Grant had not heaped added disgrace upon him by shipping him to the mostly ignored trans-Mississippi after his defeat at the Battle of Chickamauga.

Finally, the Joint Congressional Committee on the Conduct of the War might be faulted for failing to look more carefully at weapons technology and production. While the committee was involved in some fruitless controversies, it could have done some good by encouraging cooperation between government and the private arms industry.

It is difficult to estimate how much more quickly single-shot breechloaders and repeaters might have been deployed in the Union army. But if top military and government leaders acknowledged their superiority earlier, it is certain the arms could have been adopted more rapidly. As noted, War Secretary Stanton did not recommend uniform adoption until one and a half months before Appomattox, even though the earliest test results were favorable beginning two months after the war started. The failure to mobilize government and private industry into cooperative efforts and focused technological development was a mistake that would be corrected in later wars.

3

PREEMPTING
THE CIVIL WAR

The fateful chain reaction of cotton state secessions that preced-
ed the Civil War might have been aborted in January 1861.
Preemption may have been accomplished in a manner comparable to
the way President Andrew Jackson avoided a similar rebellion
against federal authority twenty-eight years earlier during the South
Carolina tariff nullification crisis.

Along with most Southerners, South Carolina had long opposed
protective tariffs. Although the Constitution authorized tariffs for
revenue, as an exporting region the South felt that tariffs designed
chiefly to protect domestic manufacturers were unconstitutional
because they favored one section of the country over another. Tariffs
became increasingly protective from 1816 through 1828. In January
1833, South Carolina "nullified" the most recent tariffs, prohibiting
federal officials from collecting duties within its borders starting
February 1, 1833. A successful nullification precedent raised the
specter of regional secession because Southern congressmen voted
64–4 against the 1828 tariff. Despite habitual sympathy for states'
rights, President Jackson sought congressional authority to compel
tariff compliance militarily. Through a combination of a show of
force and support for a compromise tariff, Jackson brought the
Palmetto State back into line, forestalling additional movement by
other states toward nullification or secession.[1]

A comparatively obscure incident in early January 1861 might have provided a similar opportunity to halt the Civil War before it started. Contrary to popular belief, the first shots of the Civil War were not those forcing the federal garrison at Fort Sumter to surrender on April 13, 1861. While conscientious Civil War students realize that Charleston, South Carolina, witnessed cannon fire three months earlier, many may not appreciate that the January 9, 1861, episode was potentially far more consequential than generally supposed.

Six weeks after Lincoln was elected president, South Carolina became the first state to secede, on December 20, 1860. Federal troops were routinely stationed in the state, including seventy-five artillerymen commanded by Major Robert Anderson at Fort Moultrie, which was at the mouth of Charleston harbor. Moultrie faced the water from the harbor's north shore and wasn't designed to withstand attack from the landward side. President James Buchanan, who would remain in office until March 4, 1861, took steps to protect the federal soldiers in Charleston even before South Carolina seceded.

On December 11, he notified Anderson to avoid aggression but to defend the forts "to the last extremity" if attacked. He further authorized Anderson to concentrate his troops at Fort Sumter if the major discovered tangible evidence of hostile intent from South Carolina. He was also prepared to send reinforcements to Anderson "at the first sign of danger." For this purpose, the secretary of war had stationed the USS *Brooklyn*, a powerful war steamer, "in Hampton Roads, to take on board three hundred disciplined troops, with provisions and munitions of war, from . . . [nearby] Fortress Monroe [Virginia.]"[2]

Accordingly, the day after Christmas 1860, Moultrie's troops quietly disabled their artillery and secretly boarded boats for unoccupied Fort Sumter. Although still under construction, Sumter was more defensible. It was on an island near the harbor's center on the edge of the main shipping channel. Sumter's artillery was also far more powerful than anything available to South Carolina's military forces.

Once Anderson concentrated his force at Sumter, South Carolina occupied the remaining harbor fortifications, which were nearly vacant. Despite pleas from his few remaining Southern cabinet members, Buchanan refused to order Anderson to evacuate Sumter

A Civil War-era map of Charleston Harbor showing its defenses. Fort Sumter is at the lower right. (*Library of Congress*)

and Charleston altogether. "This I cannot do," he said. "This I will not do. Such an idea was never thought of by me in any possible contingency." He concluded that if he were to do so, "I could travel home to [my Pennsylvania estate of] Wheatland by the light of my own burning effigies." On New Year's Day 1861, Buchanan concluded, "It is all over now, and reinforcements must be sent."[3]

It is important to appreciate that in early January 1861, South Carolina's military capability was wholly inadequate for action against Fort Sumter, or most any armed vessel that might enter the harbor. Lieutenant General Winfield Scott, commander of the US Army, would later tell President Lincoln, "It would have been easy to reinforce this fort [Sumter] down until about February 12."[4] Author Maury Klein summarizes a report, from the South Carolina militia also issued on New Year's Day, to the state's governor, Francis Pickens:

In blunt language [General James] Simons observed that Sumter commanded the line of communications for every other fort. Moultrie was "wholly untenable," lacking a single man who had ever loaded a siege gun or handled a heavy-caliber cannon. The same was true of Fort Johnson, whose force could be routed by a few shells from Sumter. The Morris Island battery was manned by cadets from The Citadel and a rifle corps, none of whom had artillery experience. *No fort was equipped to repel incoming vessels.* (Italics added.)[5]

Nor was South Carolina's military inadequacy merely the opinion of her own experts. Major Anderson and others of the Sumter garrison came to the same conclusion. On New Year's Eve, Anderson wrote to Washington, "the Government may send us additional troops at its leisure. . . . [W]e are safe. . . . [W]e can command the harbor as long as our Government wishes to keep it." In describing the situation on January 9, Captain James Chester, who was an artilleryman inside Sumter, wrote, "at that time Sumter was master of the situation." He added that should even an unarmed relief vessel have passed the cadet battery on Morris Island, "it would have been comparatively safe."[6]

Although Anderson was not eager for reinforcements after his troops were concentrated in Fort Sumter, such was not the case earlier. For example, Fort Moultrie was designed for a garrison of three hundred men, while he had but seventy-five on hand. Since Moultrie was vulnerable to attack from its landward side, his messages to Washington stressed a need for more troops unless his existing command were removed "to Fort Sumter, which so perfectly commands the harbor and [Fort Moultrie.]"[7]

As noted, the USS *Brooklyn* was on standby at Hampton Roads as a vessel for a relief expedition to provide Anderson with provisions and two hundred additional soldiers. On New Year's Eve, Buchanan told General Scott to prepare the expedition for departure. Although the ship would be ready to leave by January 3, after reflection, Scott suggested that a merchant steamer replace the *Brooklyn* for at least two reasons. First, the *Brooklyn*'s hull drew sixteen feet of water, which was close to the limit of Charleston's shipping channels. Moreover, the offshore sand bar created by silt draining from the Ashley and Cooper rivers, which meet at the tip of Charleston's peninsula to form the harbor, could be even shallower than the chan-

The sloop-of-war USS *Brooklyn*. (*National Archives*)

nels. Second, a faster steamer might more readily slip into the harbor before the Carolinians could resist.[8]

Scott may have had a third reason for declining to use the *Brooklyn*. The soldiers slated to board the ship were part of the garrison at Fortress Monroe, Virginia. A few days earlier, Scott told soon-to-resign secretary of war John Floyd (a Virginian) that the general could not spare that many troops from the garrison. Apparently he was concerned that if two hundred or so were removed, prosecession Virginians might opportunistically seize the undermanned fort.[9] Two months earlier, Scott had written to Floyd:

> [I]t is my solemn conviction there is some danger of an early act of rashness preliminary to secession; [specifically,] the seizure of some or all of the following posts: Forts Jackson and St. Philip . . . below New Orleans, both without garrison; . . . Forts Pickens and McRae [at] Pensacola [Florida]; . . . Forts Moultrie and Sumter, Charleston Harbor, the former with insufficient garrison and the latter without any; and Fort Monroe, Hampton Roads, without sufficient garrison. . . . [A]ll should be immediately so garrisoned as to make any attempt to take them . . . ridiculous.[10]

Buchanan was doubtful about the change to an unarmed merchant ship. The *Brooklyn* was a powerful warship with over twenty cannons capable of shooting nine- and ten-inch-diameter projectiles. South Carolina had nothing approaching the firepower of either

Sumter or the *Brooklyn*. Nonetheless, "with great reluctance" Buchanan deferred to Scott's judgment as the military expert. Scott was the highest-ranking officer in the US Army and was a revered figure largely because he had sealed victory in the Mexican War a dozen years earlier by occupying Mexico City.[11]

As a result of Scott's change, a paddle-wheel steamer named *Star of the West* was chartered in New York and loaded with 250 soldiers from nearby Governors Island. Also aboard was an experienced Charleston pilot to navigate the ship safely into the destination harbor. The *Star* left New York on January 5 and would arrive off Charleston harbor on the night of January 8. Anderson's New Year's Eve message, implying that he could hold Sumter indefinitely, did not arrive in Washington until the *Star* had already departed. Two days after the *Star* left New York, Buchanan learned that the Carolinians were constructing an artillery battery at the entrance to Charleston harbor's main channel. Therefore, he instructed that the *Brooklyn* also be sent from Hampton Roads to intercept the *Star*. If the *Brooklyn* arrived on time it was to instruct the merchant ship to return to New York, but if there were any trouble it was to aid the *Star*.[12]

Scott's messages informing Sumter of reinforcements were intercepted and arrived too late. However, Governor Pickens learned of the plans and decided to resist. Artillery batteries were hastily set up along the northern and southern shores of the harbor mouth. The ship channel would require the *Star of the West* to first run the batteries on the south side (Morris Island), turn west, and run those on the north shore where Fort Moultrie was now occupied by Carolinians. A signal boat was put on patrol duty. South Carolina's military unpreparedness was evidenced by the choice of Citadel cadets to man the Morris Island batteries. Then, as now, The Citadel was a military college, much like the Virginia Military Institute. Shortly after dawn, the signal boat launched flares. The cadet commander on Morris Island scanned the channel and saw the *Star of the West* moving cautiously up the channel, sounding for the bottom as it came. He instructed that a cannon be aimed to place a shot across its bow and ordered sixteen-year-old George Haynesworth to fire. The cannonball skipped over the water but, because it didn't have enough propulsion, failed to even make it as far as the front of the ship.[13]

Captain John McGowan of the *Star* was hopeful that Sumter would retaliate against the rebellious fire. To encourage such intervention, his unarmed ship was flying an oversized US flag. But the fort remained silent, even as the cadets repeatedly imperiled the ship with more shots. Eventually it was hit three times, but still Sumter made no reply. After the three hits, McGowan realized he must soon turn west and face dangers from Fort Moultrie as well. Instead, he put the *Star* in tight turn and returned to New York.

Following the cadets' first shot, drummers inside Sumter beat the long roll calling troops to battle stations. Cannons were loaded and the muzzles pushed through their firing apertures. Although the *Star of the West* was under fire from points within range of Sumter's guns, Anderson hesitated. He had no orders telling him what to do. Scott's undelivered instructions would have told him that if the *Star* was taken under fire, Sumter "may use its guns to silence such fire." Since those orders never got through, the major was acutely mindful that retaliating fire could trigger a fratricidal war between the states. Such responsibility caused Anderson to hesitate, and the *Star* retreated before he took further action.[14]

Meanwhile, Mississippi joined South Carolina in secession before sundown, followed by Florida the next day and Alabama the day after that. A week later Georgia seceded, followed the next week by Louisiana. On the first day of the next month, Texas left the Union. Three days later the seven states formed a confederacy. Thereafter, secession momentum stalled. After two additional months of stalemate, the now-inaugurated Lincoln decided to send a second relief expedition to Sumter to restock provisions and add soldiers to the garrison. Confederate president Davis, and most of his cabinet, concluded that Sumter must not be permitted to resupply. He authorized the bombardment that started on April 12 and led to the fort's surrender the following day. In response, Lincoln called for an army of seventy-five thousand volunteers to invade the rebellious states and put down "combinations too powerful to be suppressed" by ordinary means.[15]

Governors were notified of their respective state quotas. Virginia, North Carolina, Tennessee, and Arkansas refused the call and joined the Confederacy within a couple of months. Missouri, Kentucky, and Maryland also declined, but did not leave the Union. The federal commander in Saint Louis chased the Missouri governor and his militia to the southwest corner of the state. Kentucky resolved to remain neutral, until Confederate Lieutenant General Leonidas Polk unilaterally fortified a Mississippi River town inside the state, thereby tipping the sentiment scales northward on September 3, 1861. Various machinations stifled Southern sympathies in Maryland.[16]

It is interesting to ponder what would have happened if the warship *Brooklyn* had been sent as originally planned instead of the merchant steamer *Star of the West*.

Since the *Brooklyn* was under orders to deliver supplies and soldiers to Sumter, it almost certainly would have returned fire to the Carolina batteries.[17] It had the strength to fight past them and relieve Fort Sumter. Furthermore, the *Brooklyn*'s gunfire would more likely have prompted Sumter to retaliate as well. The meager Carolina batteries available in early January had no chance against such combined firepower. As noted, the *Star of the West* only abandoned its mission when it started coming within range of the batteries at Fort Moultrie while it was simultaneously moving beyond the range of those on Morris Island. Yet Moultrie was the more vulnerable of the two Carolina batteries and could have been silenced by Fort Sumter.[18]

Afterward, the *Brooklyn* could have sailed three miles upstream to the Charleston wharves, eliminating whatever resistance it might meet along the way. Once there, it could demand the city's surrender under its frowning guns. That's how it happened a year later when federal warships—including the *Brooklyn*—fought past two forts guarding New Orleans, the Confederacy's biggest city.[19]

Assuming the *Brooklyn* had left Norfolk when it was ready on January 3, the ship would have arrived in Charleston by January 6, which was three days before any other state was prepared to secede. If the *Brooklyn* and Sumter had promptly forced Charleston to accept federal authority, the rebellion may never have spread enough to take root. It could have been quickly crushed, as President Jackson had done about thirty years earlier.

Historians might condemn Buchanan for failing to follow Jackson's precedent to act forcefully and promptly to suppress South Carolina's rebellion. However, upon analysis, it is clear that he was sensitively aware of Jackson's example but believed he lacked the necessary tools to implement it. Specifically, Jackson did not use force against the Palmetto State on his own authority. He required congressional permission and promptly got it. He asked for a force bill in mid-January 1833, which Congress passed about six weeks later as a component of a compromise bill that would reduce the tariff. (In the terminology of the times, a force bill was a congressional bill authorizing the president to use military force to settle a dispute, which was the subject of the bill.) As Buchanan later wrote,

> Congress refused to revive [such authority] throughout the entire session of 1860–1861 and to confer upon [me] the same powers . . . conferred upon President Jackson. . . . [W]hilst witnessing the secession of one after another of the cotton states . . . it was the imperative duty of Congress to furnish the President . . . the means of repelling force by force . . . to preserve the Union. They nevertheless refused to perform this duty.[20]

Although reliance upon the *Brooklyn* instead of the *Star of the West* for the early January 1861 relief of Fort Sumter seems appealing in retrospect, the scenario is not without complications.

First, owing to the depth of the *Brooklyn*'s hull, it would have been required to maneuver ponderously once inside Charleston harbor. Also, as noted, the offshore sandbar might have been an even more significant obstacle. However, there was a third option, aside from the *Brooklyn* or a merchant steamer: the mission might have used a smaller warship. One example was the USS *Pawnee*, which was stationed near Washington, DC, during the first three months of 1861. Earlier it had been on a three-month cruise to Mexico, but it had returned to Philadelphia on December 12, 1860. In short, it was available.[21]

The *Pawnee* was a modern steam-and-sail-powered vessel that was only a little over a year old in January 1861. It was equipped with ten cannons, including eight with nine-inch-diameter projectiles and two smaller ones. By comparison, the *Brooklyn* had twenty nine-inch guns. However, since the *Pawnee*'s hull drew only ten feet of water, it could have more easily crossed the sandbar and would have been significantly more maneuverable once inside Charleston harbor. If it were not large enough to accommodate 250 soldiers, it could have escorted a merchant steamer carrying them. In any event, the *Pawnee* would have provided the Union forces significantly more firepower than the Carolinians had available, particularly when Sumter's armament is included. Thus, instead of the *Brooklyn* pro-

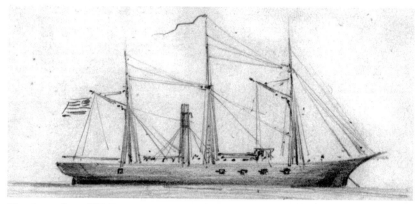

The sloop-of-war USS *Pawnee*, sometimes referred to as a "gun boat." (*Library of Congress*)

ceeding to the Charleston wharves to demand the city's surrender, it could have been the *Pawnee*.[22]

There is a second complication that might have resulted from using a warship instead of the *Star of the West* to relieve Sumter in early January 1861. While a show of force might have preemptively blocked other cotton states from seceding, it can be conversely argued that such action might have further provoked them. A number of leaders, North and South, reasoned that if the disaffected states of the Deep South were not coerced back into the Union, they would eventually return on their own, particularly once it was evident they would remain an isolated small minority unless other slave states joined them. For example, when Virginia, North Carolina, Tennessee, and Arkansas joined the gulf South after Lincoln's call for volunteers to suppress the rebellion, they doubled the white population and material resources of the Confederacy. They also nearly doubled the Confederacy's land area east of the Mississippi River.[23]

CONCLUSION

For purposes of preserving the Union, it would probably have been wiser to have selected a warship, as opposed to a merchant steamer, for the January 1861 Fort Sumter relief expedition. Since the Carolinians had nothing to match the combined firepower of Sumter and such a vessel, it is likely the warship could have forced the surrender of Charleston before any other states seceded, especially if it arrived on January 6. Although it is debatable whether the use of such force would have aborted—or encouraged—further state secessions, the use of the *Star of the West* obviously failed to prevent the Civil War.

Even in the Deep South there was considerable Union sympathy in early January 1861, which may have been fortified by decisive action against South Carolina while the state was the only one to have seceded. Decisions to leave the Union were made in the remaining gulf states in elections and conventions held from December 1860 to early February 1861. Two types of delegates were elected to such conventions. First were those favoring immediate secession, labeled "immediatists" by historian William Cooper. The second group consisted of those believing the Lincoln administration should be given a chance to demonstrate its true intentions through action before additional states should resort to secession. Cooper identifies the second group as "cooperationists."

Initially, immediatists had significant winning margins in only Texas and Florida, but even in the latter, cooperationists probably won 40 percent of the vote. In the other four gulf states, immediatist margins were narrower. Even in Mississippi, where slaves represented about half the population, only 40 percent of the vote went to immediatists, while 30 percent voted for cooperationists, and the remaining 30 percent were for candidates who did not clarify their positions. In Georgia, immediatists won 51 to 49 percent, while their victory in Louisiana was only slightly better at 52 to 48 percent. Alabama gave immediatists a 57 to 43 percent majority.

Although the comparative strength of the cooperationists vanished by the time secession convention delegates voted, those votes came after the easy repulse of the *Star of the West* gave the impression that the Union lacked the resolve to block secession. Mississippi was the first example. Despite the fact that immediatists captured only about 40 percent of the vote in December, three-fourths of the delegates voted against all efforts of cooperationists to slow secession. The final vote on January 9 was 85 percent in favor of secession. Although cooperationists maintained their strength in Alabama's final convention secession vote of 61 to 39 percent, in the other gulf states "the cooperationist minority became part of the majority [because] state loyalty conquered." One Alabamian wrote, "every feeling of patriotism" and "every sense of good judgment" compelled that "I must share my state's destiny."[24]

Although many present readers of American history are captivated by the Civil War era, its casualties and destruction were horrifying, and the war might better have been avoided. At least six hundred twenty thousand soldiers died in the Civil War, compared to four hundred five thousand American deaths in World War II, the second-largest total of war dead in US history. About 2 percent of the country's population was killed in the Civil War, which would equal more than six million deaths if applied to today's population. More than 4 percent of white Southerners were killed, which would be more than twelve million deaths if applied to the present US population.

Until each side came to regard the offenses of the other as unforgivable, nearly everyone moved reluctantly toward war. Although a minority of agenda-driven agitators confidently predicted any consequent war would quickly result in victory for their side, most statesmen correctly harbored darker suspicions. Many outside the Republican Party attempted unsuccessfully to reach a compromise over the five-month period from Lincoln's election to the bombardment of Fort Sumter. While both Lincoln and Davis acknowledged the possibility of war in their respective presidential inaugural addresses, each proclaimed a desire for peace. Lincoln famously spoke to Southerners directly:

> The Government will not assail you. . . . We must not be enemies. Though passion may have strained it must not break our bonds of affection. The mystic chords of memory, stretching from every battlefield and patriot grave to every living heart and hearthstone all over this broad land, will yet swell the chorus of the Union, when again touched . . . by the better angels of our nature.

Two weeks earlier, Davis had simply said, "our true policy is peace."[25]

It was all to no avail.

Too often, wars evolve along unpredictable paths driven by underlying and barely restrained forces propelled toward entropy. Throughout history, humanity sporadically relearns this lesson. For example, in November 1944, the US secretary of war appointed a committee to prepare an analysis of strategic bombing during World War II. In commenting on the future, the report on the European theater stated, "The great lesson to be learned . . . is that the best way to win a war is to prevent it." The quote has sometimes been abbreviated and misattributed to Nobel Peace Prize winner General George Marshall: "The best way to win a war is to prevent it."[26]

The problem with alternate histories, such as the substitution of a warship for the *Star of the West,* is that the hypothetical change of a single variable renders as speculative all subsequent actions and reactions. Consider if John Wilkes Booth's pistol miraculously failed to fire. While it might seem probable that Lincoln would live, there could be no assurance that Booth would have been unable to kill him another way.

Conversely, the value of alternate historical scenarios is that they force us to appraise past events in the context of the applicable times and circumstances without prior knowledge of the results. For example, if it was known that the Soviet Union would eventually collapse as a consequence of flaws inherent in its economic system, it would seem illogical to support a corrupted puppet régime in South Vietnam at the cost of nearly sixty thousand American lives. But in the 1960s, our leaders concluded the fall of South Vietnam would initiate a chain reaction of additional communist takeovers. Those who can remember the politics of the 1960s cannot deny the prevalence of the domino theory.

As Cuban refugee and Yale historian Carlos Eire writes, "Show me history untouched by memories and you show me lies. Show me lies not based on memories and you show me the worst lies of all." As our nation marches past the 150th anniversary of the end of the Civil War, many historians are increasingly prone to ignore the context of those times. Consideration of alternate scenarios can help correct this defect. The best Civil War history is written by those able to imagine they were present at the time without knowing the outcome. In short, hindsight handicaps history.[27]

4

TREASURY INNOVATIONS
AND MISCHIEFS

As the Civil War grew to unexpected size and length, the financing requirements of the Union and Confederacy became unparalleled. Ultimately only Lincoln's government proved to be successful. Innovations quickly adopted during the war continue presently as the foundations of American banking and finance. But the river of money flooding through the Treasury also became an irresistible temptation for some who rationalized that secretly diverting comparative trickles for personal gain would little damage the overall war effort. The interplay between federal financial innovations and their unintended temptations for corruption is an intriguing story.

QUANTUM CHANGES

As the June fiscal year data in Table 1 illustrate, average annual federal spending during the seven years prior to the Civil War was less than $80 million, which was about the same as the year before the war began. During the five years straddling the war, US government spending rose to an average of $700 million yearly and peaked at over $1.3 billion in 1865. The average annual budget deficit for seven years before the war was less than $10 million, compared to $525 million during the war. The national debt increased from $65 million at the start of the war to $2.7 billion the year it ended.

Although there was no precedent for accommodating such enormous financial needs, it is obvious they could not be managed in ordinary ways for two reasons. First was the sheer magnitude. Even though taxes increased by a factor of six, federal spending increased by a factor of nearly thirty. Consequently, the budget deficit increased sixty-five-fold. Second, the eleven states that left the Union for the Confederacy were not going to be a revenue source unless the rebellion was defeated.

Table 1. United States Government and Spending

Fiscal Years 1855–1859 (in millions of dollars)

	1854	1855	1856	1857	1858	1859
Revenue (Primarily Taxes)	80	72	81	76	54	62
Deficit Spending (Surplus)	(13)	(2)	(1)	3	33	23
Total Spending	67	70	80	79	87	85
Gross Public Debt	42	36	32	29	45	59

Fiscal Years 1860–1865 (in millions of dollars)

	1860	1861	1862	1863	1864	1865
Revenue (Primarily Taxes)	65	50	60	124	277	348
Deficit Spending (Surplus)	13	30	425	602	601	963
Total Spending	78	80	485	726	878	1,311
Gross Public Debt	65	91	524	1,120	1,816	2,681

Wartime Increases from fiscal year 1861 to fiscal year 1865:
Annual federal spending increased 29-fold
National debt increased 41-fold
Average budget deficit increased 65-fold

Source: usgovernmentspending.com

Two factors compounded the problem. First, prior to the war, the United States effectively relied on an inelastic gold standard that made it difficult to expand the money supply to meet burgeoning military and economic needs. Second, the ultimate size, and attendant financial needs, of the war only gradually became apparent. Alterations in the monetary system grew increasingly radical as the scale of the war swelled beyond expectations.

THE GOLD STANDARD

To understand the inelasticity of the gold standard it is necessary to examine the standard's fundamental characteristics. In English-speaking countries, banking evolved among merchants in the mid-seventeenth century. Shopkeepers normally stored their surplus gold in the king's mint for safekeeping, until Charles I needed money shortly before the English Civil War in 1638. The king confiscated much of the merchants' gold, calling it a loan. Although the loan was eventually repaid, merchants thereafter preferred to deposit their gold with private goldsmiths, who issued warehouse receipts to each depositor. Such receipts essentially became paper money and were preferred in many transactions in place of bulky coins.[1]

Soon goldsmiths realized that most such receipts would remain in circulation and rarely be presented for redemption. Therefore, they could loan money in the form of newly issued receipts, maintaining a gold inventory equal to only a fraction of the face value of receipts outstanding. Theoretically, once such loans were repaid, the amount of receipts remaining in circulation would be equal to the gold inventory, and the smith would have earned interest income on the loan. Pragmatically speaking, however, new loans were constantly being created as the old ones were paid off. As long as the receipts presented for redemption never exceeded the smith's gold inventory, there was no harm. But if ever a holder presented a receipt that could not be redeemed, public confidence in the smith's warehouse receipts would vanish, and the paper would no longer be accepted in transactions, except perhaps at a discount to face value.[2]

At the start of the American Civil War, about one thousand six hundred banks operated in the above manner. There was no federal requirement for minimum reserve ratios. Regulations regarding reserve ratios, interest rates, loan activities, and other matters were imposed by the states individually. About seven thousand kinds of bank notes circulated. Most were spurious.[3]

For fifteen years prior to the war, the US government was prohibited from issuing paper currency. While the US Mint coined money, the coins were normally struck in gold or silver, which is to say, specie. Taxes and other funds due the federal government were paid to the Treasury. The 1846 Independent Treasury Act specified how such funds were to be collected and held.

First, any funds due to the federal government had to be paid in the form of Treasury notes or specie. Treasury notes were typically interest-bearing short-term Treasury obligations. They were issued as debt instruments, limited in amount, and were not officially money, but were commonly used as such since they were acceptable for paying taxes. Second, funds received by the federal government had to be held in the Treasury or sub-Treasury buildings instead of banks. That provision essentially removed the US Treasury from the banking system. Third, the government was required to pay its bills through the Treasury in the form of specie but could alternately use Treasury notes. Consequently, in times of budget surplus, the Treasury tended to draw specie out of the economy, thereby reducing the money supply. Conversely, during periods of deficit spending it pumped specie into the economy.[4]

The US Mint coined gold and silver in specified ratios intended to reflect the relative bullion value of each metal. Although the legal ratios were close to the market ratios they slightly undervalued silver, thereby leading silver dollars to be driven out of circulation. Put another way, the bullion value of a silver dollar was greater than its monetary value. Therefore, silver dollars tended to be melted down and transformed into bullion, which could be sold at more attractive market rates. The effect of such arbitrage was to place the United States on a gold standard. At the start of the Civil War, the nation's money supply was primarily linked to the amount of gold coins in circulation or held in reserve by reliable banks. A small amount was available in silver coins below the one-dollar denomination.[5]

On the eve of the Civil War, the nation's total currency was about $450 million, of which only $250 million was in specie. The remaining $200 million consisted of private paper issues of questionable quality. An estimated $50 million of the paper money circulated in the South. The gross national product was about $4.3 billion, equaling about $140 per capita.[6]

SECESSION CRISIS

The earliest effect of secession was a crisis of confidence in the financial viability of the federal government. About 90 percent of federal taxes were obtained from import tariffs, which were almost certain to decline as Southern states left the Union to form a Confederacy that was likely to adopt lower duties. Not only would Confederate states avoid US tariffs, but states remaining in the Union would be tempted to smuggle goods from Southern entrepots. Consequently, the entire federal tax structure was on the brink of collapse.[7]

To complicate matters, the government needed to borrow money as a result of revenue shortages lingering from the 1857 depression. In September 1860, the Treasury floated a $10 million 5 percent bond issue, but buyers took delivery on only $7 million once Lincoln was elected. A $5 million issue was sold in December, but the interest rate had to be raised to 12 percent. In February 1861, Congress authorized a $25 million issue bearing 6 percent interest, but the Treasury could sell only $8 million and had to accept prices as low as 90 percent of face value.[8]

When Lincoln's Treasury secretary, Salmon P. Chase, took office in March 1861, the national debt stood at $75 million, of which $18 million was added during the secession crisis alone. That month Chase was able to raise only $8 million through a combination of offerings involving long-term bonds and short-term notes. He could have raised more if he would have accepted prices below 98 percent of par. His refusal to do so alienated the government's traditional bankers, who were the principal bond buyers.[9]

SUMTER CRISIS

The day after he took office, Lincoln was informed that Union-held Fort Sumter in South Carolina's Charleston harbor was running low on provisions. About a week later, on March 10, Lincoln asked his cabinet to vote on whether a resupply expedition should be sent. Five were strongly opposed out of concern that it would precipitate a war, one was in favor, and Chase was ambiguous. However, sentiment within the cabinet soon began to shift for two reasons.[10]

The first was reaction to passage of the first Morrill Tariff two days before Lincoln was inaugurated. The new duties were almost twice as high as those of the Confederacy. Northerners increasingly recognized that if the tariff was not enforced in the cotton states (which was one reason for holding Southern forts), widespread circumvention would ensue, resulting in a collapse of the federal tax structure. While many Northerners, including Lincoln, were prepared to offer safeguards to protect slavery in the states where it was then legal, almost no Republicans were willing to compromise on tariffs. Despite calls from notable Democratic Northern leaders such as Senator Stephen Douglas to reduce the increases, Republicans demanded a protectionist tariff and were ready to go to war in order to have it.[11] As historian William Cooper explains:

> Northeastern mercantile and financial interests quickly became aware of the possible negative consequences. . . . At the end of March a committee of New York merchants came to the White House to press the president on the government's policy. . . . This tariff conflict . . . caused a shift in business opinion. Before it had been almost monolithic against [forcing Southern state reunification], but now it was turning to form up behind Lincoln's inaugural pledge to collect revenue and hold the forts.[12]

The second reason sentiment within the cabinet began to shift in favor of a resupply expedition to Fort Sumter was that Postmaster General Montgomery Blair, the lone cabinet member who had voted in favor of it, introduced the president to Gustavus Fox, who was Blair's brother-in-law. Fox had a plan to resupply Sumter that had been ignored by General in Chief Winfield Scott. Lincoln thought Fox's plan was reasonable and asked the cabinet to vote a second time, on March 29. That vote was five-to-two in favor of the Fox plan. Secretary Chase voted with the majority.[13]

Fox's mission prompted the Confederates to bombard Fort Sumter into submission on April 12 and 13. Lincoln responded with a call for seventy-five thousand volunteer soldiers to put down the rebellion. Although Fox's plan failed, afterward Lincoln wrote him, "You and I both anticipated that the cause of the country would be advanced by making the attempt . . . even if it should fail. It is no small consolation now to feel that an anticipation is justified by the result." The Civil War had begun.[14]

After Sumter, four more states—Virginia, North Carolina, Tennessee, and Arkansas—joined the rebellion. In combination they contained half the white population of the augmented eleven-state Confederacy. Lincoln was fortunate that Congress would not be back in session until July because he could more readily exercise his executive powers to meet the developing war crisis until then. He was especially concerned about keeping Maryland in the Union because if it joined the Confederacy, Washington would be surrounded by Rebel states. Maryland's governor was mildly pro-Union, but most of the legislature leaned toward secession. Lincoln imposed martial law in the state, arrested prosecession residents, and shut down newspapers with antiadministration viewpoints. One arrested citizen named Merryman appealed to a circuit court under a writ of habeas corpus that he either be released or charged with a specific crime in a civil court. The sitting judge happened to be the US Chief Justice Roger Taney, who ordered Merryman released. Lincoln ignored the ruling and wrote standing orders for the judge's arrest, although they were never executed.[15]

According to Assistant Secretary of State Fred Seward, son of Secretary of State William Seward, a few months later, in September, Lincoln ordered Brigadier Generals Nathaniel Banks and John Dix to prevent prosecession Maryland legislators from attending a session where it was thought they had enough votes to pass a secession ordinance. A list of such legislators had been compiled between April and September. When their attendance was blocked, the legislators realized that without the protections of habeas corpus, they could languish in jail indefinitely if they attempted to resist.[16]

Although Lincoln's executive actions kept Maryland in the Union, Treasury Secretary Chase could not access much more funding without congressional authorization. In May he was able to raise only about $12 million in a combination of offerings for notes and bonds, some of which sold for less than 86 percent of par.[17]

War Financing

In July, Congress authorized Chase to borrow up to $250 million in a combination of bonds and notes. Leading banks soon agreed to buy $150 million of such paper scheduled at $50 million in each of August, October, and November. Although they hoped to resell most of the securities to their own clients, the banks had to keep about $100 million themselves. The average interest rate was about 7 percent. The secretary told the banks that unless they took the paper on his terms he would print paper money until it cost $1,000 to buy breakfast. By the end of 1861, New York banks refused to redeem their banknotes for specie, and the federal government followed almost immediately, as did the rest of the country's private banks. As 1862 started, private banknotes were nothing but paper money.[18]

Since gold was still required for international settlements, a gold-trading exchange opened in New York within two weeks.

Thereafter, gold quotations became a barometer of faith in the federal government. The more paper dollars required for buying a single gold dollar, the lower the faith. The low point came in July 1864, when two and a half paper dollars were needed to buy a single gold one. For some, the exchange became a gambling casino for placing bets on the fortunes of war. As always, those with superior insider information were unfairly advantaged. One famous speculator, Daniel Drew, later reminisced, "Along with ordinary happenings, we fellows on Wall Street had the fortunes of war to speculate about. . . . It's good fishing in troubled waters."[19]

Secretary of the Treasury Salmon P. Chase. (*Library of Congress*)

Unlike most bankers, forty-year-old Jay Cooke of Philadelphia successfully resold government bonds. He offered them to the public, as opposed to the traditional small group of well-heeled investors. He used newspaper ads and encouraged newspapers to write favorable editorials about the financings as a patriotic responsibility. He also had connections to Secretary Chase's home state of Ohio. Cooke's brother, Henry, published a newspaper in Columbus and moved to Washington after the war started. Even before the war began, the Cooke family lobbied Lincoln for Chase's appointment. Chase and his daughters sometimes made overnight visits to Jay Cooke's Philadelphia estate (The Cedars) as he and the young ladies travelled the business and social circuits between New York and Washington. Jay Cooke placed 34 percent of the first $50 million Treasury offering after the Battle of First Bull Run (known as First Manassas to Confederates) in July 1861.[20]

Since suspension of specie redemption reduced private banknotes to mere paper currency, Congress yielded to the temptation to permit the Treasury to print its own paper money as a means of financing the war and providing a single version of a uniform currency. The result was the February 1862 Legal Tender Act, authorizing the issuance of $150 million in US notes that informally became known as greenbacks. Some private banknotes were engraved on only one side, whereas the greenbacks were printed on both sides, with a portrait on the front and plain green designs on the back. Greenbacks were declared legal tender for all public and private debts, except for customs duties, which still needed to be paid in specie so the government could continue to pay interest on its debt in specie.[21]

As a means of bolstering public confidence in the greenback, Congress promised that the February 1862 issue would be the only one. However, once it became apparent that the notes were accepted—although at a discount to specie—Congress granted two more authorizations of $150 million each. The second was in July 1862, and the third was early in 1863. A total of $415 million was actually issued. Chase had his picture placed on the front of the one-dollar denomination, of which 2.6 million were issued. He put Lincoln's portrait on the ten-dollar denomination, of which fewer than four hundred thousand were issued. The secretary hoped to challenge Lincoln for the Republican presidential nomination in 1864. No doubt having his picture on the one-dollar version of greenbacks would raise public awareness of him.[22]

Earlier, Chase had the slogan "In God We Trust" engraved on US coins. At one meeting, the cabinet considered adding the legend to greenbacks as well. But Lincoln suggested wryly, "If you are going to put a legend on the greenbacks, I would suggest that of Peter and John, 'Silver and gold I have none, but such as I have I give to thee.'"[23]

California and Oregon defied the Legal Tender Act, although the federal government did nothing to suppress their rebellion. Like citizens everywhere, few residents of those states wanted to accept greenbacks as legal tender in place of specie, because greenbacks traded at a discount. In April 1863, as Union Major General Joseph Hooker was preparing to advance on General Robert E. Lee at Chancellorsville and Major General Ulysses Grant was crossing the Mississippi River to approach Vicksburg from the rear, the California legislature adopted a "specific contracts act" stipulating that contracts requiring payment in specie could be enforced in court. Moreover, California banks would not accept greenbacks for deposit, and the state refused to accept greenbacks as payment for taxes. California and Oregon ruled that greenbacks were violations of their state constitutions.[24]

Even though greenbacks considerably increased the money supply, Chase still needed more money. He did not ignore taxes, which increased from $42 million in fiscal year 1861 to $334 million in fiscal year 1865, but deficit spending remained the prime source of federal funding. Thus, Chase needed a reliable method of selling bonds. In autumn 1862, he granted Jay Cooke's bank a monopoly on underwriting, or selling, federal debt. Historian Dan Rottenberg writes:

> Armed with his authority as the Federal government's sole financial agent in negotiating $500 million worth of government loans, Cooke sprang into action. . . . He unleashed a barnstorming sales machine that employed brass bands, newspaper advertising, and a nationwide army of some 2,500 salesmen. . . . Eventually this team disposed of . . . nearly 75% of the Union's bond issues sometimes raising $2 million in a single day.[25]

Despite Cooke's outstanding sales job, he and Chase coveted an even more powerful method of ensuring a ready market for federal bonds, one that remains in effect today. With the aid of Ohio senator John Sherman, a brother of Major General William T. Sherman, they drove a bill through Congress that became the National Banking Act of 1863, which was followed by an amendment the next year. The acts established national banks and empowered them to issue banknotes backed by the federal Treasury and printed by the government so they all looked the same. The quantity of notes that a bank could issue was proportional to its reserve capital on deposit with the comptroller of the currency. Since such reserves included government bonds, the acts provided a powerful incentive for national banks to buy bonds issued by the Treasury and sold by Cooke. The acts also taxed the previously popular private banknotes, thereby pushing them out of circulation and establishing the present US standard of green paper money.[26]

CORRUPTION

Jay Cooke has been labeled everything from an exceptional patriot to a robber baron. During the Gilded Age, he became a scandalous railroad financier and went bankrupt in the Panic of 1873. But during the Civil War he did more than any single banker to develop a market for federal government bonds at prices acceptable to the Treasury. Because of complaints by competing bankers to congressmen, Chase canceled Cooke's monopoly on Treasury sales in January

1864. But Cooke managed to get it back after Chase went on to become US chief justice in December 1864. Cooke's original commission of 0.25 percent of par value was tiny compared to the market discounts Chase had to accept when selling bonds early in his Treasury tenure.[27]

By the end of the war, Cooke had negotiated his commission up to 0.75 percent. To many it seemed like theft from the government to pay him even that much since his firm did little more than process public money that flowed in to buy bonds, particularly after the National Banking Act essentially made such bonds a required investment for the dominant banks. Cooke started the war as a moderately successful promoter. At the end he was a millionaire whose reputation had spawned the expression "as rich as Jay Cooke." He is estimated to have invested $100,000 into Chase's unofficial 1864 presidential campaign and ranked second only to Rhode Island US senator—and Chase son-in-law—William Sprague as a contributor.[28]

As the table at the start of this chapter documents, gigantic amounts of money were flowing through the federal Treasury during the Civil War, particularly in comparison to the sums applicable before the war. Businesses associated with such a monetary flood presented temptations for exploitation, if not outright corruption. A number of high profile characters appear to have yielded to such temptations. According to Chase biographer John Niven, Henry Cooke was one:

> [Henry Cooke] used insider information to engage in a particularly flagrant speculation in army quartermaster supplies. His associates were an army captain stationed in Cincinnati and an editor of the Ohio State Journal. Cooke's role was exposed just as Chase's campaign for the Republican presidential nomination began to gain momentum in December 1863 and January 1864. War Secretary Stanton [a Chase ally] saw to it that the affair was covered up.[29]

Jay Cooke also benefitted from his brother's close proximity to Secretary Chase in Washington, where Henry managed the local office of Jay Cooke & Company. Henry Cooke came and went at the Treasury Department, much like a trusted assistant, picking up secret information, such as advance knowledge of military movements, which could be transformed into profits on the stock exchange. He telegraphed such information to Jay Cooke's Philadelphia office. After the military imposed telegraphic censorship, the brothers developed a private cipher, thereby sustaining the profitable messaging.[30]

Even Chase is not beyond suspicion, despite a historical reputation for personal honesty. When Jay Cooke opened a branch of his bank in Washington in February 1862, Chase was one of the first depositors. The secretary soon asked the financier, "How can you invest a few thousand dollars for me so as to make the best possible profit?" Evidently Chase could satisfy himself that he was merely asking for a favor instead of a bribe. He soon discovered that the profits from the morsels that Cooke set aside for him were rewarding. Cooke was even accommodating enough to loan Chase the funds required for the profitable investments if the secretary could not provide his own money. Chase biographers Thomas and Marva Belden wrote:

> Chase was not troubled by the singular manner by which Jay Cooke was [earning profits for him]. Cooke lent him capital, made the investments for him, within a few weeks reported a large return, and sent him a check. Chase did not appear even mildly curious to find out whether or not this ritual was a genteel fiction to disguise periodic gifts.[31]

Ellis Oberholtzer, the biographer selected by Jay Cooke's children shortly after the financier's death, stated:

> Throughout the year 1862, at Chase's solicitation, Cooke was investing various sums of money for the secretary, with a view to obtaining for him the largest possible income on his fortune. Every few weeks he received checks, which represented the proceeds of various speculations in railway and industrial stocks conducted with a practical banker's acumen plus a very generous regard for a friend's best pecuniary interests.[32]

Considering that Chase perpetually needed money to sustain the lifestyle demanded by a presidential aspirant, there's little doubt that the investment returns Cooke provided were a courteous form of bribery. By the end of 1862, Congress was threatening to investigate connections between the two. Although Chase's congressional friends blocked the investigation, his correspondence with Cooke quickly dropped off. When, six months later, Cooke sent Chase a check for $4,200 representing the return on an investment the financier had made for the secretary, Chase returned it with the inconsistent explanation that he could not accept "dividends" on investments he did not make himself.[33]

Chase's attitude reversal is explained by the May 1863 engagement of his eldest daughter to one of America's wealthiest men, US senator William Sprague of Rhode Island. The couple wed in November 1863, and Chase's daughter Kate wore a $50,000 tiara gift from her husband. Four blocks away at Ford's Theater, John Wilkes Booth produced the comedy *Money*, with a plot based on the question of whether a woman should give her love to a man with money or to one for whom she holds natural affection. While many assumed Kate Chase was getting both, she ended up dying a fifty-nine-year-old divorcee. Modern biographers assume she married Sprague for the money he could provide to her father's political ambitions. Even contemporary Henry Adams referred to her as Japheth's daughter, recalling the biblical king who was compelled to sacrifice his daughter in exchange for the leadership he gained from a Jehovah-granted battle victory.[34]

Chase's unsuccessful bid to replace Lincoln as his party's presidential candidate left the secretary politically vulnerable after Lincoln was renominated in June 1864. So when Chase resigned in protest over the president's intervention in a New York customs appointment, Lincoln accepted the resignation. But Lincoln still thought highly of Chase and appointed him chief justice in December 1864 upon the death of Roger Taney. Chase held the position for over eight years, until he died during the Grant administration in 1873, although he attempted to become the Democratic presidential candidate against Grant in 1868.

THROUGH THE LOOKING GLASS

Before Chase became chief justice, he was a reliable Radical Republican, but afterward some of his key opinions appeared to be mirror images of his prior viewpoints. An early example after he became chief justice was his wish that the treason indictment against former Confederate president Jefferson Davis be quashed. Next, while presiding over the impeachment trial of President Andrew Johnson, he privately disagreed with the Republican position that the president should be convicted for violating the Tenure of Office Act, because Chase believed the act to be unconstitutional. While Republicans were unsure of his private thoughts, they were enraged that he presided over the trial evenhandedly. Johnson avoided conviction by a single vote. As noted, unlike Supreme Court justices of later eras, Chase refused to set aside his presidential ambitions after becoming chief justice. It was a questionable break with decorum even at the time.[35]

Perhaps Chase's most significant opinion reversal involved the Legal Tender Act that he vigorously advocated during the Civil War. As Treasury secretary, under the act he issued $415 million in greenbacks, which could not be redeemed for specie and persistently traded below face value in relation to specie. But in *Hepburn v. Griswold* in 1870, he ruled with the court majority that the act could only be justified as a wartime necessity and was otherwise unconstitutional. The defendant, Susan Hepburn, had attempted to use greenbacks to satisfy a debt she owed to Henry Griswold, although the original loan to Hepburn was in the form of specie. The majority ruled that under the Constitution, the federal government was allowed to coin money but not transform paper currency into legal tender. Hepburn would be required to pay the debt with specie. The decision was overruled the following year after two new justices appointed by President Ulysses S. Grant had taken their seats.[36]

In *Texas v. White*, Chase ruled with the majority that the Confederate states had never been out of the Union because secession was illegal. The decision contradicted the perspective favored by Radical Republicans that the former Confederate states were conquered provinces subject to congressional rule. In the *ex parte Yerger* decision, Chase and the court majority opened the way for judicial review of the Reconstruction Acts of Congress, which were imposed by Radical Republicans. (An *ex parte* judicial decision is one in which all of the parties to a controversy are not present in court.) The Radicals responded by unsuccessfully introducing bills to deny the Supreme Court the power to overrule any acts of Congress. In *ex parte Milligan*, the court held unanimously that a president had no power to institute military trials against civilians in time of war when civilian courts were operating in the area. The decision essentially invalidated the Republican-supported wartime case against Ohio Democrat Clement Vallandingham.[37]

In 1868, Chase's political ambitions led him to some of his most glaring inconsistencies. Since Ulysses Grant was the odds-on favorite for the Republican nomination, Chase considered a presidential bid as a Democrat, even though he was a prominent pioneer of the Republican Party. The Republican platform declared that African American suffrage would be mandatory in the former Confederate states but remain a state right in the rest of the country. The Democratic platform held that it should uniformly be a right reserved to each state without geographic discrimination. At the end of the war, Chase agreed with the Republicans that the Southern states must adopt African American suffrage. But in order to have a chance at the Democratic nomination, he adopted an ambiguous stance. While proclaiming support for "universal (male) suffrage" as a basic principle, he told the press that suffrage should be conferred by the states individually. It was not enough. The Democrats selected former New York governor Horatio Seymour as their candidate to oppose Grant. Seymour's vice presidential running mate was Frank Blair, who had derailed Chase's 1864 presidential bid with accusations of corruption at the Treasury.[38]

Despite ideological flip-flops, Chase remained consistent in his needs for questionable money sources. Even after he became chief justice, Chase biographers Thomas and Marva Belden conclude:

> Cooke continued to aid Chase with investments, collect his interest, and oblige him with an occasional loan. The financier thoughtfully made certain that Chase's business transactions maintained a high rate of profit, without reference to the ups and downs of the market, and by the summer of 1867, Chase was able to anticipate a private income greater than his official salary.[39]

CONCLUSION

Salmon Chase's name is in the moniker of one of the world's biggest banks (J.P. Morgan Chase) for two reasons. First, he laid the foundation for a national currency that enabled the money supply to expand and contract in response to government policy. Second, he generally had an impeccable reputation for personal honesty.

There's no doubt that he transformed banking in the United States and successfully raised the money the Union needed to fight the Civil War. But his personal integrity collided with an insatiable presidential ambition that left him chronically short of money. While it's unlikely he blatantly took bribes, he did accept loans and gifts. His relationship with Jay Cooke & Company suggests that he willingly accepted as a polite fiction that the investment returns earned by Cooke on discretionary investments made on Chase's behalf failed to qualify as bribes. Perhaps he believed what he wanted to believe. But as H. L. Mencken warned, "It is hard to believe a man is telling the truth, when you know that you would lie if you were in his place."[40]

5

THE CAMELOT COUPLE

A week after her husband's assassination, President John Kennedy's widow was interviewed at her Massachusetts home by a then-prominent magazine. During the session, Jacqueline Kennedy compared the couple's one thousand White House days to King Arthur's mythical Camelot. She added that prior to retiring for the evening, the president often played a recording of the title song from the popular Broadway musical of the same name. To most any American who can remember the 1960s, President and Mrs. Kennedy became the Camelot couple. He was from a politically ambitious and established wealthy family. She was a stunning beauty about a dozen years younger, molded by finishing school refinement and a cultural education. On a diplomatic tour with her husband, she addressed the French in their language. Only years later would the nearly spotless public image of the Kennedy era become tainted with reports of sexual infidelity and painkiller overuse.[1]

Civil War Washington had a similar Camelot couple, William and Kate Sprague. They were married on November 12, 1863, while General Grant was preparing for an offensive at Chattanooga and little was happening militarily in the eastern theater. The groom was a thirty-four-year-old US senator from Rhode Island, while the bride was the twenty-three-year-old daughter of the politically ambitious Treasury secretary, Salmon Chase. The senator was the scion of one of America's wealthiest families. During the ceremony, the bride wore a diamond-and-pearl tiara gift from her husband worth $50,000, which would be valued at over $600,000 presently. As the bride entered, a military band struck up the "Kate Chase March," composed for the occasion. The reception displayed wedding gifts valued at $60,000, which exceeded the financial worth of the bride's family. Nearly all of Washington society attended, including President Lincoln, who stayed two hours. Mrs. Mary Todd Lincoln declined, officially because she still mourned the death of a son almost two years earlier, but more probably because the two women were bitter social rivals. One of Kate Chase's biographers wrote, "After Willie Lincoln's death . . . in early 1862, the mourning Mrs. Lincoln may have remained as the titular head of Washington society, but Kate reigned as its sovereign queen."[2]

Also attending was John Hay, one of Lincoln's youthful secretaries and later secretary of state under Presidents William McKinley and Theodore Roosevelt. He may have also been romantically interested in Kate before she married. He had been an occasional theater escort of hers and visited the Chase home. Several weeks before the wedding, he wrote to a friend:

> The town is dull. Miss Chase is so busy making her father next president that she is only a little lovelier than all other women. She is to be married on November 12, which disgusts me. She is a great woman . . . with a great future.[3]

THE CHASE FAMILY

Salmon Chase was born in New Hampshire in 1808, the same year as Jefferson Davis and a year before Abraham Lincoln. Although his family was well connected, it was not prosperous. His father died when the boy was nine, leaving a widow with ten children. A few years later, when an Episcopal bishop uncle volunteered to finish the boy's education, Salmon's mother sent him to the cleric in Ohio. Three years later, when the uncle left on a European trip to seek funding for a school that would become Kenyon College, the boy returned to New England. He enrolled at Dartmouth College, in New Hampshire, and graduated in 1826, at age eighteen. His next move was to Washington, DC, where he established a school for boys and counted the children of President John Quincy Adams's cabinet members among his pupils. Included were two sons of Attorney General William Wirt, who encouraged Chase to study law. Chase was admitted to the bar at twenty-one. The following year, 1830, he moved to Cincinnati to practice law. Chase concluded that Cincinnati had a bright future based on his two years of living in the bustling town while residing with his uncle.[4]

Chase built his legal and political career in Ohio. After repeatedly defending escaped slaves captured in Ohio, he became known as the attorney general for runaway slaves. In 1849, at age thirty-nine, he was elected to the US Senate on the Free Soil ticket. In the Senate, he would not compromise on slavery. He opposed the Kansas-Nebraska Act that authorized future states from that territory to be admitted as free, or slave, based on a popular vote by the residents. He also opposed the Compromise of 1850 that admitted California as a free state, because the compromise did not explicitly prohibit slavery in all of the territories of the Mexican Cession. He was a leader in the formation of the Republican Party on the principle of opposition to such slavery expansion. In 1855, at age forty-seven, he was elected the first Republican governor of Ohio. At the 1860 Republican presidential convention, he and New York senator William Seward were the leading contenders for the nomination, which eventually went to Abraham Lincoln as a compromise candidate. Imagining he was denied the office by unfair political bargaining, Chase coveted the presidency for most of the rest of his life.[5]

Chase was married and widowed three times. His first wife, Catherine, was from a prominent Cincinnati family. Less than a year after they married, she died giving birth to a daughter who would not survive childhood. Four years later, at age thirty, he married seventeen-year-old Eliza Smith. Their first child was a girl, named Catherine (Kate) in honor of Chase's first wife. It was this girl who became the belle of Civil War Washington. Eliza Chase gave Kate two sisters, but both died in infancy. Kate's mother died when the girl was five years old. Less than two years later, Chase married a third time. His last wife, Sarah Bella Dunlop Ludlow, was the daughter of another prosperous Cincinnati family. Known as Belle, she was the mother of Janette (Nettie), Salmon's only other child to reach adulthood. Nettie was eight years younger than half-sister Kate. Belle Chase died in 1852, less than six years after her wedding.

Little Kate did not welcome a stepmother. During her own mother's long ill-
ness, Kate drew especially close to her
father. The days began at breakfast with
Chase's sister, Alice. At the end of each
day, Kate waited eagerly for her father to
come home. In the evenings she read him
Bible verses and poems. The presence of a
stepmother disrupted the security of the
routine. Kate grew rebellious. When
daughter Nettie arrived, Chase decided to
send Kate to a boarding school. He chose
Miss Henrietta B. Haines's school in the
Gramercy Park area of New York City. It

Kate Chase Sprague. (*Library
of Congress*)

was a Spartan place. The day began with prayers and breakfast at six
in the morning. Studies included music, drawing, composition, lan-
guages, and history. Thursday nights provided receptions for mem-
orable guests. Kate was at the school for nine years.

There she learned well how to be a young society lady. She learned
the proper manners, speech, gestures, and overall deportment. She
was comfortable in high society and perceived nuances about it that
unfinished girls might only learn at an older age, if ever. She could
waltz, and ride horses at a canter in a ladylike manner. She developed
a love for fine clothes, which would evolve into a taste for expensive
living. Back in Cincinnati, her father was often dismayed at the
clothing bills forwarded to him for payment. Like Jacqueline
Kennedy, she learned to speak French, and she spoke it better than
her Phi Beta Kappa father.

Despite occasional visits from New England relatives, Kate was
lonely in New York. Nobody could take her father's place. She wanted their relationship to be similar to the one they shared before she
had a stepmother. After Belle Chase died, Kate reasoned that she
might reconstruct a more mature version of the pre-Belle father-
daughter relationship. While at boarding school, she observed that
the world of adults was driven by ambition. Consequently, she
resolved that her father's ambitions would become hers. All of her
refinements would be employed to help him achieve his goals. She
knew that he wanted to win elections, and she had little concern for
the issues of the elections, so long as he won. In such a manner she

hoped to become indispensible to him, and therefore seldom far from his thoughts and presence.[6]

When Chase became Ohio's governor in 1856, Kate returned home and joined him in Columbus. Although only sixteen, she functioned more as a mother to eight-year-old Nettie than an older sister. Chase's sister was still in the household, but Kate drew more attention in the new city than did Alice. Friends remarked on the handsome father-and-daughter couple and complimented the governor on Kate's beauty and intelligence. For her part, Kate did all she could to keep her father from becoming lonely enough to seek a fourth Mrs. Chase. She read and talked with him, and they occasionally played chess during long winter evenings. Although he failed to win the Republican presidential nomination after finishing his term as governor, he was elected to the US Senate in 1860. Consequently, he would return to Washington in March 1861 with twenty-year-old Kate. In a January 1861 meeting in Springfield, Illinois, President-elect Lincoln asked Chase if he would accept the post of Treasury secretary, presuming it were offered. Chase's words were noncommittal, but the shrewd Lincoln didn't read a man merely by his words.[7]

The Sprague Family

William Sprague IV was a grandson of the founder of the A & W Sprague Manufacturing Company, which was organized as a Rhode Island cotton mill in 1811. When the founder died in 1836, the company had already diversified into other business, including sawmills. William's father, Amasa, and uncle, William III, inherited the business and continued to expand it.

When William IV was thirteen, Amasa Sprague was murdered on New Year's Eve 1843. He was struck in the arm by a bullet and then bludgeoned to death by a rifle butt while walking alone on a cold country road. The abandoned gun was found in a nearby ditch. When the body was discovered, Sprague's wallet was untouched. It is generally believed he was killed because he persuaded the town council to decline a liquor license application near his factory. As a wealthy industrialist, Sprague had many enemies, but eventually one suspect, John Gordon, was convicted. The identity of the assailant was sufficiently controversial that Rhode Island abolished the death penalty seven years later. Gordon's defenders believe he was convicted because of religious prejudice against Roman Catholics. In 2011, Rhode Island governor John Chafee posthumously granted Gordon a pardon. Management of the business fell to young William's uncle, William Sprague III, who also became the boy's legal guardian.[8]

Aside from managing one of America's wealthiest businesses, the uncle was also active in politics. He was elected congress-man in 1835, governor in 1838, and US senator in 1842. When he died in 1856, twenty-six-year-old William IV; his brother, Amasa; and their cousin Byron

William Sprague. (*Library of Congress*)

became the principal managers of A & W Sprague. Because William started working for the business at sixteen, he had more experience than the other two. As a result, he promptly became leader of the company, which operated nine cotton mills and other businesses. Since boyhood, however, William had been fascinated with the mil-itary. In 1859, he took a European tour, supposedly to study Old World armies. However, rumors of drunkenness and flirtations soon drifted across the Atlantic to Rhode Island's capital, Providence.[9]

Upon returning to Rhode Island in January 1860, he discovered that a coalition of Democrats and other conservatives, termed the Union Party, had nominated him to run for governor against a Radical Republican. Surprised, he initially declined the honor. However, when his advocates stressed that Rhode Island's supply of cotton for its mills might be strangled by Radical Republican alien-ation of the South, he agreed to run. In an election said to have cost $100,000, thirty-year-old William Sprague became the state's gov-ernor. Politics was a family tradition, and his mills needed cotton.[10]

Together in Washington

One day after returning to the Senate on March 4, 1861, Salmon Chase learned that Lincoln had nominated him as Treasury secretary and the Senate had confirmed him, all while he was out of the cham-ber. It was simultaneously a heavy responsibility and a rich prize. Because seven seceded Southern states were no longer paying feder-al taxes, much of the responsibility for keeping the country solvent rested on his shoulders. Yet he had little experience in banking and government finance. But in an era of patronage, a Treasury secretary could dispense some of the most attractive government jobs to political friends. Chief among them was the office of the tariff collector in New York, where the bulk of such duties were paid. The appointed position was worth $25,000 to $30,000 annually in salary and fees, which was more than the president was paid. The New York customs house had hundreds of employees whose salaries were routinely assessed 2 percent for political donations to the party in power.[11]

Her father's appointment was also a boon for Kate Chase. From a social perspective, she sensed an opportunity to take the lead in the society functions of cabinet members. As biographers Thomas and Marva Belden explain:

> Because of the ill health of [Secretary of State William Seward's] wife, Kate [Chase] was in fact . . . the first lady of the Cabinet, and she knew that eventually she could become the unofficial first hostess of the national capital, that she could mesmerize Washington, become the confidante of men engaged in directing the state, be worshipped, admired, envied. But Kate was not satisfied. She and her father had failed. A great gawky giant from Illinois sat at the head of the Cabinet meetings, and a plain middle-aged woman was the hostess in that unpretentious but most desirable white house. . . . In 1864 there would be another test between desire and reality, and she was determined not to fail again.[12]

Shortly after Confederates forced the surrender of Fort Sumter on April 13, 1861, Lincoln called on all the states to provide seventy-five thousand volunteers to suppress the rebellion. It was a clear signal that war could no longer be avoided, and the states of Virginia, Tennessee, North Carolina, and Arkansas joined the seven cotton states in an eleven-member confederacy. Equally worrisome to Lincoln was the possibility that Maryland might also join the Southerners, thereby leaving Washington, DC, surrounded in hostile territory. Lincoln was desperate for Union volunteers to reach the capital before Confederate forces might occupy it. For ten days he felt like he was under siege. Marylanders cut the telegraph lines and railroad connections to the North. Unfulfilled rumors of troop arrivals drove him to distraction. Pacing the floor, he was heard to say, "Why don't they come? Why don't they come?" Troops from New York finally came on April 25. Within days, thousands of reinforcements started arriving.[13]

Among the first of the additional soldiers to arrive was the 1st Rhode Island Regiment, commanded by Colonel Ambrose Burnside. Even before Lincoln's call for volunteers, Governor Sprague offered to send a regiment and a battery of artillery. He was the first non-Republican governor to do so. Moreover, he personally lent Rhode Island $100,000 to equip the regiment. While he did not lead the regiment, he was with it when it arrived and bivouacked in Washington. Although a small man, he was a gallant figure as he dashed about in his dazzling uniform on an elegant horse, much appreciated by all of Washington. No doubt the bachelor governor would have been pleased to know that Kate Chase was among those admirers. There would not be a big battle for three months. Meanwhile, Washington was a carnival of military reviews, band concerts, and flirtations, but Sprague soon returned to Providence to raise a second regiment.

The 1st Rhode Island was composed of young men from the state's most respected families. The preponderance of wealth among them led some observers to refer to the unit as the "million dollar regiment." When Burnside was asked to requisition government supplies for his troops, he replied, "We need nothing. . . . Rhode Island and her governor will supply their wants." The soldiers enlisted for only ninety days because they expected to subdue the rebellion quickly. Within weeks nearly everyone agreed that goal could best be accomplished by capturing Richmond. In mid-July the Rhode Island regiments marched out with the rest of the Union army to confront the Confederates near Manassas Junction, Virginia, and then continue on to Richmond. Sprague went with them, although he had no official commission.

He took charge of a battery in the Union flanking movement at the First Battle of Manassas (First Bull Run), where he helped stop a Rebel counterattack with Rhode Island's second regiment. But the tide of battle went against the Union army, which was routed. Sprague was mortified. He was particularly annoyed that the elite 1st Regiment failed to show the courage of the 2nd Regiment. Returning with his troops to Washington, he took a room for himself at the Willard Hotel. Shortly thereafter, the soldiers of the 1st Rhode Island Regiment decided they had seen enough of war and shamelessly disbanded.

Although ashamed of his privileged Rhode Islanders, Sprague continued to serve in the army without a commission. He joined the Army of the Potomac during an early part of the Peninsula Campaign, where official dispatches referred to him as a scout. Brigadier General Joseph Hooker, who would later command that army at the Battle of Chancellorsville, made favorable mention of Sprague's services. But on the whole, Sprague had little impact. As a result, he wrote to Lincoln with a suggestion about combining the western and eastern forces. Lincoln gave him a pass to consult with the principal western commander, Major General Henry Halleck, at Corinth, Mississippi, in early summer 1862. Halleck listened politely but had no interest in the boy governor's ideas. Still, the trip was a turning point for Sprague. No doubt the cotton growing in the region reminded him of the needs of the economic engine that propelled the family fortune as well as much of the economy in his home state. He put away his uniform to focus on other projects.[14]

SPRAGUE'S NEW PROJECTS

For months preceding the Corinth trip, Sprague frequently saw Kate Chase because he visited Washington often to promote his business and military interests. The Rhode Island legislature gave him an opportunity to enlarge his Washington influence by electing him to the US Senate, where he would take his seat in March 1863. While his money brought him power, it was respect that he craved. He could not help but notice the envious glances other men cast in his direction whenever he was in public with Kate. "She possessed an almost mystical self-assurance which neither money, nor liquor, nor travel, nor politics had brought William Sprague. Kate had the cool self-possession of a goddess whose will determines the course of destiny. Sprague's very temerity revealed his weaknesses."[15]

But there was a second reason to court Kate Chase. Since her father was Treasury secretary, he was authorized to issue permits enabling the named holders to legally purchase cotton in Union-occupied regions of the Confederacy. Such permits were licenses to print money. The wartime hunger for cotton in New England and abroad drove commercial cotton prices from thirteen cents a pound in 1860 to a peak of $1.90 in 1864. Yet the staple could be bought for a fraction of the New York prices from destitute Southerners, or even the inventories of the Confederate government.

Sprague's first attempt to leverage his relationship with Salmon Chase for questionable purposes came shortly after Union troops occupied the cotton-growing lands near Port Royal, South Carolina, in November 1861. He influenced Chase to appoint a fellow Rhode Islander, Lieutenant Colonel William Reynolds, to manage the collection and shipment of the region's cotton to the North. But after several months of repeated rumors that Reynolds was abusing his position for personal gain, Chase dismissed him.[16]

When visiting Washington as a bachelor, Sprague normally stayed at the Willard Hotel, which was then—as now—a center of the city's political intrigue. William Russell, who was the Washington correspondent for the *London Times*, commented that the Willard probably contained more "scheming, plotting, [and] planning . . . than any building the same size . . . in the world." The hotel was at the northwest corner of 14th Street and Pennsylvania Avenue. During the secession crisis before the shooting started in April 1861, hotel management kept peace by arranging that Southerners use the 14th Street entrance while Northerners used the Pennsylvania Street entrance. The respective groups were assigned rooms on different floors.[17]

Shortly after returning from Corinth, Sprague met a Texan named Harris Hoyt at the hotel. Hoyt claimed he was thrown out of the state because of his Union loyalties. He aroused Sprague's interest when speaking of his many Union-loyal friends in Texas who were eager to sell cotton if they could get it through the blockade. Hoyt presented a note written by Lincoln's private secretary, John Hay, which said in part, "Mr. Harris Hoyt . . . is recommended to the President as a true and loyal citizen." Instead of writing that the recommendation was "*by* the President," Hay specifically wrote it was "*to* the President." Evidently, Hoyt hoped that Sprague would make little note of the difference.

Prior to meeting with Sprague, Hoyt presented Hay's "recommendation" to Secretary Chase, as well as Navy Secretary Gideon Welles, in hopes of getting a permit to slip cotton out of Texas without interference. Both men turned him down. But since Hoyt had an ear to Washington gossip, he learned of the Rhode Island governor's relationship with Kate Chase. Perhaps Sprague could help him get Secretary Chase to issue the required permit. Evidently Sprague encouraged the notion, because Hoyt returned to Chase the next day, but was turned down a second time. In a burst of anger, Hoyt mused aloud whether he should "send Chase to Sprague and his partners." The secretary irritably replied, "I wish you to understand that these gentlemen do not control me."

Undeterred, Sprague asked Hoyt to travel to Providence, where he hosted a meeting to see what might be arranged. Hoyt brought along an experienced Texas skipper named Charles Prescott, and Sprague called in William Reynolds. During the meeting, Hoyt declared that the Texas legislature authorized him to build a textile mill there if he could raise the funds. If Sprague and Reynolds would give him enough money to buy a shipload of weapons and other contraband, Hoyt would take it to Texas, sell the arms to the Confederate army, and use the proceeds to construct the mill. Mill profits would be used to buy cotton for shipment to the North. Sprague admitted that while he had thus far been unable to get a permit, he felt confident that he could eventually get one. Sprague and Reynolds agreed to finance the venture. Management of the Northern end of the business, which would become known as the Texas Adventure, would fall to Reynolds and William Sprague's cousin, Byron Sprague. Prescott went to New York to buy the necessary ships while Hoyt bought the contraband cargoes.

Although Sprague and Reynolds wrote fresh recommendations for Hoyt to use with Chase and Welles, both secretaries refused Hoyt's renewed authorization requests. As an alternative, the partners agreed that Sprague should write letters to the commander of the Union army occupying New Orleans and to the officer commanding the West Gulf Blockading Squadron. The letters Sprague wrote to Major General Benjamin Butler and Rear Admiral David Farragut commended Hoyt as a Union-loyal Texan who was returning to his home state to gather information and help other loyalists. There was no mention of cotton.[18]

The original plan was to steam into and out of Galveston. But a federal force occupied the town in October 1862, and Prescott's ships weren't ready until December. Consequently, the shipment went first to Havana and then Matamoros, Mexico, across the Rio Grande from Brownsville, Texas.

The venture supplied its backers with high-grade cotton for almost two years, until a shipment was caught by the blockade in November 1864. Although cargo ownership was disguised, English insurance records enabled investigators to trace it to Prescott, who was then living in Troy, New York. Four months earlier, Salmon Chase had resigned as Treasury secretary, but Lincoln would nominate him to be chief justice in December. On the same day Chase was nominated, Prescott gave a confession implicating Hoyt, Reynolds, and Byron Sprague. Hoyt originally hoped that Chase's court appointment would lead to his release. When it didn't, he felt betrayed and confessed everything, including Senator Sprague's involvement. Prescott independently augmented his confession to support Hoyt's version, thereby providing the two witnesses required for a treason conviction against the senator.[19]

An examination of New York customs irregularities earlier in the year disclosed that some officials colluded with selected shippers thought to be blockade runners. The top New York customs officer was Hiram Barney, who was appointed by Secretary Chase and was also a close associate of Senator Sprague's. In addition, Barney managed Chase's New York real estate and had lent him $45,000, which may have never been repaid.[20]

Also earlier in the year, Congressman Frank Blair accused Chase's Treasury Department of mismanagement that led to widespread corruption in cotton trading. From the floor of the House, Blair said "a more profligate administration of the Treasury never existed . . . the whole Mississippi valley is rank . . . with fraud and corruptions practiced there by [Chase's] agents." Blair's accusations, along with a blundering rhetorical attack on Lincoln by a small group of Chase advocates, derailed the secretary's attempt to capture the 1864 Republican presidential nomination. When he felt compelled to save face with a false public denial of any interest in the office, his son-in-law and other backers turned off the money flow that enabled him to finance his secret campaign. Sprague only slowly came to his father-in-law's defense on the Senate floor, which angered his wife and injured their already rocky marriage. Sprague could not doubt that she would be enraged by the scandal that might partially impute to Chase if the Texas Adventure became public. The average American would simply see that Sprague's textile mills prospered while her father was responsible for issuing cotton-trading permits.

But significantly, Sprague might become the first senator executed for treason.[21]

The matter was referred to Secretary of War Edwin Stanton three weeks before President Lincoln was assassinated. While Stanton took no action, it is commonly believed he declined because an inquiry would have reflected poorly on a presidential administration whose leader was martyred shortly after the secretary received the charges. Stanton may have also wanted to avoid embarrassing Chase, who had been a persistent Radical Republican ally when the two served in Lincoln's cabinet. Finally, Stanton was politically cagey. He could undoubtedly foresee advantages in having a wealthy senator obligated to him.[22]

SPRAGUE'S DILEMMA

The 1866 congressional elections gave Radical Republicans veto-proof control of the Senate and the House. Thereafter, they could disregard President Andrew Johnson's plans for reconstructing the South and impose their own. Among the bills quickly passed over the president's veto was the Tenure of Office Act. Essentially, it prevented any president from removing any executive officer appointed by a president without the approval of the Senate. It presumably followed the logic that since such officers were appointed by the advice and consent of the Senate, they should therefore not be removed without the consent of the Senate. President Johnson believed the law was unconstitutional and decided to challenge it when the Senate was not in session by replacing Secretary of War Stanton with Ulysses Grant because Stanton was liberally using the military to enforce Radical Republican policies. But Stanton refused to physically leave his office.[23]

When the Senate reconvened, it declined to accept the change and directed that Stanton be reinstated. After Johnson refused, Congress impeached him, principally for violating the Tenure of Office Act. Although the House drew up the charges, it was the Senate's responsibility to try the case. As required by the Constitution, Chief Justice Chase presided over the trial. Conviction required a two-thirds "yea" vote in the Senate. Chase privately believed the Tenure of Office Act was unconstitutional and was, therefore, not a valid justification for removing Johnson. Although his daughter may have sensed his opinion, she had another reason for favoring acquittal. If Johnson were convicted, the new president would be Ohio's senator Ben Wade, who was a habitual political enemy of Chase's. (Since there was no vice president, Wade was next in line of presidential succession because he was president pro tempore of the Senate.) On the other hand, Stanton was aware that Sprague's involvement in the Texas Adventure could convict the senator if the presently dormant case were reactivated. Since it was imprudent for Sprague to share such information with his wife, she was perplexed by his unwillingness to vote for acquittal. When the moment of truth arrived, Sprague voted for conviction. The couple had a savage quarrel, after which she left for their Rhode Island home. Johnson avoided conviction by a single vote.[24]

KATE'S CAMPAIGN

Despite sitting as the chief justice, Chase still yearned to become president when the next election year came in 1868. After Republicans nominated Ulysses S. Grant in May, it appeared that Chase would need to wait another four years to try. When the *New York Herald* hinted his ambitious daughter was encouraging him to consider the Democratic Party in a "foolish ambition" to become first lady, Chase hotly denied it. But he also wrote to a Democratic politician that if his party could accept Chase's principles, he would "not be at liberty to refuse the use of my name." As in 1864, he was not publicly a candidate, but privately he said he would accept the nomination under circumstances that made it "his duty."[25]

His daughter became his unofficial campaign manager at the July New York Democratic convention. Although she was not admitted onto the floor of Tammany Hall, she worked in private conferences and caucuses. She managed a group of young men from her Fifth Avenue Hotel suite. The main objection to Chase was his support for "universal suffrage," which would include African American males. Republicans also demanded universal suffrage in the South but reserved the question of black suffrage outside the South as a matter for the states individually. Chase tried to straddle the two positions by proclaiming universal suffrage as a basic tenet while telling the press that he thought suffrage should be awarded by the states individually. When the party platform failed to include such an ambiguity, he told friends that he did not want his name presented at the convention. Kate did not give up. She hoped for a stalemated convention that would leave the delegates "in a mood to come to us" and intended to present a letter sent from her father verifying that he would support the platform. Former New York governor Horatio Seymour chaired the convention. Although he had frustrated Republicans as governor of a powerful state during the Civil War, he flatly refused to be a presidential candidate despite many requests.[26]

Through twenty-one ballots, Kate's hopes were promising. Since Seymour was not a candidate, she had been negotiating with the New York delegation, among others, to submit her father's name. Thus far, leading candidates had been unable to win the necessary two-thirds majority. Finally, the chairman recognized an Ohio delegate. From the balcony, Kate strained to hear the man say that he "put into nomination against his inclination, but no longer against his honor, the name of Horatio Seymour." A weeping Seymour yielded as the convention stampeded him into the nomination. Kate felt betrayed. Insult was added to injury when Frank Blair was chosen as the vice presidential candidate.[27]

CLOSET SKELETON

William Sprague's Texas Adventure came out of the closet five years after the end of the Civil War, in 1870, when a Rhode Island congressman, Thomas Jenckes, sought reelection against a Sprague-backed candidate during President Grant's administration. Jenckes accused Sprague of illegally trading with the enemy during the Civil War. In response, Sprague asked for a Senate investigation to clear his name, which was launched early in 1871. Conveniently, Grant's secretary of war was the corruptible William Belknap, who later resigned for bribe taking. Suspiciously, Belknap had little interest in cooperating on the Sprague inquest. For example, he failed to locate a copy of Hoyt's full confession given years earlier to the recently deceased Stanton, which implicated the senator. Additionally, the committee did not call Jenckes as a witness until shortly before Congress adjourned, thereby leaving the congressman no time to gather corroborating witnesses who were geographically scattered. The perfunctory investigation cleared Sprague because "there was nothing in the paper[s] implicating Sprague." Unfortunately, key papers were missing, including Hoyt's confession, which Jenckes could have corroborated with witnesses.[28]

DOOM

William and Kate doomed their marriage and burdened their children through their irresponsible conduct.

It is hard to avoid concluding that Kate married William for his money. After the Civil War, America entered the Gilded Age. Selected northeastern villages, such as Saratoga, New York, Long Branch, New Jersey, and Newport, Rhode Island, were transformed into opulent resorts with luxury hotels. Caught up in the extravagance, Kate convinced William that the family should have its own mansion, which she named Canonchet after the Narragansett chief during the King Philip War. After failing to get her father nominated president in 1868, she seemed to put all her anger and energy into the mansion. Eventually it would have over sixty rooms. The house was surrounded by hundreds of acres of forest. Perhaps she believed it might one day become a summer White House. The Belden biographers provide an example of her casual disregard for William's money as well as the painstaking efforts of skilled workmen:

> As the work progressed, [Kate] hired more workmen, expanded her plans, made revisions, until the original farmhouse . . . was devoured by the relentless growth of her invention. She would give orders for a suite of rooms . . . to be done in a certain style— French provincial or Louis XIV—workmen would finish the rooms with painstaking care; furniture would be ordered and installed; Kate would step across the threshold, stare absently for a moment . . . and then abruptly turn and walk out. Calling for the foreman, she would announce that the suite was unsatisfactory, that it would all have to be done over in the style of Queen Anne.[29]

Less than three years after they married, in April 1866, she sailed for Europe with her infant son, William V; a nurse; and sister Nettie. In August the *New York World* reported, "It is reported in Providence, Rhode Island that the wife of a (not very) distinguished US Senator is about to apply for divorce." On the Senate floor, Sprague began to attack the "immoralities" of the age. Among others he condemned "Americans who travel abroad, mix and mingle in that filth and come home here to inculcate the immoralities that they have seen [abroad] upon their own society." He suspected his wife of infidelities. Whether Sprague was the father of her second child, born in 1869, "is a subject of speculation."[30]

Among her escorts to President Johnson's impeachment trial was New York senator Roscoe Conkling. She and Conkling are believed to have carried on an affair for years. The senator was a flamboyant, arrogant, and physically impressive figure. Unlike William Sprague, he eschewed alcohol and tobacco. He also had the reputation of a skilled amateur boxer. President Grant offered to appoint him chief justice, but Conkling turned it down because he had his own presidential itch. He was a prominent Republican leader during the Reconstruction era. "Although Roscoe Conkling dominated the House and Senate for almost two decades, he left practically no legacy of constructive achievement. He is remembered rather as a bitter partisan who fought civil service reform. Although he did not use public service for private gain, in an era when graft and corruption were all too common, he did work closely with the worst spoils-men in his party." Perhaps Oscar Wilde had men like Sprague and Conkling in mind when he quipped, "The husbands of the most beautiful women belong to the criminal classes."[31]

In August 1879, the Kate-Roscoe relationship became too much for William when he returned unexpectedly from a trip. Discovering the following morning at breakfast that Conkling was her house-guest, he confronted her presumed paramour with a shotgun. Pulling out his watch, he told Conkling to leave the house within thirty seconds or "I will blow your brains out." Conkling approached Kate to speak privately. "Mrs. Sprague, your husband is very much excited and I think it better for all of us if I should withdraw. If my departure puts you in any danger, say so, and I will stay, whatever the consequence." She advised him to leave. To finish with an exclamation point, William told him "if you ever cross my path again I will shoot you on sight." Three years later, the Spragues were divorced, and Conkling no longer visited her. The public might never know all the facts, but enough had been observed to conclude that two of the country's most provocative men had a vicious quarrel over a legendary beauty.[32]

For his part, Sprague went through a string of affairs and prostitutes, battling sporadically with alcoholism. Consequently, his business empire weakened until much of it was forced into bankruptcy after a multiyear economic depression gripped the nation following the Panic of 1873. Three months after his 1882 divorce, he took a vow of temperance and remarried. He died in 1916, a day before his 86th birthday. Following the divorce, his ex-wife lived in Washington in the house inherited from her father. Gradually, she could no longer afford to live extravagantly and died in meager circumstances in 1899, less than a month before her 59th birthday. Their son, William V, committed suicide in a Seattle boardinghouse in 1890 at age twenty-six. He had already been married and later divorced after discovering that his bride gave birth to a child of questionable lineage within six months of their marriage. Roscoe Conkling lost his Senate seat a few years after his confrontation with Sprague. Canonchet was destroyed by fire in 1909.[33]

CONCLUSION

Perhaps it is a mix of curiosity and *schadenfreude* that fascinates the public when celebrity lives turn tragic. By comparison to the day-to-day difficulties of nineteenth century factory workers, slaves, and farmers, William and Kate Sprague should have enjoyed rewarding lives. No doubt, ordinary Americans would have begged to switch their problems for those of the Spragues. But as Mark Twain put it, "Life does not consist mainly . . . of facts or happenings. Its consists mainly of the storm of thoughts that is forever flowing through one's head."[34] It was their misfortune that William and Kate each permitted class five tornados to become trapped inside their skulls.

SIX

THE BURNING
OF ATLANTA

When Union Major General William T. Sherman accompanied the last corps of his sixty-thousand-man army out of Atlanta on the morning of November 16, 1864, to begin their unopposed March to the Sea, which would end five weeks later in Savannah, he left behind a wrecked city. Three miles outside of town he stopped his mount on a hill near a battlefield where one of his chief subordinates and commander of the Army of the Tennessee, Major General James McPherson, had been killed nearly four months earlier. Sherman took a final look back and recalled in his memoirs, "Behind us lay Atlanta smoldering and in ruins, the black smoke rising high in the air and hanging like a pall over the ruined city." Soon a passing infantry band started playing John Brown's anthem. "Never . . . have I heard the chorus of 'Glory! Glory! Hallelujah!' done with more spirit."[1] The soldiers were proud of their accomplishments.

A little over six months earlier, they had started a campaign that culminated with the capture of Atlanta on September 2, 1864. Although suffering thirty-seven thousand casualties, they inflicted thirty-five thousand on their outnumbered opponents, who could less afford the losses. More importantly, the capture of Atlanta provided such a morale boost to the Union war effort that it virtually assured the reelection of President Lincoln. However, the soldiers' most recent achievements were questionable. Beginning in

September, they forcibly removed almost all of Atlanta's residents, although most had no destinations where shelter would be available. In November, Sherman's men burned Atlanta and several north Georgia towns, thereby compelling further civilian removal and suffering in the region.[2]

Estimates of the damage left behind vary widely. Captain Orlando Poe, whom Sherman ordered to supervise the sanctioned demolition, estimated that 37 percent of the city was destroyed. However, structures beyond the officially designated targets became unofficial victims. An Indiana soldier's diary simply records, "We have utterly destroyed Atlanta." After Sherman left, Georgia's governor sent a militia officer to prepare an assessment. The man spent four days methodically walking throughout the town. Eventually he prepared a map of every house left standing, because it was easier than mapping those that were destroyed. Within a half mile radius of downtown, only four hundred homes remained where there were once three thousand six hundred. The officer then extrapolated beyond his circle to the previously less densely populated areas, where even fewer structures remained. He concluded that four thousand to five thousand homes were in ruins, thereby implying that over 90 percent of the city was destroyed.[3]

Residents who returned after Sherman left were shocked. At least seven eyewitnesses recorded their impressions. One was a former Confederate cavalryman named Zachariah Rice, who returned just four days after the federals left. Among his observations was that "most all of the residences in the city have been burned that were unoccupied." Since nearly all residents were compelled to evacuate in September, Rice's comment implies that most homes were destroyed. Similarly, civilian James Crew returned about two weeks after the Union soldiers left. He was among an earlier delegation that unsuccessfully asked General Sherman to rescind his September evacuation order. Crew wrote to his wife on December 1, "At least two-thirds [of the city] has been destroyed." A reporter for the *Augusta Chronicle & Sentinel* wrote on December 15, "about three fourths of the buildings have been torn down or burned and about nine-tenths of the property value destroyed." Whatever estimate one chooses, the differences to city residents were mere gradations of hell.[4]

PRIOR DAMAGE

Popular understanding of the burning of Atlanta suffers from misconceptions. The spectacular scene in the film *Gone with the Wind* mistakenly portrays the principal conflagration as occurring when the Confederates abandoned the city on September 1. It is true that they destroyed selective parts of the town when they left. Once Sherman cut the last of the railroads converging on Atlanta, Confederate Lieutenant General John B. Hood felt compelled to preserve his army and evacuate with as many supplies as possible. It was a better option than staying behind, where he would eventually be surrounded and forced to surrender, similar to the fate of the Rebels at Vicksburg about a year earlier.

Consequently, Hood resolved to leave nothing of military value behind that could be used by the Union armies. Most significant among such items was the army's supply train. It consisted of five engines and eighty-one cars idling on double tracks near the eastern edge of town. Although most boxcars contained food and medical supplies, nearly thirty were loaded with munitions. When it was set on fire, the train probably created the largest explosion of the Civil War. The booms could be heard for thirty miles around. According to author Russell Bonds, "The inferno was so tremendous that it would cause the common misconception that it was the Confederates, and not Sherman, who had burned Atlanta in 1864." Fortunately, inhabitants living close to the train had been ordered away because every building for a quarter mile around it was torn up or perforated with hundreds of holes. Among the facilities destroyed were the Atlanta Rolling Mill, railroad roundhouse, arsenal shops, and a cannon factory.[5]

However, aside from military assets, the Confederate evacuation was responsible for comparatively little damage. Although explosions continued into the middle of the night, once the approved targets were demolished, a group of officers joining the retreat described the city as "dark and silent as a grave." Rebel guards posted to keep order spent a lonely and dismal night, not knowing when they should leave to avoid capture by the expected triumphant Union army. The city's remaining ten thousand residents came out the next morning bleary-eyed and dazed.[6]

After convincing a Georgia militia contingent to abandon the city, Mayor James Calhoun assembled a group of unarmed citizens,

The remains of the reserve ordnance train that was blown up on Hood's orders as the Confederate forces abandoned Atlanta. (*National Archives*)

including a black man who may have been the son of Daniel Webster, to find the nearest federal army unit and formally surrender the city. He wanted to convince the Yankees they could occupy Atlanta peaceably. Two miles outside the ramparts they found a troop commanded by an Indiana captain named Henry Scott, whom they led back into town. After a few hidden Rebels took some potshots at Scott's men, Mayor Calhoun rode ahead, where he found the stragglers and demanded that they stop shooting. When the laggards threatened to shoot the mayor, federal troops came forward and took them prisoners. It was the last confrontation of the Atlanta Campaign.

Shortly thereafter, Union soldiers hoisted regimental flags over City Hall. Within a few hours, Union Major General Henry Slocum's 20th Corps occupied the town. After the soldiers broke ranks, they began looting downtown shops and were promptly joined by local citizens and ex-slaves. Some of the soldiers also plundered homes, including those of prosperous African Americans. One victim was Robert Webster, who earlier accompanied the mayor when the civic leaders surrendered Atlanta to Captain Scott. When another black victim came to his house to commiserate, Webster lamented, "My Lord, I thought they had come here to protect us, but they have taken everything I have got."[7]

Prior to Hood's evacuation, parts of Atlanta were damaged when the town was besieged from July 20 to August 31 by two factors.

One was a combination of the military trenches set up by the opposing armies. Some outlying structures were destroyed to provide clear fields of fire and for materials to build troop entrenchments. Some homes were smashed during battlefield engagements or because they were nests for snipers of either side. Shortly after the federals' victorious occupation, historian Marc Wortman writes, "Tens of thousands . . . [of Union soldiers] built comfortable camp homes for themselves. They took planks off house and barn walls and pulled up fences to erect siding and lay floors."8

The second factor was Sherman's indiscriminate five-week bombardment of the city, which started July 20. He gave Atlanta's civilians no warning and deliberately fired into the city, as opposed to its military defenders. Although there were Civil War precedents for excluding an advance warning to enable noncombatants to leave, it is difficult to justify Sherman's omission. Given the protracted length of the cannonade, a twenty-four-hour delay would have been inconsequential from a military perspective. The day after the bombardment began, Sherman wired Chief of Staff Henry Halleck in Washington, "The city seems to have a line around it at an average distance to the center of town of about one and a half miles, but our shot passing over this line will destroy the town."

Moreover, Sherman was aware that women and children would likely be among the victims. On the third day of the shelling, his chief telegrapher wired Washington at eleven o'clock that night, "as I write our heavy artillery is at work, and large fires are burning in Atlanta." Earlier the same day, one Union artillerist wrote his wife that a "great many women and children" had entered the city as refugees from nearby areas. Owing to the presence of noncombatants, he hoped the Rebel soldiers would abandon Atlanta so that the cannon barrage could be discontinued.9

Initially civilians reacted with panic and terror. In the first few days many overwhelmed the railroad station trying to get out of town, overburdened with luggage. The first deaths probably happened within three days. Newspapers and personal letters began reporting civilian killings within a week and a half, although it is difficult to separate genuine incidents from hearsay. Nonetheless, some women and children were undeniably among the victims. After a few weeks the residents grew accustomed to the cannonade and moved about cautiously but openly. They lived in their base-

The Atlanta railroad depot, the "Car Shed," left, before its destruction, and its ruins, right. (*Library of Congress*)

ments or built shelters by digging holes in their yards covered with timbers upon which they threw three to five feet of dirt.[10]

On August 7, Sherman sought to intensify the bombardment when he telegraphed Halleck, "I have sent to Chattanooga for two thirty-pounder Parrotts [rifled cannon] with which we can pick out most any house in town. . . . One thing is certain, whether we get into Atlanta, or not, it will be a used-up community by the time we are done with it." Instead of the two Parrotts he received four siege guns of about the same caliber. They could hurl their heavy projectiles almost two miles. On August 9, the general intensified his cannonade and wired Halleck, "I threw into Atlanta about 3,000 solid shot and shell today." Brigadier General John Geary wrote his wife that the cannonade involved one hundred guns, saying, "I cannot tell how many lives were lost but the casualties among the enemy must have been numerous." It was the heaviest day of shelling during the entire siege. Less than a week later, Geary wrote his wife that fires were a nightly occurrence in the city.[11]

In order to promote such eruptions, Union artillerists experimented with incendiary shells. Some batteries kept nearby furnaces stoked so solid shot projectiles could be heated to a temperature at which they would start fires in wooden structures after impact. One officer declared the technique a "perfect success." His lookouts told him, "Large fires were visible in the city every night the hot shot was used."

As Sherman intensified the shelling, he pretended to believe there were no civilians in the city. Although normally complimentary of Sherman, historian Marc Wortman writes:

> A week and a half after General Sherman ordered the siege shelling to begin, he mentioned to Major General George Thomas, "the inhabitants have, of course, got out." He was being disingenuous. He almost certainly knew that thousands of civilians remained trapped in the city limits. Three days later, on August 13, a Union Colonel sent a report saying that one of his officers "could distinctly hear loud cries from women and children."[12]

During the five-week cannonade, historian Stephen Davis concludes, Sherman's artillery fired more than one hundred thousand projectiles into Atlanta, thereby dropping five hundred tons of Northern iron into the city. He estimates that a couple of dozen civilians were killed and scores more wounded. Finally he concludes, "Despite the intermittent intensity, and month-long duration of Sherman's artillery bombardment, one must conclude that the shelling produced no strategic benefit for Federal forces. . . . At its end, Atlanta had fallen, but the Yankees' artillery shelling of [the] city had contributed nothing to their victory."[13]

Northern newspapers sometimes sanitized the bombardment. A reporter for a Cincinnati newspaper erroneously reported two weeks after it started, "The city is now almost evacuated and scarcely a family remains." Others carefully phrased their reports to suggest doubt about the effects of the bombardment. For example, a *New York Times* correspondent wrote "the whole heavens were illuminated last night in the direction of Atlanta, and a large fire, *it is supposed*, must have been raging." (Italics added).[14]

SHERMAN'S CONFLAGRATION

Although Sherman never ordered a wholesale burning of Atlanta, the arson accompanying his army's two-day departure that started on November 15 is only superficially inconsistent with his official orders. Initially the general turned to Colonel William Cogswell, who was earlier designated Atlanta post commander, to organize a plan to destroy everything that might be militarily valuable once the federals left. Since the plan that was drawn up in October was never

The ruins of Atlanta. (*Harper's Weekly*)

signed, the author remains unknown. However, it included a detailed map that marked the structures to be destroyed. No private residences were among those marked. But at the behest of his quartermaster and commissary officers, on November 7 Sherman shifted responsibility for executing the plan from Cogswell to Captain Poe in order to prevent "irregularities." It was reasoned that Poe and his engineers would be less reliant upon explosives and fire as destructive tools. Yet six days earlier, when Poe received a hint of Cogswell's plan, he wrote his superior engineering officer in Washington that by the time his letter arrived "Atlanta will have ceased to exist."[15]

The cause of the mass destruction that followed Cogswell's plan was Sherman's acquiescence to widespread disobedience among rank-and-file soldiers. During the preceding two years or so, the general's hostility toward Southern civilians gradually escalated to the point of infecting his soldiers' attitudes.

It began when he was post commander at Memphis in summer 1862. Since he presumed that local guerrillas were responsible for taking potshots at Mississippi River cargo boats, he ordered that ten citizens be forcibly removed from the city for every incident along the river. When such an instance occurred in Randolph, Tennessee, in September 1862, he destroyed the town. He left only one house to mark its place.

Shortly after the fall of Vicksburg, Major General Grant sent Sherman to Mississippi's state capital at Jackson to annihilate everything of military value. But some of his soldiers went on a riot of demolition, informally naming the city "Chimneyville" when they left because brick chimneys were virtually the only structures left standing. Although Sherman blamed Confederates for setting some of the fires, an Illinois captain wrote in his diary, "During the day some of our men . . . after pillaging the place set fire to a great many buildings, some of which were very fine. . . . I never saw or heard of a city being so thoroughly sacked and burned as [Jackson]."[16]

More pertinent to Atlanta's story was the momentum that grew from the ruin of several towns in north Georgia in the days before Sherman's departure for his March to the Sea. One of the first victims was Cassville, about fifty miles north of Atlanta, which the general characteristically accused of harboring guerrillas. On the afternoon of November 5, residents were given only twenty minutes to evacuate the community. Within moments, "the Public Square was one vast sheet of flames [that] spread all over town" leaving nothing but chimneys.[17]

Five days later, the manufacturing town of Rome was razed. Although industrial facilities were targeted, the fire spread. A livery caught fire, filling the air with terrified animal cries and the smell of burning horseflesh. Eventually, only isolated buildings remained standing. The next day Sherman wired Major General George Thomas in Nashville, "Last night we burned Rome and in two or more days will burn Atlanta."

The next target was the railroad connecting Atlanta to Chattanooga, which had been Sherman's supply line throughout the Atlanta Campaign. Since his departure for Savannah meant he would no longer need it, the general decided to destroy miles of the line after the last train left Atlanta for the North on November 12. The following day the rail town of Marietta, within twenty miles of Atlanta, was wrecked. One lady confronting the incendiary soldiers was shocked at their youth. They reminded her of mischievous schoolboys, except they held torches. Rebuking a group, she asked if they liked burning houses. One answered, "whether we like it or not, we must obey orders." When the soldiers left Marietta, their band played "Hail, Columbia."

Major Henry Hitchcock joined Sherman's staff when the village was being burned. Young Hitchcock won the appointment partly as a result of the influence of his father, Major General Ethan Allen Hitchcock, who had been a special military adviser to Lincoln for a time. Once Marietta shops and homes got caught up in the blaze, some soldiers tried briefly, but futilely, to stop the spread. Major Hitchcock commented to Sherman:

"[The town will] burn down, sir."

"Yes," said Sherman. "Can't be stopped."

"Was that your intention?"

The general answered indirectly, "Can't save it. . . . There are men who do this," motioning to a nearby group of soldiers. "Set as many guards as you please, they will slip in and set fire."[18]

For days before the November 15 March to the Sea departure date, the scattered parts of Sherman's army north of Atlanta converged on the city, destroying railroad track and communities as they approached. By the time they arrived at the gates of the city, demolition had become customary. Wisconsin Corporal Harvey Reid wrote, "I don't believe that Sherman contemplates burning anything but public buildings, but it is very evident that acts of vandalism will be winked at. . . . [T]here are plenty who will not be slow to avail themselves of such tacit license." A few days later Reid wrote, "many soldiers set fire to the houses they had been occupying as they left them."

General Slocum, whose troops occupied Atlanta, tried to protect residential dwellings. But the provost guards under Colonel Cogswell were concentrated downtown, where Sherman would be quartered the night of the biggest conflagration. The first unauthorized fires started on November 11 near the edge of town. While some federal soldiers were ordered to extinguish the flames, they had little success. The next morning Slocum offered a $500 reward for the identity of the arsonists, but it was never collected. On November 13, when an Illinois captain marched into Atlanta with his unit, he recalled "the smoke almost blinded us." Similarly, a Connecticut captain wrote "for three days the fires have been raging like a furnace . . . and . . . have spread considerably among the residences, there being no effort to save or destroy them."

November 15 was the day of the incendiary holocaust. A doctor for the 7th Illinois Regiment who marched into town later wrote,

"Many houses had been burned and all day long the fires kept increasing in number." An Ohio captain recorded, "no sooner did we arrive than the boys commenced burning every house in [the northwestern] part of town . . . [and] . . . soon that part of the city was gone." By three o'clock in the afternoon, officers who had been distributing supplies at the commissary told soldiers to just take whatever they needed because the out-of-control fires would inevitably consume the facility. Colonel Cogswell conceded that it was hard for his guards to prevent arson in such an environment. Even Captain Poe admitted "many buildings . . . were destroyed by lawless persons." Despite his word choice there can be little doubt that the "persons" were Union soldiers because nearly all civilians had been evacuated.[19]

Most of the few remaining civilians were Union-loyal families or people connected to such families. One of Poe's sergeants from a Michigan regiment admitted to getting caught up in the enthusiasm for arson even though he knew it was officially prohibited. By the sergeant's own admission, "As I was about to fire one place a little girl about ten years old came to me and said, 'Mr. Soldier you would not burn our house would you? If you did where would we live?' She looked at me with such a pleading look that . . . I dropped the torch and walked away."[20]

Another lingering citizen was nine-year-old Carrie Berry, whose November 16 diary entry stated:

> Oh what a night we had . . . it looked like the whole town was on fire. We . . . set up all night. If we had not . . . our house would have been burnt up for . . . the soldiers were going around setting houses on fire where they were not watched. They behaved very badly.[21]

Even before the smoke cleared, Sherman's soldiers began reflecting upon what they had done. The absence of Confederate troops and the earlier forced evacuation of nearly all civilians denied Sherman the opportunity to blame the enemy as he would later do when Columbia, South Carolina, was reduced to ashes.[22]

Starting with the commanding general, many later justified their actions as military necessity. During the general's last night in the city, as the fire raged on November 15, Major Hitchcock overhead Sherman remark that Atlanta merited destruction because of its

Map from *War Like the Thunderbolt: The Battle and Burning of Atlanta* by Russell S. Bonds.

manufacturing capacity for instruments of war. "[The] city has done . . . more to carry on and sustain the war than any other save, perhaps, Richmond. We have been fighting *Atlanta* all the time . . . capturing guns, wagons, and etc. marked *Atlanta*." The same night a Union sergeant recorded, "the entire city was destroyed [but] for a few occupied houses. It reminds me of the [biblical] destruction of Babylon . . . because of the wickedness of her people." A New York captain's memoirs recalled Atlanta's destruction as "a military necessity and richly deserved."[23]

Others erroneously minimized the amount of damage. Sherman again provided an example in his memoirs, where he wrote little about the November burning beyond falsely claiming "the fire did not reach . . . the great mass of dwelling houses." But after arriving in Savannah following his March to the Sea, he congratulated his troops on their completed 1864 campaign in a field order. Among the accomplishments he itemized was that "we quietly and deliberately destroyed Atlanta."

Initially shocked by the destruction of Marietta, Major Hitchcock sensed that Sherman might be criticized for waging war on civilians later. As a result, the inexperienced officer was transformed into a defender of his ascendant commander. After the two watched the November 15 inferno together, Hitchcock recorded, "General Sherman will hereafter be charged with indiscriminate burning, which is not true . . . only such buildings as are . . . useful for war purposes" were ordered to be destroyed, speciously adding that "no dwelling was touched."[24]

Still others admitted the reality of the officially prohibited destruction but incorrectly claimed it was accidental or resulted from impersonal factors. Some claimed the fires were spread by the wind. Others alleged that many soldiers became inebriated after discovering hidden supplies of liquor. Still others reasoned more accurately that the destructive march through towns north of Atlanta habituated the soldiers to undisciplined demolition, which the troops presumed was to continue upon arriving in the city. A *New York Herald* reporter mentioned high winds. A New York captain wrote that the fire "was not intended to injure private residences, yet many were destroyed by fires ignited by flying sparks."[25]

Probably the most widely accepted justification was that war is an exercise that cannot be controlled, implying that cruelties are inevitable. Such an interpretation appeals to the perpetrators who are thereby exonerated. General Sherman set the tone when he responded to the city council's petition to rescind his early September order requiring nearly all civilians to evacuate:

> [I] shall not revoke my orders because they were not designed for the humanities of the case. . . . War is cruelty, and you cannot refine it; and those who brought war into our country deserve all the curses and maledictions a people can pour out. . . . You might as well appeal against the thunderstorm as against these terrible hardships of war. They are inevitable, and the only way the people of Atlanta can hope to live in peace . . . is to stop the war. . . . Now you must go and take with you the old and feeble . . . and build for them . . . proper habitations to shield them against the [approaching winter] weather.[26]

However, some Union soldiers were not satisfied with the various excuses. One lieutenant wrote "such wholesale destruction will load us with merited disgrace and infamy. Let the railroads be destroyed . . . and the warehouses and arsenals, but touch not private property . . . and most of all private dwellings." A Wisconsin private's diary records:

> I believe this destruction of private property in Atlanta was entirely unnecessary and therefore . . . disgraceful. . . . The cruelties practiced on this campaign toward citizens have been enough to blast a more sacred cause than ours. . . . It is not that indiscriminate destruction of private property is ordered—quite the contrary. A guard is placed at every house we pass . . . but he remains only while his division is passing—then come the . . . stragglers and they . . . ransack the house. . . . I have never heard, however, of personal violence being offered to any citizen, but they are insulted in every other way. . . . There certainly is a lack of discipline and . . . many of our soldiers seem to think that a rebel is without . . . humanity and the greater the indignity offered them the more meritorious the action.[27]

CONCLUSION

Partly because most of the source documents about Sherman's burning of Atlanta are the official records of the Union armies, the letters and diaries of Union sympathizers and soldiers, and the reports in

Northern newspapers and magazines, the story is often distorted. No Confederate units were present to file official reports during the November 1864 inferno.

To understand what happened in Atlanta after Confederate Lieutenant General Hood's army left on September 2, 1864, historians must look to other primary sources. Among them are Georgia state documents; civilian memoirs, diaries, and letters; as well as Southern newspapers. Though the approximately fifty families remaining in Atlanta by November were mostly Union sympathizers, even their words tell a different version than the records of Union soldiers and Northern newspaper reporters. While such documents are invaluable sources, it must be recognized that many are also inclined to report hearsay as well as hard facts. It can be difficult to discern truth from fiction in order to extract a coherent narrative.

In time, federal soldiers had little wish to write about the events around Atlanta and north Georgia from November 5 to 16, 1864, because there was little to inspire pride. Cassville was burned on the first date, and Sherman left a smoldering Atlanta behind on the second. During the interval, towns such as Rome, Big Shanty (present-day Kennesaw), Marietta, and others were torched. Sherman wrote almost nothing about Atlanta's November 15–16 blaze in his memoirs beyond telling the whopper that "the great majority of dwellings" were spared. Contemporary Northern newspapers also sometimes misrepresented the facts.

Although Sherman never officially ordered an indiscriminate burning of Atlanta, during the interval from Cassville to the departure for Savannah, he did little to stop many of his increasingly undisciplined soldiers from escalating targeted destruction into a riot of arson. It is difficult to avoid concluding he arranged matters so he could deny responsibility if Atlanta's destruction became morally condemned but accept credit if it was to be celebrated.

7

CHOOSING
SHERMAN OR THOMAS

A hundred fifty years after the Civil War, the most celebrated Union commanders are Generals Ulysses Grant and William T. Sherman. They fought together in the war's first epic battle at Shiloh in April 1862. By the time of Grant's triumph at Vicksburg in July 1863, Sherman was his principal subordinate. They were again together at the spectacular Union victory at Chattanooga in November 1863. When Grant was transferred to Washington to become general in chief in March 1864, and to lead the eastern armies against General Robert E. Lee's Virginia Confederates, he selected Sherman to take charge of the major federal armies in the western theater. Although Grant and Lee were stalemated at Petersburg, Virginia, by summer 1864, Sherman captured Atlanta toward the end of the summer, thereby virtually assuring the reelection of President Lincoln—and a continuation of the war.

After the war, Grant leveraged his military reputation to be twice elected president. During his first term he appointed Sherman as commanding general of the US Army. Aside from Grant, Sherman ultimately became the most admired of all Civil War Union generals. Historians came to rely upon the memoirs of both generals as authoritative first-person accounts. Moreover, as Grant's reputation improved over the past half-century, contemporary historians have likewise elevated Sherman's like a boat rising on Grant's flood tide.

Nonetheless, there are reasons to believe that the reputations of both generals have become too inflated among early twenty-first-century historians.[1]

SHERMAN'S ACCOMPLISHMENTS

In some respects, Sherman's spring 1864 offensive was more impressive than Grant's. Both began with numerical superiority over their opponents. Sherman had one hundred thousand soldiers compared to sixty-two thousand for the enemy army under General Joseph E. Johnston, whereas Grant had almost one hundred twenty thousand to oppose Lee's sixty-four thousand. Four months after starting their respective campaigns, Sherman had captured Atlanta, whereas Grant was in the early stages of a lengthy standoff with Lee at the siege of Petersburg. Moreover, Sherman had inflicted thirty-five thousand casualties at a cost of thirty-seven thousand, whereas Grant had suffered losses of sixty-five thousand compared to thirty-five thousand for Lee. Seven weeks after he started, Grant's losses in the Army of the Potomac totaled about 60 percent of the army's losses in the preceding three years (156 weeks).[2]

Sherman's losses were lighter than Grant's because he was less prone to attack than was Grant, and Johnston was less pugnacious than Lee. Johnston tried to force Sherman to assault him in entrenched positions. However, with some exceptions, for two and a half months Sherman repeatedly maneuvered Johnston out of such defenses until Johnston's withdrawals brought his Army of Tennessee into the vicinity of Atlanta. Richmond authorities must have wondered whether the tight-lipped Johnston would continue his Fabian defense until reaching Key West. Confederate president Jefferson Davis could endure no more. On July 17, he replaced Johnston with Lieutenant General John Hood, who had earlier been a hard-hitting division commander in Lee's aggressive Army of Northern Virginia. Davis correctly expected assertive action from Hood but also cautioned the thirty-three-year-old commander, "Be wary no less than bold."[3]

During the next six weeks, Sherman's army group repelled a number of vigorous attacks by Hood. The first was on July 20 at Peachtree Creek, where Rebel losses totaled two thousand five hundred compared to one thousand nine hundred for the Union. The second was two days later east of Atlanta and is increasingly referred to as the Battle of Bald Hill, where Hood lost five thousand five hundred compared to three thousand seven hundred for Sherman. Less than a week later, Hood suffered three thousand casualties while the federals endured less than seven hundred at the Battle of Ezra Church on July 28. The final assault was at Jonesboro, where Hood attempted to keep Sherman from cutting the last railroad line into Atlanta because it would force the Confederates to evacuate the city. Hood's August 31 attack failed and resulted in losses of about two thousand two hundred compared to less than two hundred federals. Consequently, following Union attacks at Jonesboro on September 1, he was forced to abandon Atlanta, and Sherman occupied the city on September 2.[4]

General William T. Sherman.
(*Library of Congress*)

Given such an accounting, it may seem unfair to criticize Sherman. But he failed in his chief mission, which was to destroy the opposing army. Grant understood, as did Hood, that enemy armies were the principal objectives. It was unlikely that the North could win as long as Rebel armies sustained organized resistance. Similarly, lengthening the casualty lists were the most likely way to motivate the North to abandon the war effort. Thus, each was inclined to attack aggressively. Although Grant was strategically more successful than Hood, both suffered disproportionately high losses. Grant could afford them, whereas Hood could not. Given such objectives, Grant might have made a better choice in the western theater by selecting one of Sherman's subordinates, Major General George "Rock of Chickamauga" Thomas, to lead the spring offensive in Georgia.

Sherman's command, termed the Military Division of the Mississippi, consisted of three armies. The largest was the Army of the Cumberland, commanded by Thomas. The second biggest was the Army of the Tennessee, which Sherman led until he was put in charge of the three army group. Upon his promotion, he placed Major General James McPherson in charge of that army. The smallest, actually a single corps, was the Army of the Ohio, led by Major General John Schofield. General Johnston's opposing army had three corps initially under Lieutenant Generals Hood, Leonidas Polk, and William Hardee.[5]

THOMAS'S RECORD

General Thomas had a commendable record. He won the Yankees their first meaningful land battle back in January 1862 at Mill Springs, Kentucky. It provided the first evidence since the Bull Run debacle six months earlier that federal troops could beat Rebels in toe-to-toe combat. Although the Confederates planned a surprise attack, as author Shelby Foote explains, "They were launching a surprise attack against a man who could not be surprised; whose emotional make-up apparently excluded that kind of reaction to any event. Imperturbable, phlegmatic, his calm was . . . unruffled in a crisis."[6]

A year later at the Battle of Stones River, Thomas again demonstrated a steadying influence that helped the Union army sustain a victory. It was a three-day engagement, and the Confederates won the better part of the first day. That night an uncertain Major General William S. Rosecrans, who then commanded the Army of the Cumberland, polled his subordinates about whether the army should retreat. Those with civilian backgrounds advised withdrawal. Thomas was the first regular army officer to respond otherwise. Upon slamming his hand on a table, he said, "This army does not retreat," and reportedly added, "I know no better place to die." Two days later the Confederates retreated.[7]

During the second largest Civil War battle, at Chickamauga in September 1863, Thomas is credited with saving Rosecrans's army from near annihilation. When a division commander in another corps left a hole in the Union defense line because of a confusing order, Confederates poured through the resultant gap in such numbers that the entire right (south) wing of the Union army was routed. By holding his ground on the left, Thomas provided the cover that permitted the disorganized Union soldiers to escape and regroup in Chattanooga. Upon learning of the details, President Lincoln said, "It is doubtful that [Thomas's] heroism and skill . . . has ever been surpassed."[8]

When Grant was summoned to Chattanooga to take command of the Chickamauga survivors, he removed Rosecrans as head of the Army of the Cumberland and replaced him with Thomas. However,

Grant had a low opinion of Thomas's army and was inclined to use reinforcements brought in from other areas when he was ready to attack the besieging Rebel army. From the east came two corps under Major General Joseph Hooker, who was under a cloud for his defeat by Robert E. Lee five months earlier at Chancellorsville. From the west came Grant's trusted subordinate, Sherman, and the Army of the Tennessee, which Grant had commanded until his present position.[9]

General George H. Thomas.
(*Library of Congress*)

Grant intended that the battle be won by a Sherman-led attack on the north flank of the elevated Confederate defenses on Missionary Ridge. Despite a four-to-one numerical advantage, over seven hours of attacks, Sherman had no success. Finally, Grant ordered Thomas's troops to take the lightly defended rifle pits at the foot of the enemy's main defense line in hopes of diverting Rebel attention away from Sherman. Since their resultant position was untenable because of Confederate fire from above, Thomas's troops spontaneously continued up the ridge to assault the Confederate center, and, with the aid of Hooker who advanced on the Rebel south flank, won the day for Grant.[10]

Grant's low opinion of Thomas is unfortunate, because there is good reason to believe that the latter would have done a better job of leading the 1864 western federal offensive than Sherman. Alluding to Sherman's disregard for a plan to cut off Johnston's retreat path recognized by Thomas at the start of the campaign, military expert Thomas Buell wrote, "The Atlanta Campaign . . . would have ended in a week if Sherman had listened to Thomas."[11] Similarly, historian Albert Castel concluded:

> Again and again from Dalton to Lovejoy's Station [Sherman] overlooked . . . and rejected opportunities to crush or fatally cripple Confederate forces in Georgia, or at least drive them from the state. . . . Had Thomas's personal relationship with Grant permitted him to command in Georgia in 1864, almost surely the Union victory would have been easier, quicker, and more complete.[12]

Before he was sent east to become general in chief in March, Grant wanted to start a winter offensive in the west. Sherman volunteered to lead a raid in the Mississippi Valley with the objective of destroying Confederate cavalry under Major General Nathan Forrest and capturing Mobile, Alabama, if possible. He accomplished little except for burning the Mississippi town of Meridian and destroying railroad track.[13]

SNAKE CREEK GAP

Meanwhile Grant, who was headquartered in Nashville, was trying to force Thomas to react to ghosts. Grant responded to bogus reports that Confederate Lieutenant General James Longstreet was receiving reinforcements from Lee's Virginia army and Johnston's Georgia army in preparation to launch an offensive in east Tennessee. Since he incorrectly reasoned that Johnston was left with only a small force in front of Thomas at Chattanooga, he ordered Thomas to send reinforcements to Knoxville in east Tennessee and launch a forced reconnaissance toward Johnston's position only thirty miles away. Thomas's advance disclosed that all of Grant's assumptions were wrong, but it also enabled him to discover a weakness in Johnston's deployment.

Specifically, Johnston was entrenched at Dalton, Georgia, anticipating an attack from Chattanooga, thirty miles to the northwest. Thomas had discovered an undefended passage through the mountains called Snake Creek Gap that debouched fifteen miles south of Dalton. If a strong federal force were to march through the gap it could cut Johnston's railroad supply line to Atlanta and also attack him from the south as other federal units held his attention to the north by attacking from that direction. Essentially, the undefended gap would enable Johnston to be attacked simultaneously from front and rear with only improbable escape paths available.[14]

After assuming command of the western offensive in March, Sherman met with Thomas, who explained the situation at Snake Creek Gap. Specifically, Thomas proposed that his army march through the gap and attack Johnston from the rear while McPherson and Schofield pinned Johnston at Dalton. Sherman rejected the plan and instead decided to advance his army group on a broad front. He envisioned that the Army of the Cumberland would pin Johnston at Dalton while McPherson and Schofield would flank the enemy west

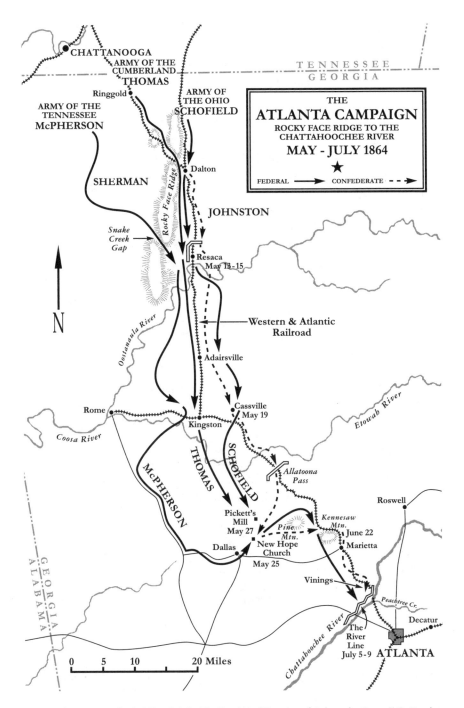

Map from *War Like the Thunderbolt: The Battle and Burning of Atlanta* by Russell S. Bonds.

and east respectively. He would not begin until early May, because he first had to build a supply base at Chattanooga. To speed things along, he forbade the issuance of rations to destitute citizens no matter how desperate their needs and despite complaints from Washington.[15]

When he finally made his move, Sherman half listened to Thomas. He sent McPherson through Snake Creek Gap but gave the subordinate discretionary orders. Essentially he directed that McPherson cut Johnston's railroad supply line but only attack Johnston if the latter attempted to retreat south. It fell short of Thomas's proposal because McPherson's force was only about a third the size of Thomas's army and lacked the cavalry Thomas recommended. As it happened, McPherson approached the railroad through the gap with twenty thousand men on May 9, but failed to cut the line, or get into a position to ambush a potentially retreating Johnston. He did not realize his numerical advantage was greater than two to one over Rebels at nearby Resaca available to defend the railroad. Since he had no cavalry for reconnaissance, his column stopped frequently to get reports back from infantry scouts.[16]

Although Sherman was dismayed that McPherson accomplished almost nothing, Thomas felt there was still time to take advantage of the situation. Since Johnston had not withdrawn from Dalton, he suggested that Hooker's 20th Corps reinforce McPherson and together they could seize Resaca. This time Sherman took the advice and sent nearly his entire army group, except a single corps of Thomas's army, through Snake Creek Gap. Unfortunately, they marched so slowly that by the time they got to Resaca on May 13, it was clear that Johnston finally understood the danger because the town was heavily defended, initially with troops that had been fortuitously arriving from Mississippi.[17]

Although Sherman's first opportunity to win a decisive victory vanished, he was quickly presented with a second chance thanks to Thomas's chief cartographer, William Merrill, who was the top graduate of his 1859 West Point class. Among the wonders worked by Thomas's pioneer (engineering) battalions was an abundant supply of pontoon bridging equipment. When the general earlier asked Merrill if he could devise a way to move pontoons more conveniently, Merrill improvised with floats that could fold in half. During the Resaca maneuvers, enough pontoons reached the area for a bridge to be built across the Oostanaula River at Lays Ferry, downstream from Resaca. Instead of using the bridge as a fresh pathway to attack Johnston at Resaca with a sizable force from the rear, Sherman planned to use it merely to attack the Rebel general should he decide to withdraw of his own volition. Sherman put only a modest force across the river at Lays Ferry and concentrated most of his troops on attacking Johnston at Resaca, where he suffered casualties of four thousand while inflicting losses of three thousand.[18]

Sherman put all the blame on McPherson for failing to leverage the march through Snake Creek Gap into a triumphant victory. In his memoirs Sherman wrote:

> [McPherson] had on hand twenty-three thousand of the best men of the army, and could have walked into Resaca, . . . or he could have placed his whole force across the railroad above Resaca, and there easily withstood the attack of all of Johnston's army. [Such action would have forced Johnston to try to escape eastward, where Sherman's army would] have captured half of [Johnston's] army and all of his artillery and wagons. . . . Such an opportunity does not occur twice in a single life, but at the critical moment McPherson seems to have been a little cautious.[19]

Sherman did not mention two reasons that McPherson failed to capture Resaca or block Johnston's anticipated retreat.

First, Sherman's orders to McPherson did not direct that the subordinate do either of those things. Second, Sherman rejected Thomas's proposal to send a much stronger force through Snake Creek Gap that could have more readily accomplished the objectives that Sherman's memoirs imagine that he (Sherman) ordered. When McPherson approached Resaca, his available force was down to about twelve thousand because he detached the rest to protect his rear and its trailing wagon train. Historian Albert Castel concludes, "Sherman's account of . . . Snake Creek Gap . . . is nothing more than an attempt to shift the responsibility for its failure to achieve what it . . . should have onto McPherson, who was not alive to defend his conduct . . . having been killed at the Battle of Atlanta [Bald Hill] on July 22, 1864."[20]

Second, Sherman's memoirs falsely suggest that he conceived the Snake Creek Gap strategy and fail to discuss his initial plan that would likely have put McPherson's army in great danger. As noted, the Snake Creek Gap idea originated with Thomas, who recommended that the force be larger and include cavalry. Additionally, Sherman originally planned to use McPherson's army in a wider flanking movement by sending it to Rome, Georgia, which was farther to the southwest. He abandoned the Rome maneuver only upon learning that the reinforcements he was expecting to add to McPherson's army would not arrive in time because they had been delayed in Louisiana's unproductive Red River Campaign, where they were on temporary loan to Major General Nathaniel Banks. Furthermore, owing to his difficulties in Louisiana, Banks discarded a plan to march on Mobile, Alabama, thereby freeing up Confederate troops in Mississippi under General Leonidas Polk to join Johnston. Polk's probable line of march would leave McPherson's isolated presence at Rome vulnerable to attack from the arriving Mississippi Rebels.[21]

NEW HOPE CHURCH AND PICKETT'S MILL

When Johnston decided to withdraw from Resaca on May 16, his army was about sixty-five miles north of Atlanta, with only the Etowah and Chattahoochee rivers remaining as natural barriers between the Yankees and Atlanta. The railroad bridge across the first river at Etowah Station was about halfway to that city. Not wanting to rely entirely upon the rivers as defensive obstructions, Johnston was eager to develop favorable opportunities to engage Sherman in battle before setting up a defense line along the Etowah. He chose a poor position at Cassville, which Yankee artillery forced him to abandon on May 20 without engaging enemy infantry. Johnston had compounded his errors on the morning of the nineteenth with a bombastic announcement to his soldiers that the army was done with retreating and would presently meet the enemy in a decisive battle to stop Sherman's advance. When he ordered yet another retreat the next morning, Confederate morale slumped.

Secretly, Johnston was also depressed by the repeated withdrawals, as he explained in a letter to his wife:

> I have seen so much beautiful country given up [to the enemy] as to be made unhappy. . . . You cannot imagine how disheartening it is, & at the same time humiliating, to see the apprehension of a people abandoned to the enemy. I'd rather have the agony of defeat as far as my own feelings are concerned.

Upon analysis, Johnston felt that a deep railroad cut at Allatoona Pass five miles south of the Etowah offered a better defensive position than the river itself. If he could hold it, Sherman could not advance closer to Atlanta without moving much of his army away from his supply line. If elements of Sherman's command were to venture far from the railroad, Johnston was hopeful of finding an opportunity to defeat the potentially scattered federal units individually in sequence. Sherman obliged, but Johnston's counter maneuvers were more defensive than offensive. The Rebel general put troops in positions where Sherman was successfully tempted to attack them.

Sherman sidled to the west in hopes of getting his armies on the south side of the Chattahoochee, well to the rear of Johnston at Allatoona. The first clash, on May 25, was at New Hope Church, where Hooker concluded that his leading corps faced a major Confederate force. Sherman was present with Hooker but presumed the corps was facing the enemy's left flank, mistakenly declaring, "There haven't been twenty rebels there today." Sherman insisted that Hooker attack. The result was a sharp repulse, with Union losses of one thousand five hundred compared to five hundred for the Confederates. Sherman refused to admit his error and claimed that the Rebels were reinforced while Hooker delayed, although Hooker sarcastically told a subordinate that such reinforcements might have amounted to fifty men.[22]

Since Hooker met stiff resistance on what Sherman assumed to be Johnston's left flank, Sherman resolved to attack Johnston's right flank near Pickett's Mill. Confederate cavalry detected the movement, enabling the Rebel defense line to be adjusted so as to present an entrenched force on what was formerly its right flank. In short, the May 26 attack was transformed into a frontal assault producing about one thousand six hundred Union casualties compared to 450 for the Rebels. Despite the fact that it was the second bloodiest Union defeat in the Atlanta Campaign, there is not a single word about the Battle of Pickett's Mill in Sherman's memoirs.[23]

Although Sherman's westward flanking movement did not get him south of the Chattahoochee, his advance units eventually occupied the little town of Acworth five miles south of Allatoona. Consequently, Johnston was forced to retreat once again. Despite a couple of tactical defeats, Sherman won a strategic victory.

KENNESAW MOUNTAIN

Yet again, Johnston resolved to force Sherman to attack him—this time at a strong entrenched defense twenty miles northwest of Atlanta—or force the enemy to move some of his units away from his rail supply line in a flanking maneuver. Such action would typically disperse Sherman's command, thereby presenting Johnston with a potential opportunity to defeat the detached enemy units individually in sequence. Sherman chose the first option at the Battle of Kennesaw Mountain on June 27. The result was a repulse that cost the federals three thousand casualties and the Confederates only seven hundred.[24]

Although Kennesaw's death toll was low compared to the corresponding bloodbath between Grant and Lee in Virginia, it was the most costly federal defeat of the Atlanta Campaign. While Sherman could not ignore it in his memoirs, he attempted to minimize his responsibility. For example, he claims that prior to the assault he "consulted Generals Thomas, McPherson and Schofield and we all agreed that we could not with prudence stretch out [our lines] any more and therefore there was no alternative but to attack 'fortified lines,' a thing carefully avoided up to that time."[25] Historian Albert Castel simply states, *"Every word of this sentence is false."* Castel continues:

> Schofield in his autobiography . . . states that he was opposed to the assault and that he believes Thomas and McPherson felt likewise, a belief that is supported by testimony from several of Thomas's and McPherson's staff officers and, in the case of Thomas, by the fact that five days prior to the assault he proposed a plan to Sherman that called for compelling the Confederates to abandon their position at Kennesaw by swinging a large force around their weakly held right flank.[26]

As for the failures at New Hope Church and preliminary action before Kennesaw Mountain, Sherman found it convenient to blame Thomas in a letter to Grant on June 18, 1864. Since he was aware of Grant's dislike of Thomas, Sherman felt that the general in chief would accept Thomas as a scapegoat. Sherman wrote, "My chief source of trouble is the Army of the Cumberland, which is dreadfully slow. . . . I have tried again and again to impress on Thomas that we must assail and not defend."[27]

FIGHTING HOOD

Once Johnston let Sherman cross the Chattahoochee and was replaced by Hood on July 17, the Confederates predictably became more aggressive. Sherman was attempting to simultaneously close in on Atlanta from the northwest, northeast, and east with the armies of Thomas, Schofield, and McPherson respectively. Thomas was the first to meet combat, at Peachtree Creek on July 20. Sherman was with Schofield in the center of the three-army Union line. He did not know until midnight that Thomas had been embattled with a superior force earlier that day, which was well after the Rebel attack had been repulsed. Instead, he mistakenly believed that the bulk of Hood's troops faced McPherson on the east side of the city. Therefore, falsely thinking Thomas would meet little resistance, about 3:30 p.m. he ordered Thomas to advance and occupy the city, "sweeping everything before [you.]" When the order arrived, most of Hood's army was still attacking Thomas, while all was quiet in McPherson's quarter.

Two days later Hood did attempt to roll up McPherson's army with an attack on its south flank and rear. The engagement became known as the Battle of Atlanta but is increasingly called the Battle of Bald Hill. Sherman mistakenly presumed that Hood's flanking movement detected the night before the attack was a general evacuation of Atlanta. Thus, he ordered McPherson and Thomas to pursue Hood, and Schofield to occupy the city. Not until eleven o'clock the next morning, July 22, did Sherman concede "we were mistaken in supposing the enemy has gone" and canceled the pursuit and occupation orders.[28]

Sherman's memoirs wrongly state that while Hood was attacking McPherson east of the city, Sherman sent repeated orders to Thomas and Schofield to push through the depleted Confederate lines on their fronts to "make a lodgment in Atlanta." But the *Official Records of the Union and Confederate Armies* contain no such orders. Schofield's autobiography denies receiving them. Similarly, Thomas's adjutant, Colonel Henry Stone, wrote thirty years later after Thomas had died, "No such orders ever came."[29]

Additionally, Sherman rejected Schofield's suggestion that the latter attack the north flank of the Rebels assaulting McPherson. The enemy flank was defended by a single brigade, which Schofield could have easily overrun with his three divisions. Such an attack

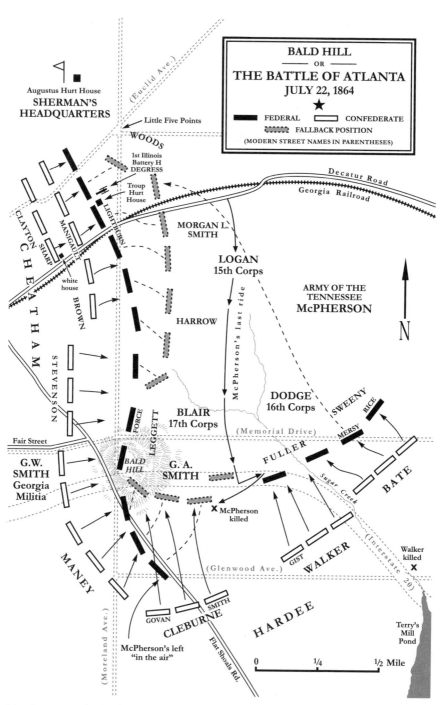

Map from *War Like the Thunderbolt: The Battle and Burning of Atlanta* by Russell S. Bonds.

might have transformed McPherson's hard-won defensive stand into a smashing Union victory capable of crippling Hood's ability to continue fighting.[30]

After Sherman finally cut Hood's only remaining railroad link between the city and the town of Jonesboro sixteen miles to the south on August 31, his memoirs erroneously blame a subordinate in Thomas's army for failing to destroy Hardee's Corps, which remained at Jonesboro after unsuccessfully attempting to drive the Yankees away from the railroad. Specifically, Sherman falsely declared that he sent "order after order" on September 1 to Major General David Stanley to "lap around Jonesboro from the east . . . to capture the whole of Hardee's Corps." He even claimed to have sent Thomas to deliver the orders verbally. When the memoir was published about fourteen years after the incident, Stanley remarked, "General Thomas [who was deceased] never came near me."

In truth, Sherman was not displeased with Stanley for failing to *obey* orders but for failing to march on Jonesboro *without* orders. Sherman ignores his own directive the previous night (August 31) that Stanley concentrate on destroying the railroad north of Jonesboro and only move toward the town at such a pace as was permitted by the demolition work. In fact, verbal orders to peremptorily deploy northeast of Jonesboro only reached Stanley by way of Thomas's adjutant about three thirty in the afternoon. Moreover, Sherman never ordered the Army of the Tennessee's three corps to attack Hardee from the west, which would be a crucial diversion for any assault from the north. At four o'clock, a single corps of Thomas's army, under the command of a brigadier with the unlikely name of Jefferson Davis, assaulted the north end of the Rebel line. Even though Davis gained a lodgment in the Confederate perimeter, most of Hardee's troops withdrew in good order to Lovejoy Station five miles to the southwest.[31]

Sherman should have devastated Hood's entire army. Shortly before five o'clock in the afternoon on August 31, Sherman received a message that Schofield and Stanley had severed the rail link about halfway between Atlanta and Jonesboro, near a place called Rough and Ready. At that point, Sherman had the bulk of a numerically superior force between two halves of Hood's army, which were separated by sixteen miles. The Confederates were badly demoralized. Their attempt to drive the Yankees from the western approaches to

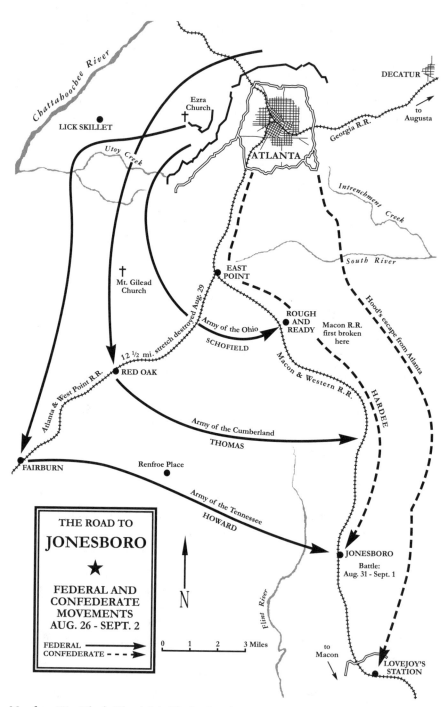

Map from *War Like the Thunderbolt: The Battle and Burning of Atlanta* by Russell S. Bonds.

Jonesboro resulted in casualties of two thousand two hundred, compared to Union losses of less than two hundred. Disillusioned by similar assaults in the past, many Confederates attacked only half-heartedly. One colonel wrote "the men seemed possessed of some great horror of charging breastworks, which no power, persuasion, or example could dispel."[32]

Confederate Private Sam Watkins wrote in his memoirs:

[W]e can see in plain view more than a thousand Yankee battle-flags waving on top the red earthworks, not more than four hundred yards off. Every private soldier there knew that General Hood's army was scattered all the way from Jonesboro to Atlanta, a distance of twenty five miles, without any order, discipline, or spirit to do anything. . . . And here [at Jonesboro] was but a demoralized remnant of Cheatham's corps facing . . . [six Yankee corps]. I have ever thought that Sherman was a poor general, not to have captured Hood and his whole army at that time.[33]

In his study of the Atlanta Campaign, *Decision in the West,* historian Albert Castel concludes Sherman had six opportunities to inflict considerably more damage on Hood during the week from August 27 to September 3. He failed to do so because he was more concerned with capturing Atlanta than on injuring Hood's army. For example, once Schofield and Stanley severed the railroad between Atlanta and Jonesboro, they could have been ordered to trap Hood in the city, where he had only a single corps and some militia. Alternately, Sherman could have followed Thomas's suggestion that Schofield and the Army of the Tennessee hold Hardee in check at Jonesboro while Thomas's army cut off his retreat at Lovejoy Station. A third example would have been to order Schofield, and/or Stanley, on September 1 to cut off Hood's retreat the following day out of Atlanta on the McDonough Road, as pictured in the preceding map.[34]

AFTERMATH

When Sherman occupied Atlanta on September 2, he left Hood's army intact to fight another day. Even though the Confederates were badly demoralized, Sherman did not pursue them. Hood was given about a month to lick his wounds, after which he seized the initiative. He reasoned that his army might suffer widespread desertions if it merely continued to retreat. Thus, he resolved to attack Sherman's railroad supply line north of Atlanta, much as Johnston had tried earlier, but merely with cavalry. This time, however, Hood used his entire army, thereby hoping to compel Sherman to follow him back into a region the federals felt they had already won.[35]

Hood's strategy worked until early November, when Sherman convinced Grant that Thomas and Schofield could be left in Tennessee (under the overall direction of Thomas) to attend to Hood, while Sherman marched an army group of sixty-two thousand through the heart of Georgia to Savannah. "If [Hood] will go to the Ohio River I will give him rations," said Sherman. "Let him go north, my business is down South." He would burn Atlanta behind him so there would be no need to defend it. That would enable Thomas and Schofield to focus on Hood's army and defending Tennessee and Kentucky from Rebel incursions. With Atlanta abandoned and destroyed, Sherman would have no further need for his supply line from Chattanooga, which would provide two benefits. First, Hood could no longer injure Sherman by attacking the railroad. Second, Thomas and Schofield would also no longer need to defend the line.

In response, Hood advanced into Tennessee, where he developed—and then fumbled—an opportunity to destroy Schofield's army at Spring Hill on November 29. In a hasty attempt to retrieve the mistake, he attacked Schofield after the latter was entrenched at Franklin the following day. The Confederates made a gallant assault over open ground, which was half again as big as Pickett's famous Gettysburg charge. It was just as bloodily repulsed.[36]

Private Sam Watkins's memoirs ominously begin a recollection of the battle as follows:

> *"The death-angle gathers its last harvest."*
> Kind reader, right here my pen, and courage, and ability fail me. I shrink from butchery. Would to God I could tear the page from these memoirs and from my own memory.[37]

After turning back the attackers, Schofield withdrew sixteen miles to Nashville, where Thomas was waiting with his own army and strong fortifications. Hood attempted to besiege the numerically superior Union force, but by mid-December, Thomas launched an attack that routed Hood's army. As it retreated to Alabama, it was saved from annihilation by the skillful rearguards of Forrest's cavalry.[38]

About a week after the Battle of Nashville, Sherman occupied an undefended Savannah, which had been abandoned by the Confederate defenders shortly after Sherman's approach in mid-December. Behind Sherman lay a forty-mile-wide swath of destruction stretching over two hundred miles back to Atlanta. He boasted of leaving $100 million in damage in his wake, of which only about 20 percent "inured to our advantage" while "the remainder is simple waste and destruction."[39]

SELECTING SHERMAN

Grant selected Sherman to lead the western offensive in spring 1864 for three reasons.

First, he had more experience with Sherman than other possible choices. Sherman was one of Grant's six division commanders at Shiloh and among the first to be attacked. Even though he was surprised by the attack, Sherman conducted himself commendably once the fighting started. Before joining Grant's army, Sherman was temporarily sent home as "unfit for duty" because of a nervous breakdown. Despite winning at Shiloh, Grant was temporarily relieved of command of the Army of the Tennessee. Aside from his being unprepared for the Confederate attack, some critics spread rumors of his drunkenness. He considered resigning from the army, until Sherman convinced him to stay. As Sherman later explained, "Grant stood by me when I was crazy, and I stood by him when he was drunk; and now, sir, we stand by each other always."[40]

Second, Grant had unjustified misgivings about Thomas. His hostility toward Thomas originated when the theater commander, Major General Henry Halleck, decided to assume field command of the united forces of the Army of the Tennessee and the Army of the Ohio in the aftermath of Shiloh in April 1862. The combined force was named the Army of the Mississippi, and Grant was given the meaningless rank of second in command. Halleck selected Thomas to lead one of two wings of the Army of the Mississippi. Thomas's wing was composed of four divisions of Grant's former Army of the Tennessee and one of Buell's Army of the Ohio. When Halleck was summoned to Washington in July to become general in chief, Thomas volunteered to return Grant's four divisions while reassuming command of a single division in the Army of the Ohio. Despite the friendly gesture, Grant remained cool toward Thomas ever after.[41]

When Thomas served under Grant at Chattanooga, he annoyed his commander by objecting to a premature order to attack the north flank of the Confederate position on Missionary Ridge on November 7, 1863. Grant ignored Thomas's objections until Brigadier General William "Baldy" Smith, whose judgment Grant respected, endorsed them. Consequently, Grant rescinded the order.[42]

The two clashed again in February 1864, when Grant was in Nashville. He tried to direct Thomas's army in Chattanooga. As noted, Grant had false information that Lee was sending reinforcements to Longstreet in east Tennessee. He also falsely believed that Johnston had sent troops to Longstreet. Therefore, Grant wanted Thomas to send reinforcements to Major General Ambrose Burnside in Knoxville and simultaneously advance on Johnston in Dalton, Georgia. Author Thomas Buell explains:

> Thomas soon confirmed that Johnston's army was intact and Grant's view of the situation delusional. . . . Grant expected Thomas to attack Johnston's mountain fortress in late February. "It is not possible to carry this place by assault," Thomas wired Grant on February 26. . . . Grant ranted from Nashville, insisting that Thomas launch an all-out assault against Johnston and offering improbable schemes to overcome obstacles. . . . Grant wired later that day that . . . Washington . . . [informed him] that Johnston had fallen back . . . and again urged Thomas to advance. . . . Out of touch with conditions at the front, Grant was frantic for Thomas to do something, anything.[43]

A third reason Grant may have chosen Sherman was that Sherman's political connections could benefit Grant's career, whereas Thomas was a Virginian whose family could have no influence in Washington. Sherman's father had been an Ohio State Supreme Court judge. Although he died when the boy was nine, the future general was raised by Thomas Ewing, a wealthy neighbor who would become his father-in-law. Ewing was also an influential US senator and served with four pre-Civil War presidents as secretary of the interior and treasury. When the Civil War started, the future general's brother, John, was one of Ohio's US senators. John introduced him to Abraham Lincoln, who got him commissioned as a colonel before the first important battle at Bull Run in July 1861.[44]

CONCLUSION

Thomas would probably have been a better choice than Sherman to lead the Union's 1864 western spring offensive for two reasons.

First, he understood that the chief objective was to destroy the Confederate Army of Tennessee. Sherman was more focused on capturing Atlanta, even if it meant leaving the Rebel army intact to continue fighting. If Sherman had concentrated on demolishing the opposing army, the Civil War might have ended in autumn 1864 instead of April 1865. Such a decision in the west would have left the Confederacy with no way to prevent the armies of Sherman, Schofield, and Thomas from quickly reinforcing Grant at Petersburg, where they could overwhelm Lee. Given such a hopeless prospect, it is reasonable to suppose the Confederacy would have surrendered shortly after its chief western army was eliminated.

Second, on two occasions, Sherman failed to act on suggestions from Thomas that could likely have annihilated, or crippled, the opposing Confederate army. The first was at the beginning of the campaign in early May at Snake Creek Gap. Sherman only partially followed the suggestion by failing to put enough soldiers into the movement to attack Johnston's rear. In time he recognized the validity of the strategy and left the false impression in his memoirs that it was his idea. The second time was during the second day of the Battle of Jonesboro, when Sherman rejected Thomas's recommendation that the Army of the Cumberland be sent to Lovejoy Station to cut off Hardee's retreat. Consequently, Hardee escaped.[45]

Nonetheless, there's no denying that Sherman's capture of Atlanta virtually assured Lincoln's reelection, confirming that the North had found the will to prosecute the war to a victorious conclusion. Moreover, Sherman won Atlanta and continued on a circuit through the Deep South, finally almost reaching the back door of Lee's army in Virginia at the end of the war. He did so by suffering far fewer casualties than Grant. However, during that march, Thomas destroyed the Army of Tennessee for him at the Battle of Nashville in December 1864.

8

THE SPRING HILL SPIES

In 2005, a ninety-one-year-old former FBI agent named Mark Felt identified himself as Deep Throat, the secret informant to *Washington Post* reporter Bob Woodward who had helped disclose the Watergate scandal that led to President Richard Nixon's resignation. Until then, Felt was perhaps the most famous anonymous American in history. For thirty-three years he struggled over whether disclosure would dishonor the FBI and his family. Ultimately, he concluded he wanted his side of the story to be told before it was too late.[1]

In December 1913, *Confederate Veteran* magazine published an article about a retired Civil War private of the 73rd Illinois Infantry Regiment, J. D. Remington, who told another secret tale that may explain one of the great mysteries of the Confederate Army of Tennessee. On November 29, 1864, the army failed to win what should have been a decisive victory when Lieutenant General John Hood stole a march on his opponent. By three o'clock in the afternoon, Hood had twenty-five thousand soldiers in position to attack the east flank of his enemy's escape path from Columbia to Franklin, Tennessee. Hood's soldiers were particularly concentrated along the first leg of the twenty-three-mile route near a village named Spring Hill, which was about halfway to Franklin.[2]

At that time, Hood reported observing a single, five-thousand-five-hundred-man enemy division of Union Major General John

Schofield's army making its getaway along the route and ordered Major General Frank Cheatham's corps to attack it. While the Yankee division should have been crushed if it was located where Hood said, Cheatham did not attack until the outnumbered enemy set up a defense line near Spring Hill. Even then he did not use most of his corps. Instead only a single division under Major General Patrick Cleburne made the assault. After a good beginning, the charge was stopped by massed Union artillery. Finally, after nightfall, the rest of Schofield's twenty-three-thousand-man command used the vulnerable route to march safely from Columbia to Franklin without enduring a second Rebel attack. At least two were ordered, but strangely never executed.

The Confederate fiasco resulted from mysterious command failures never satisfactorily explained. The after-battle reports and later writings of key generals are contradictory in crucial respects and generate more heat than light. Almost all the rank-and-file soldiers on both sides expected an overwhelming Confederate flank attack while the federals were almost helpless during their retreat. Over the ensuing night, the Rebel army was encamped so close to the road some Union soldiers accidentally wandered into the campsites and were captured.[3]

J. D. Remington's stunning explanation was that he and another spy who was his cousin spread misinformation and conflicting orders among the Confederate command. If true, his story could explain much of the Spring Hill controversy. Partly because he waited forty-eight years to tell it, the Illinois private's story has many skeptics. But Mark Felt's experience demonstrates that delay is no proof of untruthfulness. In response to critics, Remington said, "To many who have not had the experience as a spy it may seem impossible to do the things that have been done by spies." It is sometimes impossible to verify the accomplishments of spies until decades later, if ever. For example, it was not known for fifty years after the end of World War II that Los Alamos scientist Ted Hall gave atomic bomb designs to the Soviets, although his colleague Klaus Fuchs had been identified decades earlier.[4]

SITUATIONAL BACKGROUND

While there are good arguments for accepting—or rejecting—Remington's narrative, it is first necessary to put the battle in the context of the western theater after the fall of Atlanta.

There would have been no Spring Hill affair if Union Major General William T. Sherman had executed his assignment that began in May 1864. Contrary to popular belief, he was not instructed to capture Atlanta but instead was supposed to destroy the Army of Tennessee, then commanded by General Joe Johnston. On several occasions during Sherman's May-to-September maneuvers, he should have completed that mission. The most recent opportunity was at Jonesboro, Georgia, on September 1, when Hood was in command after replacing Johnston in July.[5]

As explained by historian Richard McMurry:

> [After the Battle of Jonesboro] late in the afternoon of August 31, [Sherman] stood with six corps, some 60,000 elated, victorious troops, between the two weak parts of the opposing army and in a position to crush Confederate military power in the West once and for all. The Yankee commander, however, had no taste for such decisive work.[6]

Although Hood's army was demoralized after the fall of Atlanta on September 2, 1864, Sherman allowed it an entire month to lick its wounds. In early October, Hood marched north of Atlanta to attack Sherman's railroad supply line that stretched north to Louisville, Kentucky. Sherman thereby lost the initiative and had to follow Hood, who was most successful at Dalton, Georgia, where he destroyed fifteen miles of track in mid-October. Thereafter, Hood shifted to Tuscumbia, Alabama, to prepare for a move into Tennessee, which lifted the army's morale because many of its soldiers were from that state.[7]

Sherman was frustrated. He convinced General in Chief Grant to let him wash his hands of Hood by breaking up the combined force he used to capture Atlanta. Under the overall command of Major General George Thomas at Nashville, armies commanded by Thomas and Schofield were sent north to protect the railroad and deal with Hood. Three smaller units that would later unite under Schofield were in Chattanooga and Pulaski, Tennessee, and Decatur, Alabama. Sherman got permission to take the remaining sixty thousand Atlanta Union veterans on a march through the undefended 225 miles between Atlanta and Savannah.[8]

Hood wanted to move quickly into Tennessee in order to attack Schofield and Thomas before their forces could combine. However,

Union General John Schofield, left. (*Library of Congress*) Confederate General Stephen D. Lee, right. (*Battles and Leaders*)

owing to the Confederacy's feeble economy in autumn 1864, it took about a month to supply his army. On November 20, the last elements crossed the Tennessee River heading northeast toward Nashville. Once all the federal units were consolidated, Thomas would have seventy-five thousand soldiers to oppose Hood, who had a little over thirty thousand, including cavalry. Thus, it was imperative that Hood beat the Union detachments individually before they could combine. His first opportunity would be at Columbia, Tennessee, seventy-two miles from Tuscumbia, where Schofield would be waiting with twenty-three thousand infantry entrenched on the north side of the Duck River.[9]

Hood's army was composed of three infantry and a single cavalry corps. His cavalry commander was Major General Nathan B. Forrest, and his three infantry corps commanders were Lieutenant Generals Alexander Stewart and Stephen Lee, and Major General Frank Cheatham. Hood's immediate opponent, Schofield, commanded two infantry and one cavalry corps. His cavalry commander was Major General James Wilson, and his infantry commanders were Major General Jacob Cox and Brigadier General David Stanley. As in the Confederate army, each corps typically had three divisions, but at Spring Hill the corps under Cox had only two. Typically, each division had three or four brigades.

SPRING HILL

When Hood arrived before Columbia on November 27, he developed his plot to cut off Schofield's escape path, which was the turnpike that proceeded northeast through Spring Hill and Franklin before ending at Nashville. Starting early on the morning of November 29, he left most of his artillery and two divisions of Lee's corps to fake preparations for a frontal assault on Columbia. If successful, the deception would pin Schofield at Columbia while Hood led the rest of his army unseen across the Duck River farther to the east, where it could march quickly north to occupy the pike between Columbia and Spring Hill. The maneuver would entrap Schofield at Columbia or leave him vulnerable to a flank attack while retreating.[10]

Warned by Wilson's cavalry that Confederates were crossing the Duck River in large numbers east of Columbia, Schofield began to react. He was also under orders from Thomas in Nashville to withdraw to Franklin, where it was hoped he could be reinforced by troops delayed in arriving from Missouri. During the morning he was unsure if Hood would attempt to attack his east flank in Columbia or try to block the Spring Hill Pike. His first reaction was to send his large supply train of eight hundred wagons and forty cannons to Spring Hill with one division of Stanley's corps. At eight o'clock on the morning of November 29, Stanley started for Spring Hill with Brigadier General George Wagner's division of about five thousand five hundred soldiers.[11]

At daybreak, only about two hundred federals occupied Spring Hill, but some of Wilson's cavalry started arriving before noon when four companies of J. D. Remington's 73rd Illinois Infantry Regiment also came up. Around eleven o'clock that morning, Confederate cavalry under Forrest attacked, but the federals had repeating rifles, which gave them a significant advantage in firepower per soldier. Gradually, the federals were able to build barricades and put artillery into action. By 12:30 p.m., the rest of Colonel Emerson Opdyke's brigade arrived and was followed by Wagner's other two brigades, commanded by Brigadier General Luther Bradley and Colonel John Lane respectively The arrivals gave Wagner enough soldiers to prevent Forrest from taking the town. One Union officer wrote that if Wagner had arrived only a few minutes later, Forrest would have already captured Spring Hill. Thus,

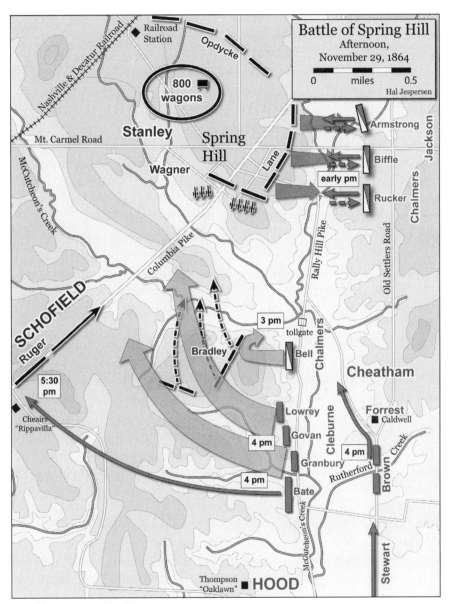

Map courtesy of Hal Jespersen, cwmaps.com.

the first Rebel attempt at blocking Schofield's retreat failed by a matter of minutes. Around two o'clock in the afternoon, Bradley's brigade took up a defensive position southeast of Spring Hill to protect the turnpike beyond the town limits.[12]

Although Forrest was unable to take Spring Hill after Wagner's escorts for the Union wagon train arrived, Forrest successfully drove most of Wilson's cavalry to Franklin, where it was too far north to be engaged. By 3:00 p.m., Forrest's men were too low on ammunition to attack Spring Hill again without assistance. Although large Confederate infantry units started arriving, this is when the first great Spring Hill mystery happened.[13]

Hood and Cheatham agreed that they held an impromptu conference near the road the Rebel army was using east of the Columbia Turnpike. Hood claimed he pointed to a Yankee division marching along the turnpike and told Cheatham to attack it with his superior numbers. He added that if required, he would soon send reinforcements that were coming up, thereby increasing Cheatham's numerical advantage. Cheatham's version of the conversation was that no troops were seen on the pike because there was no line of sight from the meeting point to the turnpike. Yet a present-day drive along the road shows that the pike was observable from several places, and a number of other contemporary witnesses said federal units were plainly seen marching along the pike for most of the afternoon.

The second major Hood-Cheatham disagreement involves the attack objective. Upon seizing the turnpike, Hood wanted the attackers to face southwest in order to block the rest of Schofield's army at Columbia from reaching Spring Hill. In contrast, Cheatham misunderstood and assumed he was to capture Spring Hill itself, which was to the northwest. The confusion became evident when Hood directed Cheatham's southernmost division, led by Major General William Bate, to take "the turnpike and sweep toward Columbia."

Simultaneously, at three o'clock in Columbia, Schofield concluded that Lee's show of force on his front was not the real threat. He directed that the last of his troops be on the turnpike for Spring Hill shortly after nightfall. Some got started by 3:30 p.m. Thus, if the Confederates were going to prevent the bulk of Schofield's army from escaping, it was imperative that they block the turnpike as quickly as possible.[14]

As Cheatham's attack evolved, the differing objectives between Hood and Cheatham conflicted. Under Cheatham's orders, Cleburne's division drove Union General Bradley's brigade off the pike and then rotated northwest toward Spring Hill. Since Bate

Confederate generals Benjamin F. Cheatham, left, and Patrick R. Cleburne, right. (*Library of Congress*)

expected to attack the pike and then pivot his division to the southwest, Cleburne's lone division was unsupported and failed to take Spring Hill when greeted by massed Union artillery. This was the second lost opportunity, because if Bate had joined Cleburne, the two divisions would probably have overwhelmed the Spring Hill defenders. A frustrated Cheatham promptly resolved to try again, but this time by coordinating all three of his divisions. He placed Major General John Brown's division on Cleburne's right and Bate's division on Cleburne's left.

The next failure occurred when Bate didn't execute either Hood's or Cheatham's plan. As Hood ordered, Bate was about to attack a vulnerable column of retreating Yankees when he received an order to join Cleburne and Brown in Cheatham's second attempt to take Spring Hill. Since he didn't want to forfeit the golden opportunity immediately to his front, he sent a message to Cheatham requesting that his commander cancel the order, but Cheatham refused. This was the third lost opportunity, because if left to his own judgment, Bate would have plunged into the nearly helpless lead elements of Schofield's remaining columns directly in front of him. The reason Bate did not participate in Cheatham's second attack is that it was controversially canceled, as shall be explained.[15]

The fourth lost opportunity resulted from Brown's failure to initiate the attack that was supposed to trigger Cheatham's second

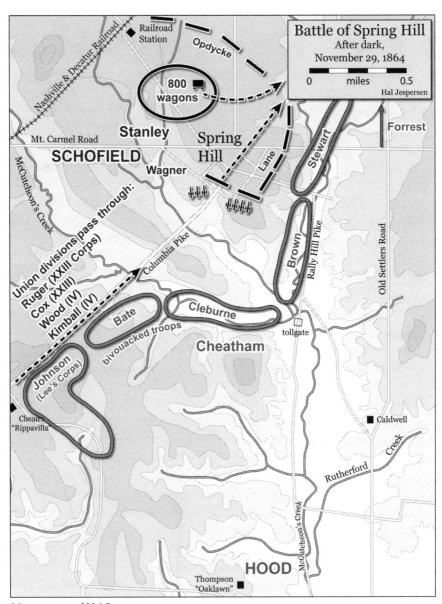

Map courtesy of Hal Jespersen, cwmaps.com.

assault, which was to include all three of his divisions as opposed to
only Cleburne's. Cleburne's division was to be in the middle, with
Brown on his right and Bate on his left. Brown delayed because he
was waiting for Stewart's corps to deploy on his right. He wanted

Stewart to take the ground because one of his brigadiers, General Otto Strahl, convinced Brown that unknown federal units were lurking there. Unfortunately, Brown did not realize the numbers of such federals were small. As shall be explained, eventually Brown did nothing because he said Cheatham ultimately suspended the attack.[16]

After the war, Cheatham explained that Hood told him to cancel the attack when Cheatham rode to Hood's headquarters with Tennessee governor Isham Harris and one of Brown's staff officers. They informed Hood about the vague presence of federals on the right flank of the proposed attack line. Hood's memoir confirms the meeting but states he voiced dismay that Cheatham had not already attacked. He further adds that Cheatham accepted much of the blame for Spring Hill failures a week later in a private conversation between the two. Since Cheatham's claim that Hood canceled the attack was triggered by the posthumous memoir, Hood could not respond.[17]

Additionally, Stewart was ordered to take a road that would enable his corps to deploy perpendicular across the Columbia Turnpike as well as be in position to protect Brown's right. However, as the preceding map illustrates, Stewart's corps ended up parallel to the pike instead of perpendicular across it. Although Hood provided a local guide to be sure Stewart took the correct roads, around twilight an unknown staff officer arrived who declared Stewart was going the wrong way. He said Hood sent him to provide correct directions. Initially, Stewart concluded that Hood must have changed his mind and followed the new directions. But eventually Stewart suspected an error. He therefore decided to visit Hood personally in the company of General Forrest about eleven o'clock that night.

Brown's opportunity was so obvious that his inaction perturbed many of his ordinary soldiers. A South Carolina colonel wrote that the troops "were in momentary expectation of moving [and] could not understand why we did not attack and every man felt and I heard hundreds remark that for some cause we were losing a grand opportunity."[18]

Unbelievably, Rebel errors compounded. For example, during the three o'clock Hood-Cheatham meeting, General Stewart's corps was nearby and could have quickly aided Cleburne's stalled attack before Spring Hill. But he was told to wait and only later ordered to march to Brown's right after Cheatham's uncoordinated assault using only Cleburne's division had already failed. When Stewart arrived at the army headquarters between eleven o'clock and midnight for clarification about the suspected erroneous change in marching orders to Brown's right, Hood told Stewart to rest the soldiers at their present location and be prepared to move in the morning. Evidently Hood did not realize that none of the ordered Rebel attacks and maneuvers successfully blocked the Columbia Turnpike. Thus, he did not realize Schofield's army was marching past the Confederate campsites unmolested. Presumably, he thought at least Forrest had blocked the pike north of Spring Hill "so in the morning we will have a surrender without a fight." This was the fifth lost opportunity.[19]

One Union captain described the nighttime march from Columbia to Spring Hill:

> We were in such close proximity to the Confederates that we could see their long line of campfires; . . . could hear the rattle of their canteens; see officers and men standing around the fires, or loitering about; while the fumbling of our wagon train on the pike, and the beating of our own hearts were the only sounds we could hear on our side.
>
> Had Hood placed a single . . . division in a fortified position across the road . . . it would have [checked the] Federal retreat, and dawn would have found our forces cut off from all hope of escape.[20]

One final chance to stop the Union army flight came after midnight. An anonymous Confederate private reported to Hood that federal columns were presently marching to safety on the pike. Hood directed Lieutenant Colonel A. P. Mason to order Cheatham to send a brigade to investigate and attack if the information was valid. Cheatham ordered Major General Edward Johnson to select one of his brigades for the task, but when Johnson arrived at the turnpike ahead of the brigade about two in the morning, the road was empty. The last of Schofield's units arrived safely in Spring Hill around four that morning. Johnson must have arrived on the pike when there was a gap between federal units. By five o'clock on the morning of November 30, only a handful of Union soldiers were left in Spring Hill. The rest had continued northeast toward Franklin, where there would be a bloody battle later that day. The federal rearguard was provided by Opdyke's brigade, which included J. D. Remington's regiment.[21]

MYSTERIES

Among the Spring Hill Confederate mysteries are the following:

1. What transpired between Hood and Cheatham when they met about three o'clock in the afternoon? It may be recalled that Hood stated that he pointed to a federal column marching along the Columbia Turnpike, which he told Cheatham to attack. Cheatham agreed they met but claimed the generals could not see any federals on the turnpike because there was no line of sight to the road from the meeting place. Although Cleburne was present, he was killed the next day and couldn't verify either version.

2. After Cleburne's unsupported division failed in the attack ordered above and Cheatham organized his entire corps to make a second charge, why did General Brown fail to trigger the second attack as ordered?

3. Why did Confederate units bivouacked parallel to the Columbia Turnpike after nightfall fail to attack the vulnerable federal columns plainly seen marching to safety?

4. Why was Hood incorrectly confident he would have an easy victory the morning after retiring on the night of November 29–30?

5. Why did Stewart's corps get conflicting directions on its march to the north end of the Rebel line?

SPY STORY

J. D. Remington's espionage account addresses the five preceding mysteries.[22] As Remington told it, he was sent on spy missions six times earlier in the war: three times at Murfreesboro, Tennessee, and three times in Georgia during the Atlanta Campaign. He was among the first federal infantry soldiers to arrive in Spring Hill with Colonel Opdycke's brigade around noon. Shortly thereafter, Opdycke supplied him with a Confederate captain's uniform and sent him to secretly learn the strength of the Rebel units threatening Spring Hill.

After riding circuitously to the southeast, he entered the same road the Confederates were using to march to Spring Hill. Soon he came upon a conferencing group of Rebel officers that happened to be the meeting of Generals Hood, Cheatham, and Cleburne and their staffs noted above. Since he had become acquainted with each general on earlier spy missions, he pretended to be a messenger from Forrest. Remington falsely told them the Confederate cavalry corps had successfully blocked the turnpike north of Spring Hill. He joined and remained with the group until it advanced to a spot where federal units marching along the Columbia Turnpike were plainly visible. Remington endorsed Hood's version of the incident by writing that Hood pointed to the federals and asked Cheatham if the Rebel corps commander could also see them. Cheatham answered affirmatively, prompting Hood to order Cheatham to attack them with all his available troops.

Hood sent Remington back to Forrest with orders for the cavalry to capture the federal wagon train Remington reported to be north of Spring Hill. Instead Remington secretly met with his cousin, who he earlier recognized during the Hood-Cheatham-Cleburne meeting. Although officially a Confederate officer, his cousin was secretly a Union spy. While the two arranged a plot to disrupt Confederate plans, Cheatham launched his attack, but only with Cleburne's single division, which was eventually stalled as noted.

While Cheatham was arranging a second coordinated attack with all three of his divisions, Remington rode into the one commanded by General Brown. There he met General Strahl, a Brown subordinate. He convinced Strahl that Cheatham's proposed attack was dangerous because Remington had discovered an unknown number of federal soldiers on Strahl's right flank. The two rode together to Brown's headquarters, where Strahl told Brown of the phantom federals. Brown sent the disinformation via two staff officers and Remington to Cheatham, and Cheatham took it to Hood with Remington in tow. Remington heard Hood tell Cheatham to rest his soldiers, thereby canceling the attack. Thus, the second mystery involving Brown's failure to assault can be explained by Remington's misinformation. It also supports Cheatham's claim that Hood called off the second attack instead of Cheatham.

Next Remington claimed he rode along the Confederate brigades parallel to the Columbia Turnpike south of Spring Hill. It must have been near or after nightfall. He wrote of telling brigade commanders that he was sent by Hood to say they should set campsites four hundred yards back from the pike and not fire on the enemy unless the enemy fired on them. Remington's claim, if true, explains the third mystery concerning why the federals were permitted to march safely past the Rebel army overnight.

Remington's story might also explain why Hood felt confident of victory on the following morning, after retiring for bed. As explained, when the spy earlier pretended to be a messenger from Forrest, he falsely reported that Forrest had blocked the pike north of Spring Hill. He also added that Forrest was expected to destroy the bridges across the Harpeth River farther north at Franklin. Additionally, after Hood completed his post-11:00 p.m. meeting noted earlier with Stewart and Forrest, Remington told Hood that he observed the federals bedding down in Spring Hill instead of continuing onward toward Franklin. Such misinformation implied that Schofield could not escape beyond Spring Hill.

Finally, Remington wrote that his cousin was responsible for falsely convincing General Stewart that his corps was taking the wrong road when it was attempting to deploy perpendicular to the turnpike on the north end of the Rebel line. This could explain why Stewart's corps ended up camping parallel to the pike, thereby leaving Schofield's escape path open. The cousin could not verify the tale because he was among the many Confederates slaughtered at the Battle of Franklin the next day.

Historians and veterans have been unable to resolve the confusion and contradictions at Spring Hill. The consensus is that Hood was responsible because he was nearby and the overall army commander. Nonetheless, it seems plausible that at least some of the complications might have resulted from a monkey wrench thrown into the army's machinery. But it is unclear whether fate or spies threw the monkey wrench.

PLAUSIBILITY

While nearly all historians ignore Remington, his story remains tantalizing for a number of reasons.

First, before it was accepted for publication in *Confederate Veteran*, the magazine's founder, Sumner Cunningham, investigated Remington and his story. Cunningham was familiar with Spring Hill partly because he was present as a member of Strahl's brigade. He was among the many rank-and-file soldiers convinced a stunning victory had slipped through the army's grasp. As publisher, he asked Remington for references.[23]

Having moved to Jacksonville, Florida, only four years earlier, Remington had few references. However, one was John N. C. Stockton, then a Democratic candidate for the US Senate. Cunningham stated, "Mr. Stockton's letter . . . cordially indorsed Mr. Remington through four years of acquaintance." Presently, Jacksonville remembers Stockton as a prominent real estate developer and citizen who distributed public relief funds during a yellow fever epidemic, chaired the Public Works Board, and served in the state legislature. Presently, the city's Ortega district has a park named in Stockton's honor.[24]

Second, Remington is mentioned eight times in R. J. Hasty's 1890 history of the 73rd Illinois Infantry Regiment. His contribution to the regimental history was in answering Hasty's interrogatories. Hasty wrote that Remington's answers, "with very few exceptions, agree with other statements" in the history. The regimental history was published twenty-three years before Remington revealed he was a spy. In short, Remington belonged to the unit as claimed and could have been a spy at the locations specified in the seven instances he cited.[25]

Third, in 1884, Remington wrote to the author of a *Confederate Veteran* article about the Battle of Franklin. The article's author was Moscow Carter, the eldest son of the Carter family whose home was a prominent structure on the battlefield. Remington wrote to Carter, stating that he recalled shooting a Confederate officer near the east door of the Carter house and asked if it was a Carter family member. Carter replied that it was not a family member but that he remembered seeing the body, which he said was a Tennessee officer. Remington could not have observed the body after the battle because the federals withdrew to Nashville, which was in the opposite direction. Therefore, his claim of having shot the man during the battle and noting where the body fell seems legitimate.[26]

Fourth, numerous Union spies were active in the western theater during much of the war. Major General Grenville Dodge had a network of more than one hundred, including many who were never revealed. When a superior threatened to cut off Dodge's funding in 1863 unless he revealed the names, General Grant intervened on Dodge's behalf. The names were kept secret even from Grant. Furthermore, there is independent evidence of other espionage during Hood's Tennessee campaign. For example, after the Confederates completed the pontoon bridge across the Tennessee River at Tuscumbia, one Union spy attempted to destroy it by cutting it loose from one end.[27]

Fifth, Remington's narrative is consistent with the incidents as reported by Confederate participants in many ways. For example, his recollection of the meeting when Hood claims to have told Cheatham to attack around three o'clock is consistent with Hood's writings. His explanations for Brown's failure to attack and Stewart's confusing deployment are consistent with the recollections of Brown and Stewart, presuming they did not know a spy created the doubts that led to their mistakes.

Sixth, in commenting on his investigation of the merits of the article, *Confederate Veteran* founder Cunningham wrote, "Mr. Remington in all the correspondence shows a spirit of absolute sincerity."[28]

Seventh, the incidents as reported by Confederate participants have important contradictions. Such scenarios often result when participants simply don't have all the facts. Covert interference by Yankee spies who never revealed their roles while the applicable Confederate leaders were living might explain the otherwise unexplainable. To his critics, Remington answered, "Hood failed to do what he wanted to do at Spring Hill; and I ask only one small word, 'Why?'"[29]

AMBIGUITIES

Despite tempting reasons for believing Remington there are also reasons for doubt.

First, Remington never provided a fully satisfying motive for waiting nearly fifty years to reveal his role. He merely said he wanted to get the story out before he passed away, and he regretted that he failed to reveal it earlier when it could have been verified by testimony of Rebel leaders while they were still alive. However, the delay also fails to be convincing evidence that the story is necessarily false. According to military historian Peter Maslowski, who wrote the article "Military Intelligence Sources during the American Civil War":

> [F]orty years [later], at least one man who was familiar with the Union's intelligence operations still feared that 'it would be impolitic to mention' the names of wartime agents. . . . In the

postwar era, spies whose identity became known suffered ostracism and persecution from those whom they had betrayed.[30]

Since a spy who was both a cousin and a Confederate officer reportedly aided Remington, the two may have had extended family in the South that would have suffered ostracism and persecution if Remington told his story earlier. However, there is no record that he ever mentioned such a point as a reason for his delay.

Second, while Remington's version generally fits with the incidents as recollected by Confederate leaders, he could have learned about such particulars by reading *Confederate Veteran* and other publications, merely shaping his story to conform to such writings. Based on his letter to Moscow Carter, it appears Remington was a *Confederate Veteran* reader almost thirty years before his story was printed.

Third, although Remington's narrative often squares with the incidents as recorded, there are important exceptions. For example, he claims to have been with General Johnson when Johnson led one of his brigades to investigate whether Union stragglers were marching along the Columbia Turnpike during the night of November 29–30. As noted, Johnson's orders were prompted by a report to Hood from a Confederate private that Union stragglers were on the pike. While Remington and Johnson agree the road was found to be empty, Remington claims the incident was before midnight, whereas other sources put it at around two o'clock in the morning.

Although participants could often disagree on the precise *time* of events, they were less likely to disagree on the sequence of them. Remington's recollection differs not only in time but also in sequence. By all accounts, the last time Hood was awakened was when the anonymous private told him Union soldiers were marching along the turnpike in the middle of the night, which was *after* Hood's meeting with Stewart and Forrest. Yet Remington states that he returned to the Union army directly after he met with Hood following Hood's meeting with Stewart and Forrest. If he returned to Union lines directly after that meeting, he could not have been with General Johnson at a later time.

Remington's claim to have been at Hood's headquarters between eleven o'clock and midnight when Stewart, accompanied by Forrest, sought clarification about Stewart's contradictory late afternoon marching orders raises a question. Since Remington had earlier represented himself to Hood as a captain with Forrest, why did Hood fail to routinely ask Forrest to verify Remington's identity while all three were temporarily at army headquarters? By Remington's account, that simply did not happen. He wrote that immediately after the Hood-Stewart meeting, he was presented to Hood, where he told the general he had infiltrated the Union lines at Spring Hill and falsely stated the federals were stopping there for the night.

Finally, Remington claims he told the Confederate brigades bivouacked along the Columbia Pike to back off four hundred yards and not fire unless fired on. Most other reports from Union and Confederate participants suggest the Rebel campfires were much closer.

CONCLUSION

Confederate failures at Spring Hill appear to have resulted from one of two factors, or a combination of both.

First is the fog of war present to varying degrees on all battlefields. The expression is derived from Prussian military analyst Carl von Clausewitz's 1837 book, *On War*, in which he describes the uncertainty of situational awareness among participants in military operations: "[T]hree quarters of the factors on which all action in War is based are wrapped in a fog of greater or lesser uncertainty. A sensitive and discerning judgment is called for . . . to scent out the truth." Perhaps the Spring Hill calamity was merely a statistically extreme example of such a fog, amplified by the characteristic hard luck of the Army of Tennessee. Like a perpetually disadvantaged athletic team, the army was so often frustrated by the failures of its valiant efforts that it may subconsciously have denied itself an easy victory out of disbelief that its habitual bad luck could change.[31]

Second, our present understanding of the fiasco might alternatively reflect a combination of missing information and deliberate obfuscation. The lasting mystery at Spring Hill is a reminder that explanations for enigmatic incidents tend to have a variety of versions but can only possess a single set of facts. Such episodes generally cease to be mysteries once all pertinent facts are known and the true, unique set is recognized.

Sometimes it is a simple matter to identify a source that might reveal such hidden facts. For example, hypothetical testimony by the

unknown courier ordered to deliver General Robert E. Lee's Special
Order No. 191 to Major General D. H. Hill nine days before the
Battle of Antietam could solve the mystery about how the famous
Lost Dispatch was misplaced. At other times, as at Spring Hill, it is
more difficult to identify likely sources of pertinent missing infor-
mation.

The contradictions between Hood's and Cheatham's stories about
whether Hood pointed out federals marching along the Columbia
Pike at three o'clock in the afternoon imply that one of them was
lying. However, many other command failures suggest that pertinent information is missing. For example, although General Johnson
acted on orders originating with Hood to advance one of his brigades
to the pike in the middle of the night to look for Union stragglers,
Hood's adjutant admitted he neglected to issue the order. Similarly,
a courier personally unknown to Stewart instructed that he take a
road that failed to move his corps to its designated deployment location.[32]

Since Grenville Dodge had a large federal spy network operating
in the western theater, and other incidents involving Union spies
were known to have occurred during Hood's advance into Tennessee,
espionage cannot be ruled out. It could be the source of misinformation acted on by Confederate leaders without their being able to
determine the origin. Whether Remington's tale is a fabrication or
only partly true, it may be impossible to discover the truth by scru-
tinizing the historical statements of Confederates for information
they could not have. If the mystery is to be solved, it may require
investigations from a new perspective and a search of unexplored
sources.

9

GHOSTS OF
THE LOST DISPATCH

The Confederacy never came closer to winning independence than in September 1862, which was seventeen months after the four-year Civil War started. Its armies were on the offensive both east and west. In the east, General Robert E. Lee's Army of Northern Virginia culminated a string of summer victories in its home state by crossing the Potomac River with hopes of winning a final show-down battle on Northern soil. In Kentucky, Rebel armies under General Braxton Bragg and Major General Edmund Kirby Smith brushed aside opposing forces at Munfordville and Richmond. They were closing in on the state capital at Frankfort, where a previously exiled Rebel state government would be reinstalled.[1]

About the same time, Confederate Major Generals Earl Van Dorn and Sterling Price took the offensive against components of Major General Ulysses Grant's army in northern Mississippi. Across the Mississippi River, Confederate Major General Thomas Hindman was preparing to launch an offensive into Missouri. The movements were as close as the Confederacy would come during the entire war to a coordinated offensive in the eastern, western, and trans-Mississippi sectors.[2]

In July 1862, the available inventory of raw cotton in Great Britain had dropped to two hundred thousand bales, compared to 1.2 million in July 1861. By the end of September 1862, the stock would be reduced to only one hundred thousand bales, while consumption was running at twenty thousand bales weekly. Unemployment in Britain's cotton textile manufacturing industry had reached 25 percent.[3]

British prime minister John Palmerston wrote to his foreign secretary, John Russell, in mid-September, asking whether a decisive Rebel victory north of Washington might constitute a sufficient basis for "England and France [to] address the contending parties and recommend an arrangement based upon separation"—that is, Confederate independence. Russell responded that "the time has come for offering mediation to the United States Government with a view to recognition of the independence of the Confederates. . . . In case of failure, we ought ourselves to recognize the Southern States as an independent state."

Victories in Kentucky, west Tennessee, and the trans-Mississippi would be icing on the cake, but another Southern victory in the east could be enough for European intervention on the side of the Confederacy and a loss of will to continue the war across the North.[4]

EASTERN SITUATION

On September 8, 1862, about a week after his Second Manassas victory, Lee was laying plans to win the war while concentrating his army at Frederick, Maryland, about forty miles northwest of Lincoln's capital. On this day, his strength is estimated by historians to have been forty thousand, excluding about ten thousand stragglers that resulted from the blistering marching pace set by the commander in order to hold the strategic initiative.[5] His chief opponent, Major General George McClellan, had eighty-five thousand troops, and an additional seventy-two thousand five hundred were in Washington garrisoned under Major General Nathaniel Banks.[6] Lee knew Washington fortifications were too strong to attack directly, but he hoped to lure McClellan into the open, where he could have a fair fight to the finish north of the Potomac.

While some historians criticize Lee's move across the Potomac as prompted by overconfidence, such a conclusion falsely discounts Lee's conviction that if the South were to win the war, it must do so quickly because the Confederacy did not have the resources to outlast the North in a lengthy one. Most such critics also ignore the influence of persistent speculation in Richmond that the South might have won independence a year earlier by immediately attacking Washington after victory at First Manassas. In short, if Lee had not risked a showdown battle in Yankee territory, he would likely have been more excoriated for declining to attempt what Generals Joseph Johnston and P. G. T. Beauregard *should* have tried after First Manassas. Finally, there was reason to believe that Southern sympathizers in Maryland might join Lee's army if he could demonstrate an ability to continue winning in the North. According to US assistant secretary of state Frederick Seward,

General Robert E. Lee.
(*Library of Congress*)

who was the son of Secretary of State William Seward, the Maryland legislature was prevented from adopting a secession ordinance a year earlier because Lincoln had the army block prosecession members from attending and even had over thirty of them arrested.[7]

McClellan entered the campaign with two serious handicaps. First, Radical Republicans in his rear were among his worst enemies. Second, he persistently overestimated the size of Lee's army.

Only about two months earlier, McClellan had advanced the largest army ever assembled in North America to within five miles of the Confederate capital at Richmond, when Lee launched a weeklong offensive that drove it back. Despite McClellan's competently managing his troops in defensive maneuvers and suffering fewer casualties than Lee, Lincoln lost faith in him because the general kept asking for reinforcements that were not available in the numbers requested. On July 30, 1862, McClellan was ordered to begin transferring his soldiers to a new Union army under Major General John Pope in northern Virginia. Over the next month, McClellan lost his command by increments as units were transferred to Pope, despite earlier promises from Major General Henry Halleck, the general in chief, that McClellan would be given overall command of both armies.[8]

Lee routed Pope's army at Second Manassas so badly on August 30, 1862, that the following day Pope wired Halleck, "I should like to know if you feel secure about Washington should this army be destroyed." Since Pope had escalated the war into the civilian sector by confiscating private properties and dealing harshly with citizens, he was a favorite among Radical Republicans. When searching for a scapegoat to explain his defeat, they convinced themselves that McClellan was the culprit. They accused the general of deliberately preventing troops in his army from reinforcing Pope in sufficient numbers to avoid the latter's defeat. War Secretary Stanton and Treasury Secretary Chase prepared a written condemnation of McClellan, which four of the seven cabinet members signed. A fifth member provided verbal agreement, a sixth was out of town, and the seventh was purposely excluded because he was a McClellan supporter. Essentially a threat to break up the administration unless McClellan was cashiered, the resolution was to be presented to the president at a cabinet meeting on September 2.[9]

But earlier that morning, Lincoln and Halleck met with McClellan to give him "command of the fortifications of Washington and all the troops for the defense of the capital." During the tumultuous cabinet meeting later in the day, Lincoln explained that McClellan had demonstrated an ability to fight defensively, and his organizing skills were "temporarily" needed, although the general "was good for nothing for an onward movement." If not directly implying that McClellan was unlikely to be his choice whenever the Union army once again went on the offensive, the president chose words that could easily be construed to have such a meaning.[10]

Although placating the Radicals, Lincoln's comments revealed an underlying weakness in the federal command. In short, McClellan could not be confident of his authority once he took troops out of Washington, although Lincoln repeatedly urged him to "destroy the Rebel army" once he was in western Maryland. For example, the general was unsure of what reinforcements he could draw from Harpers Ferry (in present-day West Virginia) or even Washington. The president proved to be a backseat driver during the whole ensuing campaign.[11]

While some historians conclude that McClellan's misgivings regarding his authority were fabricated after he lost command a second time, such conclusions do not give enough consideration to the poisonous atmosphere in the nation's capital after the rout at Second Manassas. For example, on September 3, Lincoln untruthfully assured the disgraced Pope that the president was entirely satisfied with the general's performance and that McClellan's elevation to command was only temporary. He falsely gave Pope reason to expect that he would soon be given another active command. Moreover, McClellan probably learned he was not Lincoln's first choice, since the president had earlier offered command to Major Generals Ambrose Burnside and Ethan Hitchcock, who both turned it down. Finally, according to Postmaster General Montgomery Blair, Secretaries Stanton and Chase "actually declared that they would prefer the loss of the capital to the restoration of McClellan to command."[12]

Although the showdown Battle of Antietam would eventually take shape in western Maryland, Halleck imagined that Lee was trying to lure McClellan westward so the Confederate army could return to Virginia to make a sneak attack on Washington from directly across the Potomac. As author Donald Jermann wrote:

> [Halleck] was obsessed with the idea that the Confederates were purposely luring McClellan to the west, away from Washington, with the intention of giving him the slip, crossing back over the Potomac into Virginia, making a forced march eastward down the south bank of the Potomac and seizing Washington from the south.[13]

As long as Halleck held such fears, McClellan would never get the number of troops he felt were needed to defeat Lee. McClellan's continued overestimation of the size of Lee's army compounded the problem. As long as such ghosts and fears haunted McClellan and Halleck, cooperation between the two would be difficult. Halleck was almost inviting Lee to defeat the Union armies sequentially by insisting that a sizable garrison remain idle in Washington instead of combining the two components into a virtually omnipotent force.

When McClellan was originally given command of the Union's largest army thirteen months earlier, he tried to establish a systematic intelligence network. Allan Pinkerton, who was a Chicago private detective, was hired to organize a web of informers. The two men knew each other before the war. McClellan was an executive in a railroad company that Pinkerton's agency had serviced. Pinkerton's methodical and detailed reports were authoritative looking but enormously overestimated the size of opposing forces from the beginning. Although McClellan had other sources that provided more reliable estimates, Pinkerton had earned an undeserved reputation for excellence because he had earlier discovered a plot to assassinate Lincoln in Baltimore on the president-elect's trip to his inauguration. Thus, when McClellan later came into possession of an order by Robert E. Lee that identified each Rebel unit, he forced himself to believe that each unit in the Confederate army was three times larger than comparable ones in the Union army.[14]

Lee's problem was to draw part of the Union army out of Washington for an open fight before the Yankees had a chance to recover from their low morale after the recent string of defeats. He could beat a bigger army if it was demoralized, but each day the enemy was given time to recover its confidence lengthened the odds against another Rebel victory. Lee concluded that he would cut the east-west communications in the Union by destroying a Maryland canal and key railroads in Maryland and later Pennsylvania. If done quickly it would compel the federals to leave Washington while they were still demoralized to do battle somewhere in southern Pennsylvania.

But first Lee needed to clear an invasion path into Pennsylvania by eliminating isolated Union forces in the Shenandoah and Cumberland valleys, which extended along a southwest-northeast axis. There were about ten thousand federal soldiers at Harpers Ferry and three thousand nearby at Martinsburg. On September 9, Lee gathered with his wing commanders, Major Generals Thomas "Stonewall" Jackson and James Longstreet, to devise a plan. The result became Special Order No. 191.[15]

THE LOST DISPATCH

The next day Lee issued the order, which became known as the Lost Dispatch to Southerners and the Lost Order to Northerners. It directed that Lee's army be divided into two parts on September 10. Stonewall Jackson would get two-thirds of the troops to capture Martinsburg and Harpers Ferry eighteen miles to the southwest. Lee would take the remaining one-third under Longstreet fourteen miles northwest to Boonsboro, Maryland, on the west side of South Mountain. However, once under way, Lee continued ten more miles to Hagerstown, Maryland, just shy of the Pennsylvania line, because of reports that enemy detachments were threatening Confederate supplies in the town. Upon arriving at their respective destinations, the two components of the Confederate army would be separated by

Confederate generals James Longstreet, left, and Thomas "Stonewall" Jackson, right. (*Library of Congress*)

twenty-five miles on a north-south axis. Major General Daniel Harvey (D. H.) Hill's division would operate independently as rearguard between the two. He was stationed on the west side of South Mountain in case the Union army attempted to march across the mountain to attack the scattered parts of the Rebel army.[16]

Jackson's command was further divided into three segments corresponding to the triangular perimeter of Harpers Ferry, which was shaped by the confluence of the Shenandoah and Potomac rivers. If Lee or any of Jackson's segments required help, each fragment would face at least one difficult river crossing in order to render aid.

In sum, Lee's smaller army would be temporarily divided into five fragments. If informed of the disposition of Lee's army, McClellan could almost certainly attack and overwhelm the pieces separately. But Lee anticipated the vulnerability would be brief because he expected Harpers Ferry to fall by September 12.[17]

On September 13, McClellan's army marched into Frederick, which was only fifteen miles east of the midpoint in the north-south line separating Lee from Jackson. Sometime before or around noon, Corporal Barton Mitchell of the 27th Indiana Infantry Regiment found a bulky envelope. Inside was an official-looking paper wrapped around three cigars. The document concluded "By command of General Robert E. Lee" and was signed "R. H. Chilton, Assistant Adjutant General." The paper was quickly passed up to

Brigadier General Alpheus Williams, whose staff officers included Colonel Samuel Pitman. Before the war, Pitman worked at a Detroit bank, where he frequently paid drafts with Chilton's signature because Chilton was paymaster at a nearby army post. Pitman verified that the captured copy of Special Order 191 was authentic.[18]

It was soon given to McClellan while he was meeting with a group of local citizens. He quickly dismissed the group to study the papers. Thereafter he wired Lincoln, "I have all the Rebel plans and will catch them in their own trap." He told Brigadier General John Gibbon, "Here is a paper by which if I am unable to whip Bobby Lee, I will be willing to go home."[19]

Among the citizens meeting with McClellan when the order arrived was a Confederate sympathizer. Although he did not know the specifics, he could judge from McClellan's reaction that the federals had unexpectedly learned something significant. The unknown Rebel rode off to find cavalry Major General J. E. B. Stuart, who passed the information along to Lee. In a letter after the war to D. H. Hill, Lee acknowledged that he was informed that McClellan "was in possession of the order directing the movement of our troops."[20]

Upon examining the order and the disposition of his own troops, McClellan decided that the two most vulnerable components of Lee's army were (1) those under Major General Lafayette McLaws besieging Harpers Ferry from Maryland Heights on the north side of the Potomac River and (2) Longstreet's truncated wing, presumed to be at Boonsboro based on the Lost Dispatch instructions and therefore only fourteen miles east of Frederick. McLaws and Longstreet each had about eight thousand men. However, to get to Longstreet, McClellan would have to fight his way through D. H. Hill's rearguard.

McClellan instructed Major General William Franklin to attack McLaws with his thirteen-thousand-man 6th Corps on the morning of September 14. Franklin was to proceed through Crampton's Gap of South Mountain and assault McLaws from the north while the Confederate general's force was facing south toward Harpers Ferry, which it was helping to besiege. But Franklin was cautious and did not begin his attack at the gap until mid-afternoon, despite having a fifteen-to-one numerical advantage over the few defenders sent to confront him. Essentially, September 14 became a wasted opportu-

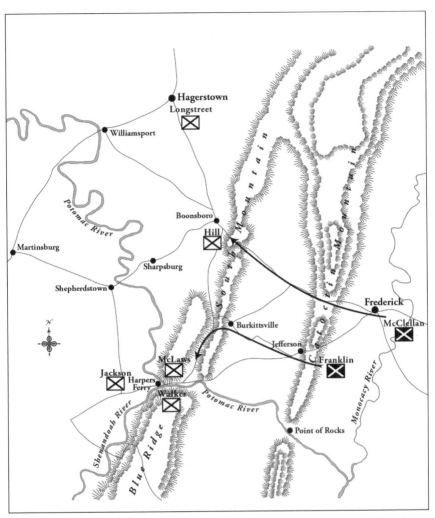

The disposition and movements of Union and Confederate armies around Sharpsburg, Maryland, at the time of the "Lost Dispatch."

nity in Franklin's sector. But if the Union defenders at Harpers Ferry could hold out another day, Franklin would have a second excellent chance on the fifteenth because he would be reinforced to twenty thousand men while McLaws's much smaller force was trapped between Franklin in his rear and a combination of the Maryland Heights cliffs, the Potomac River, and the federal garrison at Harpers Ferry to his front.[21]

Not realizing that Lee sensed something amiss, McClellan expected that Longstreet's reduced wing and D. H. Hill's rearguard would be close together at Boonsboro as directed in the Lost Dispatch. Thus, he expected to brush aside Rebel cavalry at the intervening gaps of South Mountain and descend upon the targeted Rebel units with five corps containing sixty-five thousand Union veterans.[22]

On the night of September 13–14, Lee responded to the warning provided by the sympathetic Frederick citizen earlier. He instructed Longstreet to return to Boonsboro from Hagerstown and directed that D. H. Hill defend the mountain passes through which McClellan would need to march if the federals were to try to get between Jackson and Lee. Thus it was on the morning of the fourteenth that McClellan's leading corps under Major Generals Joseph Hooker and Jesse Reno did not meet mere Rebel cavalry when they tried to force through Fox's and Turner's Gaps. Instead, at first light, D. H. Hill was present with about two thousand five hundred Confederates, and more would arrive throughout the day.[23]

The first attacks on Hill by a division in Reno's corps around nine o'clock in the morning were successful, but not enough to drive Hill off the mountain. Reno had about fifteen thousand soldiers in his entire corps and should have been able to drive Hill from the gaps by noon. However, the rest of Reno's divisions did not get to the battlefield until mid-afternoon. By then, Hill also had reinforcements and the situation was a standoff. It was not until seven hours after the battle began that the corps of Hooker and Reno launched a coordinated assault. When Hooker came up, the federals had thirty thousand soldiers on the battlefield, compared to Hill's five thousand. Nonetheless, the Confederates were able to hold on until darkness, when they retreated after suffering two thousand three hundred casualties versus one thousand eight hundred for the federals.[24]

The reason Hill was not swept off South Mountain by the crushing number of federals is because McClellan believed he was facing a much larger enemy force. Historian Jermann concludes, "Hill himself admitted that [the federals] could have [swept his force off South Mountain]. The reason [they didn't] is that the Union high command thought that they were facing 30,000 Confederates rather than 2,500. McClellan took the Lost Order at face value."

Therefore, on the morning of September 14, McClellan assumed Longstreet was close to Boonsboro instead of ten miles farther west at Hagerstown. "Furthermore," Jermann writes, "he believed that Hill's and Longstreet's divisions were much larger than they actually were." Thus, aside from Franklin's failure to attack McLaws at Maryland Heights, McClellan's own efforts (through Reno and Hooker) to capitalize on the Lost Dispatch were spooked by phantoms of imaginary Rebels compounded by a too-literal interpretation of the order. Although the federals won tactical victories at the South Mountain passes, they failed in the crucial objectives of destroying McLaws's isolated command or getting their eighty-five thousand-man army between Lee's fourteen thousand and Jackson's twenty-six thousand, which were separated by twenty-five miles.

Nonetheless, Lee's army remained widely scattered. The following morning presented the Yankees with excellent prospects for a second chance.[25]

By nightfall September 14, 1862, it was clear to Lee that McClellan's discovery of an unknown Confederate order had made his opponent uncharacteristically aggressive. He immediately perceived that McLaws's was the most vulnerable of his units. At eight o'clock that evening, he sent couriers to Jackson and McLaws, directing that they abandon their siege of Harpers Ferry and ordering the Maryland components of the Army of Northern Virginia to concentrate at Sharpsburg in preparation for crossing the Potomac River ford at Shepherdstown (in present-day West Virginia), where they would combine with Jackson on the Virginia side. McLaws attempted to reply with several couriers, but none got through. Nonetheless, he did not believe that he could escape and decided to defend his position against a likely renewal of Franklin's attack on his rear the next morning.[26]

Initially, Lee decided to move Longstreet and D. H. Hill only part way to Sharpsburg, to a place where they could protect McLaws's flank. But when Jackson responded that he believed the federals besieged at Harpers Ferry would surrender the next morning, Lee told Hill and Longstreet to go all the way to Sharpsburg and deploy defensively behind Antietam Creek, where they should await the outcome at Harpers Ferry. Owing to Jackson's optimism, Lee permitted the siege to continue. If Jackson and McLaws were successful, he would concentrate his entire army at Sharpsburg and make a stand against McClellan's combined army on Maryland soil.[27]

As Jackson predicted, Harpers Ferry capitulated the following morning, September 15. Cheering that rose up among the Confederate ranks, including those of McLaws, paralyzed Union General Franklin, who failed to renew his attack from the preceding day. He falsely believed McLaws outnumbered him two-to-one, whereas it was actually he who had a four-to-one numerical advantage. By the end of the day, Lee had fifteen thousand Confederates deployed in battle line west of Antietam Creek near Sharpsburg. They comprised only three infantry divisions augmented by a single cavalry brigade. One of the divisions was D. H. Hill's, and the other two were Longstreet's. As McClellan examined them through field glasses, he already had four times their number on the scene.[28]

Owing to a morning fog, McClellan declined to attack at Antietam (Sharpsburg) the next day, September 16. Lee's army gained strength to twenty-seven thousand as reinforcements arrived from Harpers Ferry, including McLaws's command. Finally, McClellan launched the Battle of Antietam early on September 17. It was the bloodiest single day of the Civil War, or any American war to date. McClellan had seventy-two thousand troops on hand, whereas Lee had fewer than thirty-five thousand until late in the afternoon. At the end of the day, McClellan suffered twelve thousand four hundred casualties, while inflicting ten thousand three hundred. But the Confederate defense line held. The armies glared at one another the following day before Lee withdrew to Virginia on September 19. McClellan is generally faulted for failing to use his superior numbers effectively. Instead he attacked different segments of the Rebel line sequentially, thereby enabling Lee to rush reinforcements to threatened points from units that were temporarily idle.[29]

LOSING THE DISPATCH

Although historians know how Special Order 191 was discovered, verified, and ineffectively used by the Union, it is not known how it got lost, or even if it got lost instead of stolen.

There are three extant copies of the Lost Dispatch. One was delivered to Richmond and now is in the National Archives. A second addressed to D. H. Hill is in Stonewall Jackson's handwriting and was held by Hill until his death in 1889. It is presently in the North Carolina State Archives. A third copy, also addressed to Hill, originated in Lee's headquarters and was the one found by Corporal

Mitchell of the 27th Indiana Infantry. The third copy is in the McClellan Papers at the Library of Congress.[30]

D. H. Hill was sent two copies because of his ambiguous reporting status. His division did not participate in the Battle of Second Manassas. Instead it came up from North Carolina afterward to augment Lee's army for the trans-Potomac invasion. When it caught up at Chantilly, Virginia, on September 2, Hill was not assigned to either Jackson's or Longstreet's wings but reported directly to Lee. Two days later it was the first of the Rebel divisions to cross the Potomac River at Leesburg, Virginia. Shortly thereafter Jackson crossed the river, and Hill reported to him because Lee had not yet arrived on the north bank. Because Jackson was recently injured in a riding accident, on September 6 he temporarily put Hill in command of all soldiers on the north shore, and Hill directed the seizure of Frederick.[31]

As noted, Special Order 191 was written at Frederick three days later, on September 9. Colonel Chilton, who was Lee's adjutant, signed the copies for delivery to the seven generals designated in the order: Jackson, Longstreet, D. H. Hill, McLaws, John Walker, Stuart, and William Pendleton, who commanded the artillery reserve. Brigadier General Walker was included because his division formed the third side of the planned triangle to surround Harpers Ferry, while the other two sides were to be formed by the commands of McLaws and Jackson.

Hill was among the recipients designated by Chilton because his division was to act independently as a rearguard. Additionally, Lee evidently regarded Hill's division as unattached to either Jackson or Longstreet once Lee himself arrived on the left side of the Potomac because that was Hill's status when he was on the right bank. However, when Jackson received his copy, he wrote out a second copy for Hill, presumably because he felt that Hill's division remained, or may have remained, part of his command. It was a tragic confusion because Hill claimed his brother-in-law Jackson's copy was the only one he ever received and the other one addressed to Hill from Lee was the one that fell into General McClellan's hands.[32]

Over the years, Hill went to great trouble to document that it was not his fault that Union soldiers captured one of the copies addressed to him. After the war, his chief of staff swore an affidavit stating the dispatch from Lee's headquarters never arrived. Similarly, in postwar correspondence with McClellan, Hill learned that the Lost Dispatch was found inside an envelope, which Hill presumed was the one it was delivered in.[33] He also obtained letters from two former Union officers stating that the Lost Dispatch was found two miles from Hill's campsite.[34] But even if the order were discovered miles away, it could have been dropped as Hill's unit marched out of Frederick the next day.

Confederate leaders were only certain about the identity of the captured document six months after it was lost, when in March 1863, McClellan testified before Congress. Partly because of the delay, Lee never had a formal investigation, although General Stuart and other officers became indignant with Hill when they learned his name was on the captured copy. Among his self-defensive writings after the war was a magazine article in which Hill claimed the Lost Dispatch was not so damaging as supposed because it indicated that Longstreet was closer to Hill's rearguard on September 14 than was actually true. Hill was implying that McClellan attacked the South Mountain passes more cautiously than he otherwise would have if he had known Longstreet's true location was more distant. The article annoyed Lee, who is reported to have said he could "not suppose the order was lost by a courier [because] couriers were always required to bring a receipt to show that written orders were safely . . . delivered." It was twenty-four more years before the detail about the three cigars became generally known.[35]

It seems logical that Chilton, Hill, or their staffs were likely responsible for losing the copy of the Lost Dispatch from Lee to Hill. Since it was half a year before Chilton learned which dispatch copy was lost, he claimed he could not recall the name of the selected courier. Although he did not maintain an operational log containing messenger names and noting when their receipts were returned, he insisted couriers were required to get signed receipts. Upon inquiry from Jefferson Davis after the war, he replied that failure to receive a receipt would undoubtedly have prompted a follow-up. Yet nobody from Hill's staff admitted signing one.[36]

At one point Hill suggested the variances between his and Chilton's accounts could be reconciled if the courier were a spy.[37] But it seems implausible that a spy would leave the order in an open field where it might only be discovered by accident, as opposed to delivering it directly to a responsible Union officer.

An article prepared for the *New York Times*'s *Opinionator* blog by the author summarizes a likely scenario:

> Since it was customary for delivery envelopes to also function as stock for signed receipts, some historians argue that the discovery of the order inside an envelope is convincing evidence that the copy from Chilton never reached Hill. But that scenario has problems.
>
> For one thing, there's no evidence the envelope was sealed when discovered; Corporal Mitchell's first sergeant claimed it was discovered unsealed. Yet the order was probably originally put in a sealed envelope so it could not easily be secretly examined and replaced by unauthorized readers. Moreover, if the envelope had indeed been sealed, it is unlikely Chilton would have wrapped the order around three cigars.[38]

CONCLUSION

The differing Chilton and Hill accounts cannot be reconciled. But if responsibility for losing Lee's order can't be affixed to one officer or the other, it remains possible, at least circumstantially, that they share the blame. Both men had other incidents of bad judgment and an unwillingness to accept the consequences of their actions.

Just before the Battle of Chickamauga the following year, Hill was at least partly responsible for the lost opportunity at McLemore's Cove. His commander, General Braxton Bragg, had set one of the best traps of the war to crush an isolated Yankee division, yet Hill failed to attack as ordered. He offered various mysterious explanations, including that a perfectly healthy subordinate, Patrick Cleburne, was too ill to lead the attack. Similarly, Chilton prepared and delivered questionable orders during the Peninsula Campaign and the Battle of Chancellorsville.[39]

Ultimately it seems likely the Lost Dispatch was an unlucky consequence of Lee's hurried movements following the Battle of Second Manassas. In order to hold the initiative, his marches challenged the hardest soldiers to keep up. Many simply could not and straggling became almost epidemic. Evidently, administrative officers were also hard pressed to keep up with demands.

Perhaps when Chilton's courier arrived, he learned that Hill had already otherwise received the orders and thereby assumed his copy was [merely] a . . . duplicate. With no need to leave the orders and believing them [to be superfluous] . . . he may simply have obtained a perfunctory receipt and kept the envelope and enclosure to hold his own cigars. It is the sort of thing anyone might do, and if he were one of the thousands of men killed in the ensuing battle, his story would never be heard.[40]

Alternatively, upon realizing his copy was lost, a surviving culprit may have felt too ashamed or fearful of punishment to reveal his guilt. A tale about Robert E. Lee famously repeated in the PBS documentary *The Civil War* by Ric Burns illustrates the point:

Once [a soldier] was brought before [Lee] for an infraction of the rules. . . . [T]he young man was trembling and Lee said, "You need not be afraid. You'll get justice here." And the young man said, "I know it general, that's what I'm scared of."[41]

Only the ghosts of those involved know the truth of how the Lost Dispatch came to be misplaced. But given the burgeoning access to historical information enabled by the Internet, more theories are surfacing. They range from the bizarre to the thought provoking. Perhaps you, dear reader, shall discover the answer.

FLORIDA AFTER
VICKSBURG

On January 10, 1861, the day after South Carolina artillery turned back the federally chartered merchant ship *Star of the West* sent to supply and reinforce the Union garrison at Fort Sumter in Charleston harbor, Florida became the third state to leave the Union. Its population of one hundred forty thousand, which included sixty-two thousand slaves, was smaller than the city of New Orleans. Despite its virtual tie with Virginia as geographically the largest Rebel state east of the Mississippi River, Florida contained less than 2 percent of the population and wealth of the Confederacy.[1] Yet fifteen thousand Floridians fought for the Confederacy—more than the number of its residents who voted in the 1860 presidential election. Most fought beyond state lines because Florida was located far from the fields of glory.[2]

However, the state became more important after the fall of Vicksburg, Mississippi, in July 1863. Once the Union gained control of the Mississippi River, the Confederacy was cut in two. In combination with the ocean blockade, federal gunboats patrolling the river blocked most supplies in the trans-Mississippi and blockade-immune Mexico from reaching needy troops to the east.[3] Foremost among such provisions were Texas cattle. Consequently, the Confederacy increasingly looked to Florida as a source of beef for its armies.

Although presently known for sand, sun, oranges, and amuse-
ment parks, Florida on the eve of the Civil War had nearly five times
as many cattle as people. The state's bovines were the first in North
America. Because beeves were not native to the Western Hemisphere
they were brought over as early as 1521 by expeditions of Ponce de
Leon. Ranching began sometime near the end of the sixteenth century near Saint Augustine, which was founded in 1565 and is the
oldest surviving settlement in North America. When Florida
became a US territory in 1821, it had abundant herds of wild cattle.
Upon Lincoln's election, the state ranked second to Texas in the per
capita value of livestock in the South. While Texas had 3.3 million
cattle in 1860, by 1863, Florida's comptroller estimated the state
had six hundred sixty thousand. The central and southern parts of
the peninsula were open range. Exports of live cattle to Cuba became
important in the 1850s, but were curtailed during the Civil War by
the Union blockade and official—but sometimes violated—
Confederate export prohibitions.[4]

Drovers were called "crackers" because of the distinctive sound
made by their twelve-foot-long whips. Cattle immediately responded to the discipline threatened by the sharp cracks. Cowboys rode
rugged, undersized horses known as "cracker ponies." They also used
dogs to find, round up, and protect the herds. The open range and
wild livestock provided opportunities for financially strapped pio-
neers to build profitable herds. But crackers had a tough life punc-
tuated by violence. Since vigilante justice was the typical antidote to
frequent cattle rustling, nearly all men carried firearms. The violent
culture was exemplified by an incident involving one saloon owner
who shot three riders attempting to enter his tavern while mounted,
although such arrivals were not an uncommon practice.[5]

About a month before General Braxton Bragg's Army of Tennessee
received reinforcements from General Robert E. Lee's Virginia army
in an effort to reverse sagging Confederate fortunes in the western
theater at the September 1863 Battle of Chickamauga, Bragg's chief
commissary officer was running short of beef when he learned that
Florida might have an abundant supply.[6] Simultaneously, General P.
G. T. Beauregard faced the beginning of a protracted siege at
Charleston, South Carolina, which prompted him to seek improved
logistics. He soon also focused on Florida as a storehouse of pork,
fish, molasses, sugar, and salt in addition to beef.[7]

Originally the Richmond-headquartered Confederate Commissary Department employed agents to sweep the country for supplies, but in April 1863, the Confederate Congress required that each state have its own commissary officer. Florida selected Major Pleasant White. By early October 1863, Bragg's commissary wrote White, "All other resources are exhausted. . . . [W]e are now dependent upon your state for beef." Simultaneously, White's counterpart for South Carolina wrote "we are almost entirely dependent upon Florida. . . . [O]ur situation is full of danger for want of meat."[8] The situation was equally severe in Virginia, but Georgia and South Carolina would likely require all that Florida could supply, especially after the Andersonville prisoner of war camp began adding demands in February 1864.

Cattle herds in the northern part of the state had been exhausted earlier in the war. Future rations would need to tap the south half of the peninsula, requiring drives of about a month to cover the three hundred to four hundred miles to Georgia railheads. At the end of 1863, the region accounted for 75 percent of the cattle leaving the state, which was averaging about one thousand five hundred head a week. Except for Key West and Tampa, only about three thousand five hundred of the state's residents lived south of present-day Disney World. It was wild territory containing no railroads and practically no roads of any kind. In addition to being a home for pioneering cattlemen it was also a haven for rustlers, deserters, runaway slaves, draft evaders, and others seeking to avoid the restrictions of an unwanted government.[9]

As Pleasant White pleaded for beef to supply out-of-state Rebel armies, the commanders of Union forces near the Florida peninsula became aware of the state's enlarged enemy supply role. Brigadier General Daniel Woodbury, who commanded the federal garrison at Key West, resolved to disrupt the supply flow by establishing a base on the mainland from which to launch forays against the cattle drives. He also believed such an outpost would encourage a portion of the rugged individualists in south Florida to join the Union army. Finally, he reasoned that it could serve as an export station for herd owners preferring to sell beef for greenbacks, or even gold from Cuban buyers, instead of Confederate scrip. Ironically, Florida beef was one item the federals were pleased to let escape through the maritime blockade. Any cattle shipped to Cuba, or elsewhere, would be unavailable to aid the Confederacy. By December 1863, Woodbury had selected Fort Myers as his mainland outpost, transforming it into the southern-most settlement on the peninsula along the gulf coast.[10]

BATTLE OF OLUSTEE

Simultaneously, Major General Quincy Gillmore, who commanded Union soldiers along the Atlantic coast from the Carolinas to Florida, learned of Florida's increased role in supplying Charleston. If that wasn't enough reason to consider invading Florida, Gillmore was soon given a second: Abraham Lincoln wanted to quickly establish a Union-loyal government in the state.[11]

In December 1863, Lincoln's "Proclamation of Amnesty and Reconstruction" specified that all Rebel states (except Virginia) could be readmitted to the Union individually by essentially holding elections and adopting constitutions that outlawed slavery. Elections could be authorized after merely 10 percent of the number of 1860 registered voters took the required loyalty oath. Lincoln wanted Florida, Louisiana, Tennessee, and Arkansas admitted on such terms before the June 1864 presidential nominating convention, where they would presumably deliver reliable Lincoln delegates. On January 13, 1864, Lincoln asked that Gillmore assist the president's personal secretary, John Hay, who had been sent south as a uniformed major to spearhead the formation of a Union-loyal Florida government.[12]

At the end of January, Gillmore formally provided to a skeptical General in Chief Henry Halleck the four objectives of his plan to occupy Florida between the Saint John's and Suwanee rivers. First was to enable cotton and other commodities from the area to be marketed to Northern and overseas buyers. Second was to cut off Florida commissary supplies to out-of-state Rebel armies. Third was to recruit resident slaves into the Union army. Fourth was to assist Hay in forming a Union-loyal state government. Shortly thereafter Gillmore directed that the invading force of six thousand five hundred be led by one of his division commanders, Brigadier General Truman Seymour.[13]

Seymour's men occupied Jacksonville, Florida, after arriving in transport ships. Although two-thirds were white soldiers from the Northeast, about one-third were blacks, including the Hollywood-

Confederate General Joseph Finegan, left, and Union generals Quincy Gillmore, center, and Truman Seymour, right. (*Library of Congress*)

famed 54th Massachusetts Infantry Regiment, as well as a regiment of former North Carolina slaves, and the 8th United States Colored Troop (USCT) Regiment from Pennsylvania. To oppose them the Confederate commander in east Florida, Brigadier General Joseph Finegan, had only about one thousand five hundred soldiers. Finegan quickly requested reinforcements from his district commander, General Beauregard in Charleston. Prompt movement would likely have enabled Seymour to secure enough territory to encompass more than 10 percent of the state's population, control much of the 165-mile railroad from Jacksonville to the state capital at Tallahassee, and cut off cattle supplies to Rebel armies farther north.[14]

Instead, during the first ten days in Florida, Seymour launched a series of raids to destroy provender and other Confederate-government-owned supplies at various depots within sixty miles of Jacksonville. Although he was forced to abandon captured goods on one raid at Gainesville after being driven away by Confederate guerrillas, the other forays were isolated successes.[15] However, the sorties also gave Finegan's reinforcements time to arrive. When the two armies later met in battle, the numbers were about equal at five thousand five hundred, partly because some of Seymour's soldiers were left behind to garrison outposts captured on the raids.[16]

Thinking Floridians were ready to rejoin the Union, Seymour began a march west on February 17, along the Jacksonville-Tallahassee railroad. His objective was to destroy the Suwanee River bridge because he believed it would prevent the enemy from getting reinforcements quickly enough to resist the invasion. On the morning of the twentieth, his leading mounted troops met scattered resistance until confronting heavy fire two miles short of Olustee Station around two o'clock in the afternoon, when they were about fifty miles west of Jacksonville. [17]

Armed with Spencer repeaters, the 7th Connecticut Infantry Regiment advanced to aid the mounted troopers. Initially, their superior rifles devastated an opposing Georgia regiment, killing all Rebel field officers.[18] However, owing to a logistics failure, the Connecticut soldiers could not promptly replace their soon-exhausted ammunition and had to withdraw. As the 7th New Hampshire and the 8th USCT Regiments replaced them, a pattern of Union errors began to emerge. First, as evidenced by their modest casualties, the mounted troops were far less often in the front lines compared to their artillery and infantry comrades. Second, when adding supporting infantry units to the fight, General Seymour did so in a piecemeal fashion that insured each would be outnumbered if they could not hold their ground until reinforcements came up.[19]

In contrast, the Confederate field commander, Brigadier General Alfred Colquitt, rapidly deployed new units forwarded by Finegan from Olustee Station. He organized the perimeter in a slight concave shape that enabled shooters to focus a concentric fire on the hapless Yankees. The 7th New Hampshire quickly disintegrated, partly because some members had been issued defective rifles and partly because of a confusing deployment order. The 8th USCT stood longer, but mostly only to absorb Rebel bullets. The recently formed regiment did not have enough target practice to reply effectively.[20]

After the 7th New Hampshire and 8th USCT Regiments were driven from the field, or were collapsing, unprotected federal artillery began rapidly falling prey to Confederate small-arms fire. Arriving to save them, a brigade of three New York regiments advanced to positions where they too became victims of the convergent Confederate fire. Soon thereafter the 7th Connecticut rejoined the fight after replenishing the cartridges required for their repeaters. When it appeared that the New Yorkers and 7th Connecticut could take no more, black soldiers of the 1st North Carolina and 54th Massachusetts Infantry Regiments entered the battle. Both advanced to the front, but the former slaves of the Carolina regiment were more vulnerable near the center of the enemy's convergent fire, whereas the 54th Massachusetts was on the left (south) end.[21]

Although the concave firing line was generally a Confederate advantage, it also had weaknesses. Given the equal size of the respective armies, the geometry resulted in fewer Confederate soldiers per unit length on the perimeter, thereby inviting a Yankee counterattack to focus superior numbers on a potential breakthrough point. The flaw was amplified during a thirty-minute period of inactivity when the Rebels had depleted their ammunition. One brigade commander helped relieve the shortage by sending his own staff officers to Olustee Station with orders to return with replenishments themselves.[22]

Around six o'clock in the evening, Seymour's army began a mostly well ordered retreat, but not before suffering about one thousand nine hundred casualties, compared to only 950 Confederates. At 34 percent of the troops employed, the casualty rate at Olustee was one of the highest endured by a Union army during the war. The comparative rates at better known battles such as Stones River, Chickamauga, and Gettysburg were 31 percent, 27 percent, and 25 percent, respectively. Less than 10 percent of federal Olustee casualties were among the mounted and artillery units, while over 90 percent were infantry. Like the composition of the army about two-thirds of casualties were whites and one-third blacks.[23]

Rebel infantry pursued the retreating federals for a few miles but halted after nightfall. Although criticized for failing to continue the chase, Colonel Caraway Smith, who commanded the Confederate cavalry brigade, claimed a nighttime pursuit would have been more confusing than effective. Nonetheless, the Rebels captured five of the Union army's sixteen cannon. The road back toward Jacksonville was strewn with Yankee guns, knapsacks, and blankets.[24]

General Seymour reported that 158 black soldiers were missing, compared to 346 whites.[25] Missing soldiers of a defeated army are normally captured because they are often too wounded to join a retreat. Several reports indicate that black combatants remaining on the field were murdered. There are even accounts that slaves accompanying the Rebel army participated in the slaughter.[26] However, when questioned by an investigating congressional committee, Seymour's chief of staff, John W. Turner, testified that he did not believe there were any outrages, that white and black captives were treated equally.[27] Nonetheless, given similar complaints at other battles later in the year such as Fort Pillow and Poison Springs, it seems likely that about twenty-five to fifty captured black soldiers were killed.[28]

General Beauregard was disappointed that Finegan's army failed to pursue the defeated federals. He especially lamented a jurisdictional entanglement that prevented him from sending more reinforcements to Finegan in time to win an even more decisive victory. Specifically, Beauregard had long urged that the isolated rail networks between Florida and Georgia be joined by constructing a connecting line between Live Oak, Florida, and Lawton, Georgia, but civil action in Florida courts blocked access to the necessary iron rails.[29]

FLORIDA'S YANKEE RAILROAD

Owing to the low value-to-weight ratio of railroad iron, blockade runners carried almost none of it. Therefore, the Confederacy could maintain its essential lines only by taking rails from less important ones. In principle, the transpeninsula link owned by the Florida Railroad Company that connected the Atlantic port of Fernandina to Cedar Key on the Gulf of Mexico was a good source for such rails because both endpoints were occupied by Union troops early in the war. But states' rights were taken seriously in the Confederacy. Therefore, the Richmond government could not legally seize the company's rails without legal due process.[30]

The matter was complicated by the fact that one of the company's founders was former US senator David Yulee of Florida, who resisted attempts in (Confederate) Florida courts to remove the rails. Furthermore, the company's largest shareholders were Northerners who simultaneously used their influence to protect the line from federal confiscation. Yulee and his Northern investors wanted to preserve the line owing to its profit potential upon the return of peace because the line provided a valuable shortcut for shippers between Atlantic and gulf ports such as New York and New Orleans. The first train to complete a transpeninsula journey did so only about a month and a half before the opening shots at Fort Sumter. [31]

Yulee organized the company eight years before the Civil War but depended on funding from the North to finish it, despite generous subsidies from the state of Florida. In 1858, controlling interest in the company was purchased by a partnership composed primarily of New Yorkers Marshall Roberts and Edward Dickerson. Roberts owned the United States Mail Steamship Company. He was interested in the railroad partly as a means of winning a postal contract to carry mails between New York and New Orleans. Among his vessels was the *Star of the West*, mentioned earlier in the Fort Sumter rescue attempt. Dickerson was a patent attorney, inventor, and business rival to John Ericsson, who designed the USS *Monitor*. After the war, Dickerson was involved in a number of high-profile lawsuits, including one that helped Bell Telephone become dominant in its industry.[32]

Shortly after the war started, Yulee had the Northern investors legally declared enemy aliens and thereby obtained control of the railroad within Confederate jurisdictions. However, in less than a year, the railroad's terminal points at Cedar Key and Fernandina fell to Union invaders. In April 1862, Confederate secretary of war George Randolph asked permission of Governor John Milton of Florida to appropriate rails from Yulee's company. Although Milton agreed, Yulee won a court injunction against seizure. Through a combination of similar legal actions, Yulee delayed removal of the iron long enough to prevent connecting Florida's railroads to those in Georgia until a month before Appomattox.[33]

Meanwhile, Roberts and Dickerson tried to prod Lincoln's government to aid their interests by sending troops into the north central part of Florida's peninsula. Since they wished to avoid the appearance of self-interest, they backed an initiative led by Eli Thayer, an abolitionist and former Massachusetts congressman. Thayer hoped to get twenty thousand soldiers to invade the state and upon victory become Florida citizens. Then they would raise cotton and establish a Union-loyal government. Although Vice President Hannibal Hamlin was involved in the plan, it ultimately failed to win approval despite receiving Lincoln's sympathies for a time.

Dickerson and Roberts engaged a crooked tax commissioner, L. D. Stickney, to represent their interests in Florida and pay federal taxes owed by the Florida Railroad Company. Their action enabled the railroad to avoid possible federal confiscation. But Stickney was motivated by self-interest. He sold company assets for personal profit and generally exercised poor stewardship. Consequently, at the end of the war, the legal status of Florida Railroad was ambiguous.[34]

Owing to his early advocacy of secession, Yulee was imprisoned for nine months after the war. Roberts and Dickerson used their influence to keep him confined until satisfied that he would cooperate in their postwar ownership scheme. By autumn 1866, the state of Florida had gained title to Florida Railroad because the company failed to pay interest owed to an Internal Improvement Fund established by the state prior to the war to subsidize construction of the railroad. Although the state originally provided subsidies of about $3.2 million, in October 1866, the company was sold for about $325,000 to a partnership managed by Dickerson. Yulee's cooperation was presumably obtained by his prison release and by permitting him to be a minor shareholder.[35]

CATTLE WARS

After the defeat at Olustee, Union efforts to thwart Florida cattle drives shifted to Fort Myers. Refugees began to arrive within days of the December 1863 Union occupation. Although originally organized into an irregular force of Florida Rangers, the men were soon incorporated into a new regiment named the 2nd Florida (Union) Cavalry. Gradually General Woodbury brought in Union infantry as well, including detachments of African Americans. During the final year of the war, companies affiliated with Fort Myers participated in numerous cattle raids as well as more ambitious expeditions. One was the destruction of Tampa's defenses at Fort Brooke. Another was an attempt to capture Florida's capital at Tallahassee, which was repulsed at the Battle of Natural Bridge in March 1865.[36]

In March 1864, Major Pleasant White received a letter from his south Florida cattle procurement agent, James McKay of Tampa. McKay told White the region would be unable to supply cattle in the next season unless a dedicated force was formed to confront challenges from Fort Myers. White forwarded the suggestion to the War Department in Richmond, where it was approved. Command of the unit was assigned to Major Charles J. Munnerlyn, who was busily organizing the 1st Battalion, Florida Special Cavalry, in early July. Composed of experienced cowhands, the unit informally became known as the Cow Cavalry or Cattle Guard Battalion.[37]

Munnerlyn was a wealthy Georgia slaveholder and a former Confederate congressman defeated at reelection because he advocated military conscription. Upon losing the election he enlisted as a private but was soon promoted and given special assignments where his ability and influence were better employed.

For example, he persuaded a personnel-stingy General Joe Johnston, who commanded one of the biggest Rebel armies, to provide a volunteer core of experienced drovers. Since Cow Cavalry members were draft exempt, the major received applicants from all over Florida. But he was selective because inexperienced cowboys were worse than useless. Eventually, the Cow Cavalry consisted of nine companies totaling eight hundred men and was active from Fort Myers to Georgia. By patrolling a three-hundred-mile stretch of dusty trails and open range, the Cow Cavalry enabled cattle drives to be resumed.[38]

Munnerlyn's troops also rounded up deserters, assisted in blockade running, and protected salt production. Salt was a valuable commodity throughout the South because it was the only practical way to preserve edible meat.

By October 1864, the Confederacy was desperate for more troops in the major war theaters. The shortage was so pronounced there was even growing discussion about admitting African Americans as soldiers. In such an environment, Richmond concluded that Florida's Special Cavalry Battalion could be more valuably employed in Georgia or Virginia. But Commissary General Lucius Northrop successfully appealed to Secretary of War James Seddon to leave it in place by writing "nowhere in the Confederacy can services of these few detailed men be so valuable as in the present organization."[39]

By February 1865, the success of the Cow Cavalry led to rumors among Confederates that Fort Myers might soon be abandoned. Since Munnerlyn had been promoted to lieutenant colonel in December, command devolved to Major William Footman. With two hundred troops from companies at Tampa and points farther south, Footman decided to give the approximately three hundred Yankees remaining in the fort a shove.

Footman originally planned a surprise attack, but after capturing five soldiers outside the compound who told him about the presence of women and children inside it, he decided to send a surrender demand. The demand was refused. The resulting southernmost "battle" of the Civil War east of the Mississippi evolved into a long-range skirmish with small arms and a few light artillery pieces, with few casualties on either side. Unable to take the fort by force, the Rebels retreated into the bush. The federals unilaterally abandoned the place a few weeks later.

The Fort Myers area was not long unpopulated. The following year, permanent settlers used lumber from the vacant structures to build new homes. Simultaneously, nearby Punta Rassa became the northern terminus of a telegraph line to Havana that facilitated commercial transactions, and the area became a leading export station for cattle. Less than twenty years later, Thomas Edison bought waterfront acreage for a winter home. Henry Ford and Harvey Firestone joined him when the three emerged as some of the leading American industrialists in the early twentieth century.[40]

CONCLUSION

Ultimately, the Union invasion that culminated in the Battle of Olustee accomplished little. It only briefly disrupted the Confederate supplies from Florida. Fewer than a hundred former slaves joined the Union army. (By the end of the war, more white Floridians than blacks were fighting for the Union.)[41]

Politically, the campaign failed to wrest Florida from the Confederacy. The Northern press blamed Olustee on President Lincoln's political ambitions. The *New York World* wrote, "[N]o military purpose took an army into Florida . . . as . . . it would . . . no more . . . put down the rebellion than would the occupation . . . of Coney Island." The influential *New York Herald* concluded, "[T]he Florida expedition was undertaken to bring the state back into the Union so that Mr. Lincoln might have three more delegates . . . in the nominating convention and Mr. Hay might go to Congress."[42]

Although some Union cattle raids were successful, the bigger factor restricting the flow of Confederate beef was an endemic reluctance among Florida cattlemen to participate. With little use for slaves, most were anxious for the restoration of peace in order to renew normal cattle exports to Cuba. During Reconstruction, Florida's cows-for-gold commerce helped enable the state's economy to recover earlier than other parts of the South.[43]

LINCOLN AND
MCCLELLAN

U ltimately, Civil War students must take a position on Major General George McClellan. It is necessary to decide whether Lincoln was correct in growing impatient with him or whether the general was driven to a natural resentment of the president—and especially Radical Republican leaders—by their unfair treatment of him. While most modern historians side with the Republicans, McClellan apparently had powerful endorsements among experts contemporary to his time.

One example was Helmuth von Moltke, the leader of the Prussian armies that won the 1870–1871 Franco-Prussian War, which paved the way for the creation of a unified German state. George Curtis, who was co-counsel to Dred Scott when the slave's case reached the Supreme Court in 1857, cited a conversation Moltke had with another American whom Curtis "had no reason to doubt." The American said, "Some of us in America do not estimate McClellan so highly as we do some of our other generals." Moltke replied, "It may be so, but let me tell you that, if your Government had support-ed General McClellan in the field as they should have done, your war would have ended two years earlier." However, since Moltke met with McClellan in 1868 when the latter visited Europe, it may be presumed that the Prussian was influenced by whatever information McClellan provided.[1]

Similarly, during the last summer of his life, Robert E. Lee visited his cousin Cassius Lee and they reminisced. Cazenove Lee, who was Cassisus Lee's twenty-year-old son, claimed to be present. Cazenove Lee later told Robert E. Lee Jr. that he had asked the former Rebel leader "which of the Federal generals he considered to be the greatest." According to Cazenove Lee, the old general answered, "McClellan, by all odds."[2]

While both the Von Moltke and Cazenove Lee incidents cannot be absolutely verified, they were told under circumstances that suggest validity. But whether or not they are true, a case for McClellan or Lincoln can be made independently of the statements.

Following defeat at the First Battle of Bull Run on July 21, 1861, the principal federal army in the east was in disarray. Lincoln called upon thirty-four-year-old George McClellan to take command, bring order out of chaos, and prevent the capital from being captured by the jubilant Rebels. The president chose McClellan for two reasons. First, he was familiar with him from before the war because Lincoln did legal work for the Illinois Central Railroad when McClellan was an executive in the company. Second, news reports had generally credited McClellan with winning four small victories in the western mountains of Virginia during the preceding month or so. In truth, the victories were actually won by subordinates, although McClellan had overall command. Nonetheless, they had the effect of separating the strategically important western part of Virginia from the Confederacy.[3]

The general arrived in Washington toward the end of July. Within a week he wrote the president that his objective was to crush the rebellion "at its very heart." He wanted to organize an army of such overwhelming strength that the South would quickly perceive "the utter impossibility of resistance." His goal was to end the war quickly by a decisive blow. About three months later, on November 1, the president elevated him to general in chief of all Union armies. He replaced the aged Major General Winfield Scott, whom McClellan complained was a hindrance. After renaming the defeated Bull Run army the Army of the Potomac in August, McClellan gradually transformed it into a disciplined organization as it was strengthened during the ensuing autumn months by numerous reinforcements. The new leader was also receptive to technological innovation. For example, he selected a committee to investigate the mer-

General George B. McClellan and President Abraham Lincoln. (*Library of Congress*)

its of repeating rifles, which resulted in a favorable report before the end of 1861, long before such weapons were deployed in even moderate numbers.[4]

Although the promotions indicate that Lincoln was gaining confidence in the youthful general, McClellan was simultaneously beginning a pattern of errors that would eventually lead to his undoing. Foremost among them was a tendency to greatly overestimate the size of the opposing Confederate army. A month after arriving in Washington, he imagined the nearby enemy to be one hundred fifty thousand strong, although the actual number was only about forty-one thousand. When Lincoln appointed McClellan general in chief, the president assured him that he would be given time to fully prepare his army before fighting but also warned that growing public impatience "was a reality and should be taken into account."[5]

In order to enlist support for removing General Scott, in October McClellan met with two Radical Republican senators who were eager for the army to start moving. McClellan successfully prompted Michigan's Zachariah Chandler and Ohio's Ben Wade to encourage Lincoln to replace Scott. In December, Wade would chair the Joint Congressional Committee on the Conduct of the War, which evolved into a politically motivated star chamber perpetually seeking scapegoats for Union battlefield setbacks. Wade soon became dissatisfied with McClellan's post-Scott-removal hesitancy to advance the army. Therefore, he called the general as the first witness to testify before the committee. A date was set for December 23.[6]

Unfortunately, McClellan came down with typhoid fever before he could testify. Recovery could take up to six weeks. Since Treasury Secretary Chase had previously averred that the war could not be financed beyond February 1862, Lincoln called a series of meetings before mid-January to decide what to do with the army. The meetings included selected cabinet members and two of McClellan's subordinates. In preparation for the last meeting, Lincoln asked that McClellan's subordinates arrange presentations explaining their own viewpoints about how the army might advance. One declined to say much because he did not believe the general in chief should be bypassed. The other was Major General Irvin McDowell, who commanded a division of the Army of the Potomac and had earlier led the initial federal army to disaster at First Bull Run.[7]

Edwin Stanton, who was maneuvering to get himself appointed secretary of war, warned McClellan about the final meeting. In response, the general rose from his sickbed to challenge the interference in person. Despite McClellan's attendance, McDowell was allowed to present his plan, which was a variation of the one that failed at First Bull Run. In early December, McClellan had explained to Chase the outlines of a turning movement to avoid entrenched Confederate defenses south of Washington. The amphibious movement to Urbanna, Virginia, would allow the Union army to reach Richmond, where the Rebels were unprepared to fight. He anticipated his plan would enable him to conclude the war with a climactic battle near the Confederate capital. At the January meeting, Chase asked McClellan to elaborate, but the general declined unless ordered to do so by the president. He complained that more amplification would result in publication of the scheme in a New York newspaper, thereby implying leaks in the cabinet. Finally, Lincoln merely asked if McClellan had a date certain in mind for getting started. The general replied affirmatively, and the president adjourned the meeting.[8]

The incident educated McClellan to the conspiratorial nature of politicians, which was soon amplified with betrayals by Stanton, who replaced Secretary of War Simon Cameron a few days later. As a means of fighting the general's political enemies, Stanton urged him to occasionally reveal selected information to a powerful newspaper. McClellan chose the *New York Herald.* In a three-hour January interview with the *Herald*'s Malcolm Ives, he disclosed much of what he had withheld from Lincoln and Chase. He would continue to plant stories with Ives "to throw dust in the eyes of the enemy." Ironically, Stanton would soon become one such conniving political enemy. When commenting on Stanton's character, historian Ethan Rafuse wrote, "Stanton did not hesitate to lie, double-deal, bully, or play the sycophant to get what he wanted."[9]

McClellan's Urbanna plan was a good one. Unfortunately, the opposing Confederate commander, General Joseph Johnston, recognized the danger and moved farther south before the plan was put into action. Nonetheless, McClellan launched a variation of it on March 17 and was within five miles of Richmond a little over two months later, having suffered comparatively few casualties along the way. Historian John Waugh explains the revised scheme, which became known as the Peninsula Plan because it would result in a Union advance on Richmond from the southeast by proceeding up the peninsula between the York and James rivers of Virginia:[10]

> McClellan would steer his huge armada toward Fort Monroe. . . . The line of operation, after landing, would run from Yorktown . . . to Richmond. [At Yorktown] he would marshal his army and march it, under cover of naval guns, up the peninsula between the York and James rivers. . . . No time, he vowed, would be lost in marching this force . . . to the very gates of Richmond . . . [where] the decisive battle would be fought . . .
>
> McClellan was banking on two . . . indispensible conditions. First, [in addition to his 110,000 troops he] would need 60,000 more [from Fort Monroe and the Washington area]. . . . Second, naval support was critical.[11]

Nonetheless, McClellan's army moved up the peninsula more slowly than he implied it would. Among his reasons for the delay was the denial by the president of the sixty thousand additional soldiers that the general considered indispensible to his plan. At the beginning of the campaign, Lincoln relieved McClellan as general in chief, ostensibly to enable him to focus on the Army of the Potomac. While the post was vacant, the president more frequently asserted his own judgment on military matters, including those involving interdepartmental troop deployments. When McClellan departed Washington, Lincoln detached ten thousand troops from the Army of the Potomac to be sent to the Shenandoah valley. By McClellan's reckoning, the general had left seventy-three thousand soldiers to protect the capital, including thirty-five thousand in the Shenandoah. It should have been enough, particularly considering that Rebel General Johnston burned the bridges over the Rappahannock River when he withdrew from the vicinity of Washington. Since Johnston was presently south of the Rappahannock, he would have difficulty backtracking to attack Washington. McClellan correctly reasoned that Washington was safe, but Lincoln and Stanton were not satisfied. By early April it was clear that McClellan would not get the additional soldiers he expected.[12]

Although the facts are consistent with McClellan's complaint, it was not a satisfactory excuse for the army's slow advance. His tendency to greatly overestimate the numerical strength of his opponent was a bigger factor. He estimated there were about one hundred fifty thousand Rebel troops blocking his way to Richmond, but it would be mid-May before the Confederates had as many as sixty-three thousand soldiers on the peninsula. When McClellan decided to besiege—instead of attack—the heavily outnumbered Rebels at Yorktown early in the campaign, Johnston commented, "No one but McClellan could have hesitated to attack."[13]

Much as McClellan predicted, once his army got close to Richmond, vigorous, if not pivotal, fighting began. Johnston felt compelled to try to push the Union army back by attacking on the last day of May. The resulting Battle of Seven Pines—only five miles from Richmond—was a tactical standoff, but it demonstrated the validity of McClellan's notion that the campaign would end with climactic fighting at the gates Richmond. Johnston was wounded at Seven Pines and replaced by Robert E. Lee. About a month later, Lee launched a weeklong series of attacks. Although Lee suffered a greater number of casualties, he forced McClellan to backtrack and kept him on the defensive.[14]

Washington pessimistically assumed the campaign was defeated. In mid-July, Lincoln appointed Major General Henry Halleck as general in chief. Halleck met with McClellan on the peninsula to ask if McClellan could launch an offensive with twenty thousand rein-

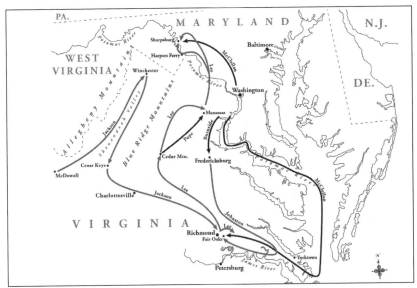

Confederate and Union movements and battles in the East, 1862.

forcements instead of the then-requested fifty thousand. McClellan responded by proposing that he cross the James River to attack the vital railroad junction at Petersburg south of Richmond. Halleck rejected the plan as too risky. During the first week of August, Halleck ordered that McClellan evacuate the peninsula. He was to send his soldiers to reinforce a new army that was operating in northern Virginia under the command of Major General John Pope. But Halleck promised that McClellan would command the combined forces if the armies were speedily united.[15]

On August 24, McClellan arrived with the trailing elements of his army at Aquia Creek, forty-five miles south of Washington and only about twenty-five miles from Pope's army. Meanwhile, Pope had battled Confederate Major General Stonewall Jackson at Cedar Mountain on August 9 and was trying to catch Jackson, who was rampaging on his supply lines, a second time. The result was the Second Battle of Bull Run, August 28–30. After joining Jackson the preceding day, Lee launched a surprise attack on the battle's final day that resulted in a decisive Rebel victory. Although three corps of McClellan's six-corps army had been attached to Pope in time for the battle, Radical Republicans, and even the president, believed that McClellan was intentionally slow in providing reinforcements to

Pope. While the fighting raged, McClellan commanded no troops except his staff officers.[16]

Radical Republicans had another reason for condemning McClellan, which would increasingly influence Lincoln as well.

General Pope's policies toward civilians were aligned with those of the Radicals, whereas McClellan's were not. McClellan believed the war was waged to restore the Union and not to attack private property, including slavery. He believed that after being defeated in a pivotal battle, Southerners could be persuaded to rejoin the Union with their institutions and property intact. His views would later be summarized in a familiar phrase of Lincoln's opposition political parties, "The Constitution as it is, the Union as it was, and the Negroes where they are." In contrast, Pope sought to confiscate slave property whenever possible and wage war on Southern civilians, as well as Confederate soldiers.[17]

Historian Bruce Catton summarizes Pope's civilian policies:

> Citizens of occupied territory would be held responsible for damage by guerrillas; the guerrillas . . . would be executed as would everyone who aided them. . . . Disloyal citizens [presumed and genuine] would be driven outside the army's lines and if they returned they would be treated as spies [subject to execution]. Inhabitants . . . who did not leave must take a [loyalty oath], and any who violated . . . [it] . . . would be shot.[18]

Those who condemn McClellan for his slowness often point to his hostile comments about Pope as evidence of deliberate reluctance. But such remarks are inconclusive. McClellan's resentment of Pope was natural because of the latter's earlier criticism of McClellan. When Pope arrived in Washington from the western theater in June, he began romancing Radical Republicans and argued that McClellan's "incompetency . . . [was] so great that he must be removed at once" and his soldiers attached to Pope's army.[19]

Over the objections of Radicals such as Stanton and Chase, who considered McClellan treasonous, after the Second Bull Run rout, Lincoln put McClellan back in charge of all the troops defending Washington, which included Pope's refugees. Following the battle, Secretary Stanton and General Halleck considered the city lost. They ordered that all of the arms and ammunition in Washington's arsenal be sent to New York, and that steamers be kept ready to evacuate the cabinet. McClellan immediately had the orders counter-manded.[20]

Eventually, the leadership change would lead to the Battle of Antietam on September 17, which ended Lee's first invasion of the North. It would also prompt Lincoln to issue the preliminary Emancipation Proclamation on September 22. But McClellan's performance during this period remains controversial. Critics continue to complain that he moved too slowly, fought poorly at Antietam, and persisted in wildly overestimating the enemy's strength.

Certainly the last criticism is valid and contributed to his cautious movements, but the political enemies in his rear must share the blame. Radical Republicans reacted with such hostility to his reappointment that the general could never be confident of his status. When the president announced the decision to select McClellan a second time, his cabinet nearly revolted. Lincoln appeased them by emphasizing that the general's authority was limited to defending the capital. He added that he did not welcome the necessity of making the appointment but felt he had no choice after other generals, such as Burnside, had turned it down.[21]

When Senator Wade asked him to sack the general, Lincoln replied, "If I relieve McClellan, whom shall I put in his place?"

"Why, anybody!"

"Wade, *anybody* will do for you, but not for me. I must have *somebody*."[22]

Thus, McClellan claimed he marched off to confront Robert E. Lee with uncertain authority for soldiers beyond the Washington perimeter. Halleck would later testify before Wade's committee that Lincoln verbally gave McClellan power to command troops in the field a few days after the tempestuous cabinet meeting where the president stressed that McClellan's authority was limited to defending Washington. Whether with or without field authority, McClellan left behind a hornet's nest of political animosity. For example, one of his friendly corps commanders who reached Pope in time for Second Bull Run would be falsely convicted—but later exonerated—in a court-martial for failing to cooperate with Pope.[23]

On September 17, McClellan confronted Lee's army on the left bank of the Potomac River in western Maryland near the town of Sharpsburg. Lee was still consolidating his army along a north-south axis parallel to the river. McClellan faced him from the north and east, with many of the Yankee soldiers located on the eastern side of Antietam Creek. The creek roughly paralleled the Potomac River. McClellan's plan was to first attack Lee's left flank at the north end of the enemy line. Once that attack showed progress, Burnside's corps was to cross Antietam Creek at a lower bridge, thereby cutting off Lee's retreat to the only nearby ford across the Potomac. As soon as the attacks on the ends achieved their objectives, McClellan would hit the Rebel center with everything else.

It was a good plan that broke down in the execution. Burnside's force was not completely across the lower Antietam and prepared to attack the south end of Lee's army until about three o'clock in the afternoon. When he finally attacked, the last remnants of Lee's army were fortuitously arriving from Harpers Ferry, whose Union garrison had surrendered two days earlier. They successfully repulsed Burnside's assault. In between the morning attack at the north end of the enemy line and Burnside's belated one on the south end, other Yankee assaults got mixed up. One attacking division directed at the north end accidentally hit nearer the center of the Rebel line because of confusion resulting from fog and battlefield smoke. Thereafter the charges along Lee's front were not the simultaneous concentration of troops McClellan intended but sequential and piecemeal. Thus, Lee was able to send reinforcements from one threatened point to another. Nonetheless, at the end of the day, Lee's army lacked the strength to counterattack, and it withdrew to Virginia two days later, after McClellan had declined to attack on September 18.[24]

Three weeks after taking command of a shattered army, McClellan had saved Washington and turned back the Confederate invasion, but Lincoln was not satisfied. He wanted the commander to immediately pursue Lee's army, which the president believed should have been destroyed during its retreat. (A little less than a year later, Lincoln would criticize the victorious federal commander at Gettysburg for the same reason.) But out of fear for its safety, Lincoln and Halleck kept over seventy thousand troops in Washington, compared to the eighty-five thousand with McClellan in the field. Partly because he consistently overestimated the size of the enemy's force, McClellan was reluctant to promptly pursue Lee. Yet if Halleck and the president had released more soldiers from Washington, the general might have won more decisively at Antietam, or at least pursued Lee more promptly.[25]

On October 26, McClellan's reinforced army of one hundred thousand began crossing the Potomac. Although Lincoln remained dissatisfied with the general, he was reluctant to remove McClellan, who was a Democrat, before completion of the 1862 midterm elections. On November 5, Lincoln replaced him for two reasons. First, the last of the important midterm elections were over. Second, Lee maneuvered a part of his army more rapidly than McClellan and blocked the Union army's path to Richmond through Culpeper, Virginia.[26]

CONCLUSION

The prevailing tendency among historians is to judge McClellan for what he did not do as opposed to what he did. Thus, he is not admired for accomplishing in a matter of three weeks the transformation of a defeated Union army into one that stopped Robert E. Lee's first invasion at Antietam. He is not applauded for immediately cancelling the orders of Stanton and Halleck to ship the weapons in Washington's arsenal to New York and keep a steamer ready to evacuate political leaders in the panicked aftermath of Second Bull Run. Nor is he credited with earlier reaching the gates of Richmond before the Battle of Seven Pines by suffering only modest casualties and inflicting more casualties on Lee than Lee did on him during the ensuing fighting on the peninsula. Two years later, Grant would sacrifice over sixty thousand soldiers to put Petersburg under siege and force the surrender of the Confederate capital. Grant's maneuver was much like the one proposed by McClellan in July 1862 but overruled by then General in Chief Halleck.

In contrast, there is little scrutiny of Lincoln's mistakes. For example, he should not have recalled McClellan from the peninsula. Instead, Pope's army—as the augmented successor to McDowell's corps—should have marched overland to Richmond from Washington as originally planned while McClellan's presence on the peninsula held Lee's army in check. It was only after Lee learned on August 13 that McClellan was withdrawing that he felt free to take most of the defenders away from Richmond to attack Pope.[27]

Additionally, Lincoln erred when keeping more than seventy thousand soldiers in Washington while McClellan was closing in on Lee in western Maryland during the pursuit to Antietam. By keeping the Union forces separate, Lincoln invited Lee to defeat them individually in sequence. Probably as many as fifty thousand Washington troops could have been sent to McClellan without endangering the capital. Such an additional numerical advantage might have prompted McClellan to attack Lee's center at Antietam late in the day when it was most vulnerable, instead of declining to throw in his last reserves. Finally, Lincoln's selection of Burnside to replace McClellan was about as bad a choice as choices can get. It validated Brigadier General John Gibbon's prediction upon learning of the change that the switch was worth as much to the South as a battlefield victory, which was demonstrated a little over a month later when Burnside was defeated at Fredericksburg.[28]

There are probably two reasons why Lincoln's errors are minimized while McClellan's are spotlighted. First, Lincoln was martyred and is arguably our country's greatest president. Second, McClellan was arrogant and not in harmony with Lincoln's central idea, which only became clear after the Emancipation Proclamation. Partly, if not mostly, in order to avoid a fatal rupture in the infant Republican Party, the president transformed a war to restore the Union "as it was" into one to transform the nation as he felt "it ought to be"—free of slavery and dominated economically by the North.[29]

Ultimately, Lincoln's purpose was to end all resistance to the federal government, after which he could dictate peace terms. He would make no deals. In contrast, McClellan presumed the war's objective was to restore the Union with a minimum of bloodshed. The difference is underscored by the fact that the two men became opposing candidates in the 1864 wartime presidential election. Thus, a common mistake is to judge McClellan's military strategy within the context of Lincoln's frame of reference.

However, it cannot be denied that McClellan's biggest error was consistently overestimating his opponents' numerical strength. The false belief repeatedly constrained him from taking swift and aggressive military actions that probably would have often succeeded. Moreover, it is unlikely that the president could have ever provided the general with enough soldiers to overcome McClellan's delusion that he was perpetually outnumbered. It was the general's fatal flaw that would eventually have necessitated his dismissal under any likely alternate scenario.

AFTERWORD

Three realms of research where further analysis might reveal additional examples of Civil War scandals and controversies are summarized below, with examples from each sector.

The first area centers on the fluctuation of public opinion caused by variable battlefield results. In this context, consideration of alternate scenarios can be enlightening. For example, the earlier "Preempting the Civil War" chapter explores the potential consequences of substituting a warship for the commercial *Star of the West*, which was the ship used in the first—but failed—attempt to relieve Fort Sumter in January 1861. Too often authors write history as if results could not have been different, but overreliance on hindsight handicaps historical writing. Such literature often fails to explain why leaders took actions that appear to be inconsistent with those results, or concludes that such actions were necessarily prompted by faulty decisions. Additionally, it tends to overlook—or at least minimize—scandalous interdictions that may have suppressed alternate scenarios. The analysis of fluctuating border state sympathies provided below is one example.

Second, the enormous flows of money through the US and Confederate Treasuries required to finance the war as well as the near fifteen-fold increase in the price of cotton from 1860 to a peak in 1864 were huge temptations for corruption. The example below inspects evidence that Ulysses Grant may have been involved in cotton trade, either directly or indirectly. While the indications are inconclusive, they suggest that future biographers and other historians should not casually dismiss them.

Third, the war resulted in legal actions and interpretations that differed markedly from convention. Some interpretations were internally inconsistent and produced long-term unintended consequences, nationally and internationally. The attempt to adapt accepted maritime rules of warfare to an American war between states is one example.

BORDER STATE SYMPATHIES

Slavery was legal in the border states of Delaware, Maryland, Kentucky, and Missouri. While none showed any indication of wanting to abandon the institution, all desired to remain in the Union if their sovereignty was respected. There were so few slaves in Delaware that the state never seriously considered secession, even though it refused to abolish slavery, even if compensated. (Delaware voted against the Thirteenth Amendment that freed the slaves.) The situations in the other three border states were more varied. Each was significantly influenced by battlefield results and the coercive actions of the Union and Confederate governments respectively, where applicable.

At the outset of the secession crisis, Missourians were predominantly Union loyal. However, many were quickly alienated by heavy-handed federal actions. Two weeks after Lincoln took office, the state's secession convention voted three-to-one to remain in the Union. But Lincoln's call for volunteers after Fort Sumter strengthened Southern sympathies. The president's political connections in the state aggravated the situation by getting the impulsive Brigadier General Nathaniel Lyon appointed military commander.

Lyon soon provoked a tragic incident when his inexperienced troops fired into a Saint Louis crowd composed mostly of women and children. In response, the state legislature promptly handed pro-Southern governor Claiborne Jackson complete control over the Missouri Militia. Jackson renamed it the Missouri State Guard and appointed former governor Sterling Price to lead it as a major general. Earlier Price chaired the convention that voted to keep Missouri in the Union. However, like most delegates, he felt the Union was voluntary and that states should not be coerced to remain in the Union or choose sides.[1]

Conditional Unionists quickly joined the guard by the thousands. Although three-fourths of the white Missourians who eventually fought sided with the North, sentiment in the Show-Me State was much different during the first year and a half of the fighting. Lyon seized the state capital and chased Price's State Guard and Governor Jackson into the southwest corner of the state, where regular Confederate troops under the command of Brigadier General Ben McCulloch reinforced Price. Over twice as many Missourians (five thousand six hundred) fought with the South as fought with Lyon's Union army when the opposing forces clashed at the state's first battle on August 10, 1861, at Wilson's Creek. Lyon's command was composed mostly of volunteers from Kansas and Iowa, as well as soldiers from the regular prewar US Army. Much to Price's disappointment, after winning the battle, McCulloch withdrew to Arkansas, partly out of respect for Missouri's sovereignty until the state officially declared which side it would join.[2]

After Wilson's Creek, Price led the State Guard to capture a federal post with about three thousand defenders at Lexington on the Missouri River toward the end of September. Embellished with the Wilson's Creek victory, Price received an estimated fifteen thousand recruits, thereby increasing his force to twenty thousand. Many of the late summer volunteers proved to be sunshine patriots after Price retreated a second time to southwestern Missouri, thereby demonstrating he could not hold central Missouri without support from the Confederacy. Nonetheless, the recruiting surge during the march to Lexington suggested that Southern sentiments were substantial. If a better-supplied regular Rebel army were to combine with Price in an attempt to win the state for the Confederacy, such latent support might be transformed into reliable reinforcements.[3]

That was precisely the objective of Confederate Major General Earl Van Dorn when he took charge of the combined Price and McCulloch forces in northwest Arkansas in early March 1862. He sought to destroy the opposing Union army by attacking it from the rear and cutting off its retreat. With a rare Confederate numerical advantage, Van Dorn laboriously circled around the Union army under Lyon's successor, Brigadier General Samuel Curtis, at the Battle of Pea Ridge, Arkansas. Partly because he ran out of ammu-

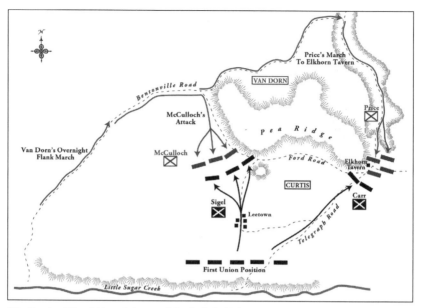

The Battle of Pea Ridge, Arkansas, March 6–8, 1862.

nition by failing to keep his ordnance train nearby, he was defeated. However, the number of Missourians fighting for the South at Pea Ridge was again larger than those fighting on the Union side. The bulk of Curtis's ten-thousand-five-hundred-man army was composed of units from Iowa, Illinois, and Indiana, whereas nearly seven thousand of Van Dorn's sixteen thousand soldiers were Missourians.[4]

Although a Rebel ammunition shortage helped save Curtis's army, the battle might have been a Union disaster. Cut off from supplies and an escape path to Missouri, Curtis, if defeated, would have been forced to surrender, or retreat to the south or west. Going south would take him deeper into enemy territory, while the Indian nations to the west offered scant forage. Either way, Van Dorn's larger army would likely have pursued, thereby requiring Curtis to fight again, probably against even longer odds. As Bruce Catton put it in *Terrible Swift Sword*, "[I]f the final Union counterattack had not cleared Telegraph Road, [the escape path to Missouri,] the [Union] army would have been almost helpless.[5]

With Curtis's army taken off the board, Van Dorn could have proceeded with his plan to threaten Saint Louis. Like Price, who gained fifteen thousand recruits during his follow-up victory at Lexington after winning at Wilson's Creek six months earlier, a victorious Van Dorn army may have swelled with reinforcements. If they had merely equaled those attracted to Price the previous September, a Rebel army of thirty thousand could likely have captured the state capital and seriously challenged Union control of the state in spring 1862. Missouri might even have joined the Confederacy.[6]

When a Confederate army tried a third time to gain control in Missouri at the December 7, 1862, Battle of Prairie Grove, Arkansas, Missourians fighting for the South again likely outnumbered those in the opposing Union army. The Union army had nine Missouri regiments, battalions, and batteries, whereas the Confederate army had fourteen.[7]

A variety of questionable machinations helped keep Maryland in the Union. Like Missouri, the state was initially overwhelmingly pro-Union. Even two weeks after Sumter surrendered, the state's legislature declined to consider secession. It also voted fifty-three to thirteen against authorizing a secession convention. However, the lower house passed a resolution condemning the war that "the federal government had declared on the Confederate States" and proclaiming its "determination to have no part . . . in its prosecution." Essentially, Maryland tried to be neutral. But since it bordered the nation's capital on three sides and would have tens of thousands of Union soldiers occupying its territory, neutrality would be virtually impossible.[8]

After the Union defeat at First Bull Run in July 21, 1861, pressure mounted to recall the legislature so that the matter of secession might be reconsidered. Secession sentiment was growing in the wake of the Confederate victory. Since the governor opposed secession, he ordered the legislature to meet for the last time that year in September at Frederick, which was in a pro-Union part of the state. But, as described by historian James McPherson, Lincoln was taking no chances that secessionists might prevail:

> [T]he administration was alarmed by [false] reports for a simultaneous Confederate invasion of Maryland. Lincoln decided to take drastic action. Union troops sealed-off Frederick and arrested thirty-one secessionist members . . . all were imprisoned for at least two months, until after the election of a new legislature in November . . . [and some] remained in prison [for over a year.]

Although Lincoln justified the prolonged detention of these men on grounds of "tangible and unmistakable evidence" of their ". . . unmistakable complicity with those in armed rebellion," the government never revealed the evidence or brought any of the prisoners to trial.[9]

However, according to Assistant Secretary of State Fred Seward, son of Secretary of State William Seward, it was not merely the arrested legislators who were prevented from voting. Many other lawmakers were discouraged from even attending because of the presence of the armed Union soldiers making arrests on the roads to Frederick. Otherwise, according to Fred Seward, Maryland's legislators would likely have voted for secession. If the younger Seward's judgment was correct, it further underscores how secession sympathies in the border states could be swayed by public perceptions regarding which side was winning the war.[10]

In order to insure favorable results in Maryland's statewide elections on November 6, 1861, the Republicans resolved to steal it. Opposition candidates were referred to as "peace party" members. Historian William Marvel explains:

> Most of the peace party candidates had already been [jailed] in Fort McHenry. . . . Roving patrols of Union soldiers threatened to raid peace party rallies on the grounds of perpetrating an "act of open hostility to the Government." . . . Army headquarters ordered military commanders to post guards at each polling place for the ostensible purpose of protecting the rights of Unionists voters . . . [but] those guards had instructions to arrest "disunionists" who dared approach the polls and Unionist citizens stood by to point out all suspects—which proved easy enough since the anti-administration parties were distributed ballots of a different color from those of the "loyal" parties. . . . Soldiers arrested disgruntled Marylanders all day long before they could cast ballots against Lincoln's war.[11]

The capricious arrests and imprisonment of many Marylanders by Union military authorities together with the enforced closure of opposition newspapers outraged many of the state's citizens. Among them was the man who would later murder President Lincoln. Eventually, however, because it stayed in the Union, about two-thirds of the state's white soldiers fought for the North.[12]

Like Missouri and Maryland, Kentucky tried to remain neutral, but it had a better chance of succeeding than did the other two. Lincoln was less inclined to impose federal power out of fear of alienating the state. He could not as readily suppress resistance because there was no equivalent to Missouri's Lyon in Kentucky and because, unlike Maryland, the state avoided the nearby presence of the tens of thousands of Union soldiers guarding Washington City. Prior to Lincoln's call for volunteers after Sumter, Kentucky's sympathies were decidedly against secession. They partly reflected the status of the state's traditional contributions to compromise, most famously personified in Senator Henry Clay, who had died nine years earlier. However, contemporary Kentucky leaders such as John J. Crittenden carried on the tradition of mediation. Even after Sumter's surrender, the state remained predominantly Union loyal, as the June and August 1861 elections demonstrated. But those election results probably also reflected the fact that federal troops "committed no overt crimes against the state, as they did in Missouri."[13]

Kentucky's neutrality was shattered on September 3, 1861, when Confederate Major General Leonidas Polk occupied and fortified the bluffs on the Mississippi River town of Columbus. By a three-to-one ratio, the state legislature voted that since Kentucky had been "invaded by the forces of the so-called Confederate States . . . the invaders must be expelled." It also invited Union forces to help repel the Rebels. About 60 percent of the state's citizens choosing to fight would side with the North, but the 40 percent siding with the South would be the largest percentage of any of the four border states.[14]

Although Confederate armies occupied much of Kentucky for about a month in late summer 1862, they gained few recruits. As Price's experience in Missouri showed, after the shooting started, border state citizens were unlikely to side with the Confederacy until the Rebels demonstrated they could hold such states indefinitely. In Kentucky, that meant at least defeating a major federal army. Despite earlier, smaller victories at Richmond and Munfordville, the Confederacy lost that chance at Perryville in early October. Nonetheless, Kentuckians became increasingly resentful of federal outrages after Union occupation. Historian Jeffrey Hummel explains:

> Federal authorities declared martial law; required loyalty oaths before people could trade or engage in many other daily activi-

ties; censored books, journals, sermons, and sheet music, and crowded the jails with Rebel sympathizers. By 1862 the military was interfering with elections, preventing candidates from running, and dispersing the Democratic convention at bayonet point. The net result was that Kentucky felt greater solidarity with the rest of the South at the war's end than at its beginning.[15]

In sum, sentiments in the border states fluctuated based on the changing fortunes of war as well as resentments to sometimes extralegal conduct by the Confederate and Union military authorities.

COTTON TRADING

Rhode Island US senator William Sprague's Texas Adventure, described earlier, is only one example of corruption in the wartime intersectional cotton-trading market. While my earlier book, *Trading with the Enemy*, provides additional examples, recent discoveries by historian Frank Varney suggest that General Ulysses Grant may have been a beneficiary. Varney's findings provide a new possible explanation for Grant's notorious order banning Jewish traders from his military district in 1862. In *General Grant and the Rewriting of History*, Varney discloses finding some "very strange letters" of William Truesdail's, who was, for a time, the chief of military police in Nashville.

Truesdail was writing Major General William S. Rosecrans to volunteer information about why General Grant was hostile to Rosecrans. Varney summarizes:

> Grant's anger toward Rosecrans may have begun with the actions of a committee Rosecrans headed to investigate illegal black-market cotton speculation . . .
>
> Why this should have caused problems with Grant is unclear; but it is known that his father, Jesse Grant, was rumored to have been involved in the black market. There is also Grant's infamous General Orders no. 11 to be considered, in which he banished Jews from his area of authority on the ground that they were engaged for profit in illegal activity . . . including cotton smuggling . . .
>
> At the same time, Jesse Grant had just taken money from a [Jewish] Cincinnati firm that desired him to use his influence to secure a permit for it to do business in the Department of

Missouri. . . . If Grant's family, friends, or even Grant himself had been engaged in the illicit purchase of cotton, he might well have been concerned with the activities of the commission. In that context, his attempt to remove Jews might be seen as an effort to reduce competition.

In order to clarify matters, Professor Varney searched for the commission's records but could not find them, which raises the possibility that they may have been destroyed. One of Truesdail's letters reports that Grant sent an officer to collect the report and all papers relating to it. Truesdail wrote Rosecrans that he did not approve of turning over the papers to Grant's representative and was "fearful the records . . . will be lost."[16]

Unfortunately, Truesdail soon became ill and died two years after the war ended. But there is additional evidence that Grant family members participated in interbelligerent cotton trading. For example, on December 15, 1863, President Lincoln signed a pass for a former Kentucky congressman, Samuel Casey, to travel multiple times to Shreveport, Louisiana, and be given safe passage when returning with cargo. Shreveport was a major cotton-trading center at the time, and Casey was a brother-in-law to Grant. Casey arranged to buy twenty thousand bales at a bargain price directly from the Confederate government. According to historian Craig Symonds, "Without question, this was trading with the enemy. The Rebels would get $2 million in much needed specie, but . . . New England mill owners would get fifteen times that much in value of cotton." With a fifteen-to-one value ratio, there was plenty of room for profits to Casey. [17]

Similarly, toward the end of the war when Grant was trying to starve Lee's besieged army at Petersburg, Virginia, he convinced Lincoln that military considerations demanded that interbelligerent trading east of the Appalachian Mountains be prohibited. Lincoln appeared to be surprised by the demand, telling his former law partner and present bodyguard, Ward Hill Lamon, "I wonder when General Grant changed his mind on this subject. He was the first man, after the commencement of the war, to grant a permit for the passage of cotton through the lines, and that to his own father."[18]

Nothing in Varney's discoveries and the incidents cited above is proof that Grant personally benefitted from wartime cotton trade.

Nonetheless, the episodes provoke enough curiosity to merit additional investigation, particularly considering that biographers normally represent the general as consistently and vigorously opposing trade with the enemy.

VALIDATING THE BLOCKADE

When Lincoln decided to blockade Southern ports less than a week after Fort Sumter surrendered, he not only created a monumental task for the Union's small navy but also quickly found himself tangled up in a confusing maze of international maritime law. His adaptations sometimes contradicted traditional American naval policies, were internally inconsistent, and would have consequences stretching well into the twentieth century. To understand such matters it is first necessary to examine the background and accepted international conventions applicable to maritime commerce during wartime.

During the nineteenth and much of the twentieth centuries, the British navy ruled the oceans. Whenever the country went to war, it typically announced a blockade of the enemy's ports. In the era before steam power, such blockades were difficult to enforce systematically because ship propulsion was at the mercy of the wind. Consequently, Britain might not physically maintain blockading patrols but merely use the announcement of a blockade to board neutral vessels anytime and anywhere wind conditions permitted in order to confiscate contraband cargoes. The practice could become rife with abuse, and it tormented neutrals.[19]

Britain's weaker opponents typically retaliated by authorizing privateers to raid British commerce on the high seas. Privateers were privately owned vessels permitted to wage such war under letters of marque issued by the authorizing government. They were allowed to sell the captured cargoes and keep the proceeds for themselves. Although privateers were legally required to put a crew aboard a captured ship in order to take it to a neutral port, where their rights to the cargo would be determined by the judgment of a prize court, some did not always comply. Therefore, the British often considered privateers to be indistinguishable from pirates. In both the American Revolution and the War of 1812, the United States was one of the nations that responded to a British blockade with privateering.[20]

In an attempt to balance the differing objections of Britain and the lesser European naval powers, fifty-five signatories agreed to a new treaty, termed the Declaration of Paris, at the end of the Crimean War in 1856. It had four major points. First, privateering was prohibited. Second, cargo could not be captured from a ship under a neutral flag unless the cargo was contraband. Third, freight owned by a neutral party could not be seized from an enemy ship unless such cargo was contraband. Fourth, paper blockades were illegal; blockades could only be binding if physically effective (meaning capable of being reliably enforced).[21]

The treaty was not binding on countries that did not sign it. Among such countries was the United States, which wanted to retain its tradition of privateering. After Lincoln announced his blockade, Jefferson Davis promptly authorized privateering. Secretary of State Seward asked Britain and France if the United States could belatedly sign the declaration but was told the prohibition on privateering could not be applied to the present (pre-existing) situation. Lincoln responded by announcing that captured privateers would be executed as pirates. When the lawyer representing one captured crew in New York argued that his clients were innocent because the Confederacy issued letters of marque as an independent country, Seward threw him in jail. Davis retaliated by declaring that Union war prisoners would be reluctantly executed in equal numbers for each captured privateer executed. Lincoln backed down and failed to proceed with any executions because he knew Davis would respond by executing Union prisoners in the same number. He later reciprocated with Davis's quid pro quo stance when he would not permit Union prisoners to be exchanged for Confederate ones unless captured Union African American soldiers were treated as prisoners of war on the same basis as white Union soldiers.

The bigger question was the matter of the blockade's legality. Captured vessels soon started pleading for release by arguing in court that the blockade was illegal. A blockade is an act of war, but no war had been declared. (That's why the 1962 Cuban blockade was officially referred to as a "quarantine" by President John Kennedy.) Lincoln was caught in a legal dilemma. Although a blockade is an act of war against a foreign nation, Lincoln insisted that the Confederacy did not exist as a nation. Such reasoning implies that he should have closed the ports as opposed to blockading them.[22]

But there were two problems with closing the ports. First, the US Constitution required that all ports be treated equally. A president lacked the authority to close some and leave others open. Second, unlike the well-defined terms of the Paris declaration, there were no internationally recognized rules for selective port closures within a given nation. The absence of such rules was thought likely to increase the probability of armed confrontation with a neutral vessel. If such a vessel belonged to Britain or France, the confrontation might provoke those powerful countries into siding with the Confederacy.[23]

Since the Constitution did not address disunion, there were no good legal options. All choices had potential consequences. In the end, the choice of a blockade permitted Great Britain and France to grant belligerent status to the Confederacy, even if they did not recognize it as an independent country. The British reacted in May 1861, with the Queen's Proclamation of Neutrality, which classified the Confederacy as a belligerent, but not a diplomatically recognized country. Thus, Rebel ships in British and colonial ports were thereafter allowed to obtain fuel, supplies, and repairs. The commerce raiders *Alabama*, *Florida*, and *Shenandoah* were examples. As a belligerent, the Confederacy was also permitted to buy weapons and supplies from neutral countries, including Great Britain. However, Queen Victoria clarified that the 1818 Foreign Enlistments Act, which prohibited British subjects from joining a belligerent navy and signified that any British ship running a blockade did so at its own risk, would also apply to the situation in America. Consequently, her government would not seek the release of captured blockade runners.[24]

Fortunately for the United States, other European powers followed Great Britain's lead and ignored the provision in the Paris declaration that blockades were legal only if they could be reliably enforced. For much of the war—certainly the first year or two—the federal blockade failed to be effective because too few ships were available to enforce it dependably. Although Confederate foreign commissioners correctly argued that the blockade did not meet the required standards of legality, Britain and the rest of Europe disregarded their pleas. Thus, blockade running became a separate business in which European deep-water vessels carried cargo to centers like Nassau and Bermuda, where the last leg of the trip into the Confederacy was executed by specialized carriers that assumed the risk of capture.

Britain concealed its chief reason for failing to recognize the illegalities of the blockade. Essentially, it was not merely thinking of the present war in North America but of potential future European conflicts. The Paris declaration had never been popular with leaders whose prime interest was the prominence of the British Empire. It reduced the flexibility of the British fleet to protect its interests. In fact, that was the precise objective of the Continental powers sponsoring the declaration. Essentially, the British could not optimally employ their fleet in a future war if it was required to effectively blockade mile after mile of enemy coastlines, such as, hypothetically, the combined Atlantic and Mediterranean shorelines of France. If signatories of the Paris declaration generally acquiesced to Lincoln's implementation of the blockade, it would become a legal international precedent that would effectively nullify the treaty provisions most objectionable to the British navy.[25]

In sum, according to the Paris treaty, the blockade of the Southern ports was illegal. Although the United States was not a signatory, Lincoln and Seward deliberately chose to model their blockade on the treaty, which led to inconsistencies. For example, while the declaration enabled them to regard privateers as outlaws, it also implied that the Confederacy was a separate nation, which they denied. Furthermore, the blockade was not "effective" by the treaty terms, which meant that compliant US warships were not permitted to seize neutral vessels whenever and wherever they wanted, such as when the ships were voyaging from one neutral port to another. Nonetheless, there were a number of such incidents, particularly around Matamoros, Mexico, and in the West Indies. Finally, Britain's acquiescence to the United States' ineffective blockade provided a legal precedent it would use to its advantage in the twentieth century. As Yale historian Samuel Bemis noted, during World War I, Britain "profited beyond measure by her far-sighted decision not to protest the blockade during the Civil War."[26]

The incidents cited above are only isolated examples of scandals and controversies that might be discovered by searching within the realms identified at the beginning of this chapter. For example, in terms of the consequences of the varying fortunes of war, the harsh treatment of Southern civilians became increasingly pronounced as circumstances made it progressively unlikely that Confederate armies could retaliate to the same extent. It is an obvious point that receives little attention. Additionally, little has been written about corruption resulting from staggering increases in money flowing through the treasuries to finance the war, but it is hard to believe that some of it failed to be diverted for personal gain. Counterfeiting of Confederate currency is one example. While much more has been written describing how the war shifted power from the sovereign states to the federal government, there is comparatively little discussion about the suppression of minority opinions among the public. All could be fertile grounds for more exploration.

NOTES

AUTHOR'S NOTE

1. Civil War Trust, "Civil War Casualties," http://www.civilwar.org/education/civil-war-casualties.html._

ONE: THE BIGGEST CONFEDERATE ERROR?

1. Burton Hendrick, *Statesmen of the Lost Cause* (New York: Literary Guild, 1939), 202.

2. Ibid., 204.

3. Frank Owsley, *King Cotton Diplomacy* (Chicago: University of Chicago Press, 1931), 8–9 and 12; Gene Dattel, *Cotton and Race in the Making of America* (Lanham, MD: Ivan R. Dee, 2009), 37.

4. Robert V. Bruce, *Lincoln and the Tools of War* (Urbana: University of Illinois Press, 1989), 50; Robert Futrell, "Federal Trade with the Confederate States, 1861–1865" (PhD diss., Vanderbilt University, 1950), 36.

5. William C. Davis, *A Government of Their Own* (New York: Free Press, 1998), 198.

6. Owsley, *King Cotton Diplomacy*, 289; Philip Leigh, *Trading with the Enemy* (Yardley, PA: Westholme, 2014), 12.

7. Ibid., 12.

8. Rembert Patrick, *Jefferson Davis and His Cabinet* (Baton Rouge: Louisiana State University Press, 1944), 221–222; Owsley *King Cotton Diplomacy*, 43–44.

9. Patrick, *Jefferson Davis*, 222.

10. Hendrick, *Statesmen*, 211–212.

11. Alexander Stephens, *A Constitutional View of the Late War Between the States* (Philadelphia: National Publishing, 1870), 2:783.

12. Ibid.

13. Raimondo Luraghi, *History of the Confederate Navy* (Annapolis, MD: Naval Institute Press, 1996), 90; Owsley, *King Cotton Diplomacy*, 439

14. Stephens, *Constitutional View*, 2:784–785.

15. Joseph E. Johnston, *Narrative of Military Operations* (New York: D. Appleton, 1874), 422.

16. Paul Studenski and Herman Krooss, *Financial History of the United States* (New York: McGraw Hill, 1952), 137–138; usgovernmentspending.com, "Spending by Decade, 1860s," http://www.usgovernmentspending.com/year_spending_1860USbn_16bs2n#usgs302.

17. Johnston, *Narrative of Military Operations*, 424.

18. Bryan Taylor, "The Confederate Cotton Zombie Bonds," Global Financial Data, https://www.globalfinancialdata.com/gfdblog/?p=2274.
19. Hendrick, *Statesmen*, 205–206.
20. Ibid., 206–207; Owsley, *King Cotton Diplomacy*, 263.
21. Owsley, *King Cotton Diplomacy*, 385.
22. Ibid., 386, 387–388.
23. Ibid., 394.
24. Dattel, *Cotton and Race*, 190; Hendrick, *Statesmen*, 225
25. Philip Leigh, "The Cotton Bubble," *New York Times Opinionator*, January 30, 2013, http://opinionator.blogs.nytimes.com/2013/01/30/the-cotton-bond-bubble/?_php=true&_type=blogs&_r=0.
26. Hendrick, *Statesmen*, 231.
27. Jay Sexton, *Debtor Diplomacy* (Oxford: Oxford University Press, 2005), 166–167.
28. Owsley, *King Cotton Diplomacy*, 405.
29. Ibid., 406–407, 410, 414.

Two: The Biggest Federal Error?

1. Richard Rhodes, *The Making of the Atomic Bomb* (New York: Touchstone, 1988), 425; Peter Wyden, *Day One* (New York: Simon & Schuster, 1984), 55–58.
2. Rhodes, *Making of the Atomic Bomb*, 425, 490; Steven Sheinkin, *Bomb: The Race to Build—and Steal—the World's Most Dangerous Weapon* (New York: Roaring Book, 2012), 124, 133; *Anderson County, Tn., Multi-Jurisdictional Hazard Mitigation Plan 2011 Update*, 1–2, http://www.andersontn.org/Emergency management/HMP IMAPFinalOakridge122711.pdf.
3. Wyden, *Day One*, 131–132.
4. Bruce, *Lincoln and the Tools*, 101; E. Porter Alexander, *Military Memoirs of a Confederate* (New York: Charles Scribner & Sons, 1907), 53.
5. Earl J. Hess, *The Rifle Musket in the Civil War* (Lawrence: University Press of Kansas, 2008), 75.
6. Bruce, *Lincoln and the Tools*, 114.
7. Ibid., 54.
8. Ibid., 290; Hess, *Rifle Musket*, 56–57; Edwin Coddington, *The Gettysburg Campaign* (New York: Charles Scribner & Sons, 1968), 258.
9. Andrew Bresnan, "The Henry Repeating Rifle," RareWinchesters.com, http://www.rarewinchesters.com/articles/art_hen_01.shtml; Joseph Bilby, *A Revolution in Arms* (Yardley, PA: Westholme, 2006), 44, 56; Bruce, *Lincoln and the Tools*, 101; Thomas Tate, *General James Ripley* (Booksurge.com: 2008), 49.
10. Bilby, *Revolution in Arms*, 37–38; Bruce, *Lincoln and the Tools*, 112.
11. Bruce, *Lincoln and the Tools*, 110–111.
12. Ibid., 25–27.
13. Ibid., 35, 50, 53, and 155; Albert Castel, *General Sterling Price* (Baton Rouge: Louisiana State University Press, 1968), 24; Spencer Tucker, *American Civil War* (Santa Barbara, CA: ABC-CLIO, 2013), 6:2535.
14. Bruce, *Lincoln and the Tools*, 113–114.
15. Bilby, *Revolution in Arms*, 74.
16. Ibid., 76–77; Hess, *Rifle Musket*, 56.

17. Bilby, *Revolution in Arms*, 78.

18. Ibid., 81–82.

19. Ibid., 88–90.

20. Steven Woodworth, *Six Armies in Tennessee* (Lincoln: University of Nebraska Press, 1998), 24; Bruce, *Lincoln and the Tools*, 255.

21. Glenn Tucker, *Chickamauga* (Dayton, OH: Morningside House, 1992), 115.

22. Ibid., 290, 304; Bruce, *Lincoln and the Tools*, 286.

23. Bruce, *Lincoln and the Tools*, 286–288.

24. Richard McMurry, *Atlanta: 1864* (Lincoln: University of Nebraska Press, 2000), 116.

25. Bilby, *Revolution in Arms*, 64–67.

26. Ibid., 94, 130–132; Jack Coggins, *Arms and Equipment of the Civil War* (New York: Fairfax, 1962), 35–36.

27. Bilby, *Revolution in Arms*, 132–134, 174, 195, 219.

28. Ibid., 138–139.

29. Ibid., 52.

30. Bruce, *Lincoln and the Tools*, 50, 116.

31. Terry Jones, *Historical Dictionary of the Civil War* (Lanham, MD: Scarecrow, 2011), 1173.

32. Bilby *Revolution in Arms*, 148.

33. Gerald W. Brock, *The Second Information Revolution* (Cambridge: Harvard University Press, 2009), 36; Herbert Johnson, *Wingless Eagle* (Chapel Hill: University of North Carolina Press, 2009), 114.

THREE: PREEMPTING THE CIVIL WAR

1. Jeffrey Hummel, *Emancipating Slaves, Enslaving Free Men* (Chicago: Open Court, 1996), 15–19; US House vote no. 81, April 22, 1828, Govtrack.us, https://www.govtrack.us/congress/votes/20-1/h81.

2. James Buchanan, *Mr. Buchanan's Administration on the Eve of the Rebellion* (New York: D. Appleton, 1866), 165–166.

3. James Chester, "Inside Sumter in '61," in *Battles and Leaders of the Civil War*, ed. Robert Underwood Johnson and Clarence Clough Buel (New York: Thomas Yoseloff, 1956), 1:61.

4. Maury Klein, *Days of Defiance* (New York: Vintage, 1997), 175–176, 191.

5. Buchanan, *Mr. Buchanan's Administration*, 178.

6. Klein, *Days of Defiance*, 200.

7. Ibid., 192; Chester, "Inside Sumter," 61.

8. Klein, *Days of Defiance*, 108.

9. Ibid., 191; Bruce Catton, *The Coming Fury* (Garden City, NY: Doubleday, 1961), 177.

10. Benson Lossing, *Pictorial History of the Civil War* (Mansfield, OH: Estill, 1866), 1:126.

11. Buchanan, *Mr. Buchanan's Administration*, 103.

12. Ibid., 189; Catton, *Coming Fury*, 177.

13. Catton, *Coming Fury*, 178; Klein, *Days of Defiance*, 191–192.

14. Webb Garrison, *Friendly Fire in the Civil War* (Nashville: Rutledge, 1999), 172; Douglas Bostick, *The Union Is Dissolved* (Charleston, SC: History Press, 2009), 63; Catton, *Coming Fury*, 178–181.

15. Catton, *Coming Fury*, 180–181.

16. Curt Anders, *Hearts in Conflict* (New York: Barnes & Noble Books, 1999), 24, 31, 39; "Secession Acts of the Thirteen Confederate States," Civil War Trust, http://www.civilwar.org/education/history/primarysources/secessionacts.html.

17. Jonathan White, *Abraham Lincoln and Treason in the Civil War* (Baton Rouge: Louisiana State University Press, 2011), 11; William Brooksher, *Bloody Hill*, (Washington, DC: Brassey's, 1995), 41–42, 83–85; James McPherson, *Battle Cry of Freedom* (Oxford: Oxford University Press, 1988), 276, 296–297.

18. Klein, *Days of Defiance*, 191.

19. Chester, "Inside Sumter," 61.

20. David J. Eicher, *The Longest Night* (New York: Simon & Schuster, 2001), 238.

21. Buchanan, *Mr. Buchanan's Administration*, 93, 158.

22. Naval Historical Center, *Dictionary of American Naval Fighting Ships*, http://www.history.navy.mil/danfs/p3/pawnee-i.htm; Abner Doubleday, "From Moultrie to Sumter," in *Battles and Leaders of the Civil War*, ed. Robert Underwood Johnson and Clarence Clough Buel (New York: Thomas Yoseloff, 1956), 1:44.

23. Doubleday, "From Moultrie to Sumter," 1:44.

24. Hummel, *Emancipating Slaves*, 141; McPherson, *Battle Cry*, 252.

25. William J. Cooper, *We Have the War upon Us* (New York: Alfred Knopf, 2012), 131–135.

26. Abraham Lincoln, first inaugural address, March 4, 1861, *Avalon Project*, Yale University, http://avalon.law.yale.edu/19th_century/lincoln1.asp; Jefferson Davis, inaugural address, February 18, 1861, *Avalon Project*, Yale University, http://avalon.law.yale.edu/19th_century/csa_csainau.asp.

27. General Richard Myers, "Why We Serve," 118th Alf Landon Lecture, April 26, 2000, http://www.k-state.edu/media/newsreleases/landonlect/myerstext400. html; *United States Strategic Bombing Survey (Europe) Summary Report* (Washington, DC: Government Printing Office, 1945), 17.

28. Carlos Eire, *Waiting for Snow in Havana* (New York: Free Press, 2003), Preambulo.

Four: Treasury Innovations and Mischiefs

1. Murray N. Rothbard, *A History of Money and Banking in the United States* (Auburn, AL: Ludwig von Mises Institute, 2002), 57.

2. Ibid., 57.

3. J. G. Randall and David Donald, *The Civil War and Reconstruction* (Boston: D. C. Heath, 1961), 340.

4. Studenski and Krooss, *Financial History*, 119–120.

5. Craig K. Elwell, *Brief History of the Gold Standard in the United States* (Washington: Congressional Research Service, 2011), 3.

6. Studenski and Krooss, *Financial History*, 137–138.

7. Kenneth Stampp, *And the War Came* (Baton Rouge: Louisiana State University Press, 1970), 232–233.

8. Studenski and Krooss, *Financial History*, 138–139.

9. Ibid., 139.

10. Doris Goodwin, *Team of Rivals* (New York: Simon & Schuster, 2005), 337.

11. Charles Adams, *When in the Course of Human Events* (Lanham, MD: Rowman & Littlefield, 2000), 25–26; Cooper, *We Have the War*, 248; Stampp, *War Came*, 162–164.

12. Cooper, *We Have the War*, 248.

13. Goodwin, *Team of Rivals*, 340.

14. Ibid., 345, 348; Cooper *We Have the War*, 263.

15. Hummel, *Emancipating Slaves*, 142–143.

16. Frederick Seward, *Reminiscences of a Wartime Statesman and Diplomat* (Boston: G. Putnam & Sons, 1916), 175–178.

17. Studenski and Krooss, *Financial History*, 140.

18. Ibid., 141–143.

19. Ibid., 143; H. W. Brands, *Greenback Planet* (Austin: University of Texas Press, 2011), 13.

20. John Niven, *Salmon P. Chase* (New York: Oxford University Press, 1995), 262, 353; Rothbard, *History of Money*, 133.

21. Studenski and Krooss, *Financial History*, 144.

22. Rothbard, *History of Money*, 124,130.

23. Thomas Belden and Marva Belden, *So Fell the Angels* (Boston: Little, Brown, 1956), 65.

24. Ibid., 127–129.

25. Dan Rottenberg, *The Man Who Made Wall Street* (Philadelphia: University of Pennsylvania Press, 2001), 67.

26. Rothbard, *History of Money*, 134–135; Studenski and Krooss, *Financial History*, 155.

27. Rottenberg, *Man Who Made Wall Street*, 70.

28. Ibid., 70; Rothbard, *History of Money*, 134.

29. Niven, *Salmon P. Chase*, 353.

30. Belden and Belden, *So Fell the Angels*, 36.

31. Ibid., 38.

32. Ellis Oberholtzer, *Jay Cooke: Financier of the Civil War* (Philadelphia: George Jacobs, 1907), 1:210.

33. Belden and Belden, *So Fell the Angels*, 81, 84.

34. Ibid., 96, 122, 270; Peg Lamphier, *Kate Chase and William Sprague* (Lincoln: University of Nebraska Press, 2003), 52–53, 274.

35. Margaret Leech, *Reveille in Washington* (New York: Harper & Brothers, 1941), 531; Niven, *Salmon P. Chase*, 416.

36. Niven, *Salmon P. Chase*, 438–439; Belden and Belden, *So Fell the Angels*, 244, 178.

37. Belden and Belden, *So Fell the Angels*, 243.

38. Ibid., 205–206, 213.

39. Ibid., 172.

40. James Ford, *If You're Lucky, Your Heart Will Break* (Somerville, MA: Wisdom, 2012), 131.

FIVE: THE CAMELOT COUPLE

1. Seymour Hersh, *The Dark Side of Camelot* (Boston: Little, Brown, 1998), 103, 234; Theodore White, "For President Kennedy: An Epilog," *Life*, December 6, 1963.

2. Niven, *Salmon P. Chase*, 343–344; Lamphier, *Kate Chase*, 49; "Notes," The Sprague Project, http://www.sprague-database.org/genealogy/getperson.php?personID=I44956&tree=SpragueProject.

3. Michael Burlingame, *At Lincoln's Side: John Hay's Civil War Correspondence and Selected Writings* (Carbondale: Southern Illinois University Press, 2000), 67.

4. Belden and Belden, *So Fell the Angels*, 8–11; Goodwin, *Team of Rivals*, 37–39.

5. Goodwin, *Team of Rivals*, 18–21, 23–24; Niven, *Salmon P. Chase*, 137–138, 212, 220–221.

6. Belden and Belden, *So Fell the Angels*, 14–16.

7. Ibid., 21–25; Niven, *Salmon P. Chase*, 211–212.

8. Belden and Belden, *So Fell the Angels*, 52–53; "Notes," Sprague Project.

9. Belden and Belden, *So Fell the Angels*, 54.

10. Ibid., 54–55.

11. Niven, *Salmon P. Chase*, 239.

12. Belden and Belden, *So Fell the Angels*, 54.

13. David Donald, *Lincoln* (London: Jonathan Cape, 1995), 298.

14. Belden and Belden, *So Fell the Angels*, 42–52.

15. Ibid., 82–83.

16. Willie Rose Lee, *Rehearsal for Reconstruction* (New York: Vintage, 1964), 19, 141; Leigh, *Trading with the Enemy*, 13.

17. Lamphier, *Kate Chase*, 46; "Hotels and Other Public Buildings: Willard's Hotel," Mr. Lincoln's White House, Lincoln Institute, http://www.mrlincolnswhitehouse.org/inside.asp?ID=184&subjectID=4.

18. Belden and Belden, *So Fell the Angels*, 56–62.

19. Ibid., 142, 147–148.

20. Peter Andreas, *Smuggler Nation* (Oxford: Oxford University Press, 2013), 173.

21. Niven, *Salmon P. Chase*, 347, 349; Belden and Belden, *So Fell the Angels*, 116.

22. Belden and Belden, *So Fell the Angels*, 148–149.

23. Randall and Donald, *Civil War and Reconstruction*, 591, 603–604.

24. Niven, *Salmon P. Chase*, 424; Belden and Belden, *So Fell the Angels*, 181, 185, 190.

25. Belden and Belden, *So Fell the Angels*, 198–199.

26. Ibid., 202, 208–209; Niven, *Salmon P. Chase*, 429–430.

27. Belden and Belden, *So Fell the Angels*, 212–213.

28. Ibid., 252–253, 255–258.

29. Ibid., 219.

30. Ibid., 164, 227–228; Niven *Salmon P. Chase*, 443.

31. John Oller, *American Queen* (Cambridge, MA: Da Capo, 2014), 198, 218; "Roscoe Conkling," Oneida County Historical Society, http://www.oneidacountyhistory.org/PublicFigures/Leaders.asp.

32. Belden and Belden, *So Fell the Angels*, 306–308.

33. Ibid., 163–164, 284; "Canonchet, Sprague Home Burned," *New York Times*, October 12, 1909, 18; Niven, *Salmon P. Chase*, 443; Leech, *Reveille in Washington*, 551; Lamphier, *Kate Chase*, 223, 232.

34. Mark Twain, *Autobiography* (Berkeley: University of California Press, 2010), 1:256.

SIX: THE BURNING OF ATLANTA

1. William T. Sherman, *Memoirs* (New York: D. Appleton, 1876), 1:178.
2. Russell Bonds, *War Like a Thunderbolt* (Yardley, PA: Westholme, 2009), 291, 316, 318–319.
3. Ibid., 358–359; Theodore Upson, *With Sherman to the Sea* (Bloomington: Indiana University Press, 1958), 133; Stephen Davis, *What the Yankees Did to Us* (Macon, GA: Mercer University Press, 2012), 409, 420, 425.
4. Davis, *What the Yankees Did*, 405–406, 414.
5. Bonds, *War*, 280–281; Marc Wortman, *The Bonfire* (New York: Public Affairs, 2009), 311.
6. Bonds, *War*, 281–284; Wortman, *Bonfire*, 311–312.
7. Wortman, *Bonfire*, 314–315, 318–319.
8. Davis, *What the Yankees Did*, 105, 149–150; Wortman, *Bonfire*, 333.
9. Davis, *What the Yankees Did*, 96, 116–118, 130–131.
10. Ibid., 127, 152, 165, 186; Wortman, *Bonfire*, 291.
11. Davis, *What the Yankees Did*, 168–169, 171–172, 187–188.
12. Wortman, *Bonfire*, 292, 289.
13. Davis, *What the Yankees Did*, 247–249.
14. Ibid., 223.
15. Ibid., 365, 370–373.
16. *Official Records of the Union and Confederate Armies* (Washington, DC: Government Printing Office), ser. 1, vol. 17, pt. 1, 144–145; John Walters, *Merchant of Terror* (Indianapolis: Bobbs-Merrill, 1973), 63–64, 97.
17. Frances Elizabeth Gains, "We Begged to Hearts of Stone," ed. Frances Black, *Northwest Georgia Historical and Genealogical Quarterly* 20, no. 1 (Winter 1988): 3.
18. Bonds, *War*, 343, 345–346.
19. Davis, *What the Yankees Did*, 389–395.
20. Sergeant Allen Campbell to his father, December 21, 1864, quoted in Mark Hoffman, *My Brave Mechanics* (Detroit: Wayne State University Press, 2007), 242–243.
21. Davis, *What the Yankees Did*, 404, 421.
22. Sherman, *Memoirs*, vol. 2, http://www.gutenberg.org/files/4361/4361-h/4361-h.htm#ch23.
23. Davis, *What the Yankees Did*, 398–399.
24. Ibid., 398, 403; Sherman, *Memoirs*, 1:177.
25. Davis, *What the Yankees Did*, 400.
26. William Sherman to the representatives of the City Council of Atlanta, September 12, 1864, http://gathkinsons.net/sesqui/?p=6819.
27. Davis, *What the Yankees Did*, 401.

SEVEN: CHOOSING SHERMAN OR THOMAS

1. Scott Janney, "A Bull Market for Grant, A Bear Market for Lee: History's Judgment of the Two Civil War Generals Is Changing," *New York Times*, September 30, 2000; James McPherson, *This Mighty Scourge* (Oxford: Oxford University Press, 2007), 123–124.
2. Thomas Buell, *The Warrior Generals* (New York: Crown, 1997), 357; Anders, *Hearts in Conflict*, 479; Eicher, *Longest Night*, 660; McPherson *Battle Cry*, 742–743; McMurry, *Atlanta*, 196–197.

3. Wortman, *Bonfire*, 260.

4. Bonds, *War*, 106, 172, 200–201, 265.

5. Buell, *Warrior Generals*, p. 357, 376.

6. Shelby Foote, *The Civil War* (New York: Random House, 1958), 1:178.

7. Peter Cozzens, *No Better Place to Die* (Urbana: University of Illinois Press, 1991), 173; Anders, *Hearts in Conflict*, 310.

8. Tucker, *Chickamauga*, 314; Foote, *Civil War*, 2:768.

9. Buell, *Warrior Generals*, 277, 284.

10. Craig L. Symonds, *Stonewall of the West* (Lawrence: University Press of Kansas, 1997), 169; Woodworth, *Six Armies*, 204–205.

11. Buell, *Warrior Generals*, 361.

12. Albert Castel, *Decision in the West* (Lawrence: University Press of Kansas, 1992), 565.

13. Buell, *Warrior Generals*, 254.

14. Ibid., 354–358

15. Ibid., 358–361.

16. Ibid., 362; McMurry, *Atlanta*, 64–65.

17. McMurry, *Atlanta*, 64–69.

18. Buell, *Warrior Generals*, 363; Castel, *Decision*, 188; McMurry, *Atlanta*, 70–72.

19. Sherman, *Memoirs*, 2:34

20. Albert Castel, *Winning and Losing in the Civil War* (Columbia: University of South Carolina Press, 1996), 96–97.

21. Ibid., 94–95; McMurry, *Atlanta*, 55.

22. McMurry, *Atlanta*, 82–89.

23. Ibid., 90–91; Castel, *Winning and Losing*, 96–97.

24. Castel, *Decision*, 319–320.

25. Sherman, *Memoirs*, 2:60.

26. Castel, *Winning and Losing*, 97.

27. Castel, *Decision*, 284–285.

28. Castel, *Winning and Losing*, 98–99.

29. Sherman, *Memoirs*, 2:77, 80; Castel, *Winning and Losing*, 100.

30. Castel, *Winning and Losing*, 100.

31. Ibid., 102–103; Castel, *Decision*, 513–515, 570.

32. Castel, *Decision*, 503–504.

33. Sam Watkins, *Co. Aytch*, intro. and annot. Philip Leigh (Yardley, PA: Westholme, 2013), 298.

34. Castel, *Decision*, 506, 539–540.

35. Steven Woodworth, *Jefferson Davis and His Generals* (Lawrence: University Press of Kansas, 1995), 291–292.

36. Shelby Foote, *The Civil War* (New York: Random House, 1974), 3:613–616, 669–674.

37. Watkins, *Co. Aytch*, 251.

38. Foote, *Civil War*, 3:673, 702, 707–709.

39. Bruce Catton, *Never Call Retreat* (New York: Random House, 1965), 415–416.

40. John Marszalek, *Sherman* (New York: Free Press, 1993), 422–423; Burke Davis, *Sherman's March* (New York: Random House, 1980), 16.

41. Larry Daniel. *Shiloh* (New York: Simon & Schuster, 1997), 311; Benson Bobrick, *Master of War* (New York: Simon & Schuster, 2009), 115.

42. Peter Cozzens, *The Shipwreck of Their Hopes* (Urbana: University of Illinois Press, 1994), 107–108; Brooks Simpson, *Ulysses S. Grant* (Boston: Houghton Mifflin, 2000), 223.

43. Buell, *Warrior Generals*, 354–357.

44. Davis, *Sherman's March*, 14–16.

45. Castel, *Decision*, 121–123, 506–507.

EIGHT: THE SPRING HILL SPIES

1. John O'Connor, "I'm the Guy They Called 'Deep Throat,'" *Vanity Fair*, July 2005, http://www.vanityfair.com/politics/features/2005/07/deepthroat200507.

2. J. D. Remington, "The Cause of Hood's Failure at Spring Hill," *Confederate Veteran* 21, no. 12 (Dec. 1913): 7–9; Winston Groom, *Shrouds of Glory* (New York, Atlantic Monthly Press, 1995), 137–138.

3. Groom, *Shrouds of Glory*, 140, 143–146, 152–153.

4. John Bakeless, *Spies of the Confederacy* (Mineola, NY: Dover, 1970), 299–300; Sheinkin, *Bomb*, 230–231.

5. Alfred H. Burne, *Lee, Grant and Sherman* (Lawrence: University Press of Kansas, 2000), 121, 137.

6. McMurry, *Atlanta*, 173.

7. Ibid., 135–136; John B. Hood, *Advance and Retreat* (New Orleans: Hood Orphan Memorial Fund, 1880), 327.

8. Groom, *Shrouds*, 111–112.

9. Eric Jacobson and Richard Rupp, *For Cause and Country* (Franklin, TN: O'More, 2006), 50; Groom, *Shrouds*, 111, 123.

10. Groom, *Shrouds*, 133; Hood, *Advance*, 218.

11. Groom, *Shrouds*, 138–139; Jacobson and Rupp, *For Cause*, 90–93.

12. Jacobson and Rupp, *For Cause*, 93–98.

13. Groom, *Shrouds*, 140.

14. Jacobson and Rupp, *For Cause*, 105–109.

15. Groom, *Shrouds*, 146–147.

16. Jacobson and Rupp, *For Cause*, 126.

17. Ibid., 136–137; Hood, *Advance*, 286–289.

18. Jacobson and Rupp, *For Cause*, 140–142, 149–151, 154–155.

19. Groom, *Shrouds*, 151–154; Jacobson and Rupp, *For Cause*, 162.

20. Jacobson and Rupp, *For Cause*, 132–133.

21. Ibid., 168–171, 177–178; Groom, *Shrouds*, 154.

22. The following discussion of Remington's espionage account is based on Remington, "Cause of Hood's Failure," 7–8.

23. Jamie Gillum, *Twenty Five Hours to Tragedy* (Spring Hill, TN: James Gillum, 2014), 343; Remington, "Cause of Hood's Failure," 9.

24. Remington, "Cause of Hood's Failure," 9; "A Yankee Spy Claimed He Saved His Army," *Nashville Tennessean*, December 6, 1964, 7-G; Metro Jacksonville, Old Ortega Historic District, http://www.metrojacksonville.com/article/2010-jun-old-ortega-historic-district#.U_89SUu3ahM.

25. R. J. Hasty, *A History of the Seventy-third Regiment of Illinois Infantry Volunteers* (Authority of the Regimental Reunion Association of Survivors of the 73rd Illinois Infantry Volunteers, 1890), 448–450.

26. *National Tribune*, December 11, 1884, http://www.midtneyewitnesses.com/eyewitness-book-series/franklin/civilian.

27. Thomas Allen, *Intelligence in the Civil War* (Washington, DC: CIA, 2004), 22–23; Groom, *Shrouds*, 128.

28. Remington, "Cause of Hood's Failure," 9.

29. *Nashville Tennessean*, "A Yankee Spy," 7-G.

30. Peter Maslowski, "Military Intelligence Sources during the American Civil War," in *US Army Military Intelligence History*, ed. James Finley (Fort Huachuca, AZ: US Army Intelligence Center, 1995), 30–31.

31. Carl von Clausewitz, *On War* (Princeton, NJ: Princeton University Press, 1989), 103; Steven Woodworth, *The Loyal, True, and Brave* (Lanham, MD: Rowman & Littlefield, 2002), 2002.

32. Jacobson and Rupp, *For Cause*, 169–170.

NINE: GHOSTS OF THE LOST DISPATCH

1. Douglas Freeman, *Lee's Lieutenants* (New York: Scribner's, 1971), 2:718; Steven Woodworth, *Davis and Lee at War* (Lawrence: University Press of Kansas, 1995), 186–188; Woodworth, *Jefferson Davis*, 144–148.

2. William Shea, *Fields of Blood* (Chapel Hill: University of North Carolina Press, 2009), 19; Foote, *Civil War*, 1:717–719, 720–736.

3. Owsley, *King Cotton Diplomacy*, 361.

4. Dean B. Mahin, *One War at a Time* (Washington, DC: Brassey's, 1999), 128.

5. Donald Jermann, *Antietam: The Lost Order* (Gretna, LA: Pelican, 2006), 44–45.

6. Stephen Sears, *Landscape Turned Red* (New York and Boston: Houghton Mifflin, 1983), 102.

7. Woodworth, *Davis and Lee*, 76; Frederick Seward, *Biography of William Seward* (New York: Derby & Miller, 1891), 613; McPherson, *Battle Cry*, 289–290.

8. Stephen Sears, *To the Gates of Richmond* (New York: Ticknor & Fields, 1992), 110, 353; Ezra Carman, *Maryland Campaign of September 1862* (El Dorado, CA: Savas Beatie, 2010), 1:124.

9. Sears, *Landscape*, 9–12.

10. Gideon Welles, *Diary* (Boston: Houghton Mifflin, 1911), 1:104–105; Carman, *Maryland Campaign*, 1:125.

11. Sears, *Landscape*, 89, 158.

12. Carman, *Maryland Campaign*, 1:142–143, 147–148.

13. Jermann, *Antietam*, 89–90.

14. Sears, *Landscape*, 23; Donald, *Lincoln*, 277; Jermann, *Antietam*, 140; Edwin Fishel, *Secret War for the Union* (Boston: Houghton Mifflin, 1996), 53.

15. Sears, *Landscape*, 64–68.

16. Hal Bridges, *Lee's Maverick General: Daniel Harvey Hill* (Lincoln, NE: Bison Publishing-University of Nebraska Press, 1991), 93. D. H. Hill, who was only temporarily with Lee's army, is not to be confused with Ambrose Powel (A. P.) Hill, who rose to a higher rank and was with Lee until a week before the army was surrendered.

17. Ibid., 93–94.

18. Colonel Silas Colgrove, "The Finding of Lee's Lost Order," *Battles and Leaders of the Civil War*, ed. Robert Underwood Johnson and Clarence Clough Buel (New York: Thomas Yoseloff, 1956), 2:603; Stephen Sears, *Controversies and Commanders* (Boston: Houghton Mifflin, 1999), 114–115.

19. Sears, *Landscape*, 113–115.
20. Sears, *Controversies*, 124; Joseph L. Harsh, *Taken at the Flood* (Kent, OH: Kent State University Press, 1999), 248.
21. Jermann, *Antietam*, 73–75, 165–167.
22. Sears, *Landscape*, 129.
23. Ibid., 128–129.
24. Sears, *Landscape*, 128–143; Jermann, *Antietam*, 161.
25. Jermann, *Antietam*, 151–153.
26. Sears, *Landscape*, 150–151; Harsh, *Taken at the Flood*, 284–285, 288–289.
27. Sears, *Landscape*, 150–151; Harsh, *Taken at the Flood*, 292–294.
28. Sears, *Landscape*, 155–156; Jermann, *Antietam*, 205–206.
29. Sears, *Landscape*, 162–163, 173–174, 176, 295–296; Harsh, *Taken at the Flood*, 366.
30. Harsh, *Taken at the Flood*, 152–153.
31. Bridges, *Lee's Maverick General*, 90–91.
32. Harsh, *Taken at the Flood*, 152.
33. D. H. Hill to McClellan, April 17, 1869, McClellan Papers, Library of Congress.
34. Bridges, *Lee's Maverick General*, 97.
35. Sears, *Controversies*, 119, 122; Freeman, *Lee's Lieutenants*, 2:718–719.
36. Sears, *Landscape*, 114, 349.
37. Bridges, *Lee's Maverick General*, 98.
38. Philip Leigh, "Lee's Lost Order," *Opinionator* (blog), *New York Times*, September 12, 2012, http://opinionator.blogs.nytimes.com/2012/09/12/lees-lost-order/?_ph p=true&_type=blogs&_r=0.
39. Ibid.
40. Ibid.
41. Geoffrey C. Ward with Ric Burns and Ken Burns, *The Civil War: An Illustrated History* (New York: Alfred A. Knopf, 1992), 271.

TEN: FLORIDA AFTER VICKSBURG

1. slaverebellion.org, "Population of Florida, 1860," *Population Database*, http://slaverebellion.org/population.php?state=Florida&year=1860&submit=view.
2. David James Coles, "Far from the Fields of Glory: Military Operations in Florida during the Civil War: 1864–1865" (PhD diss., Florida State University, 1996), 1.
3. Jefferson Davis, *The Rise and Fall of the Confederate Government* (New York: D. Appleton, 1881), 2:240–241.
4. US Department of the Interior, *Agriculture of the United States in 1860: Compiled from the Original Returns of the Eighth Census* (Washington, DC: Government Printing Office, 1864), cxvii; William H. Nulty, *Confederate Florida: The Road to Olustee* (Tuscaloosa: University of Alabama Press, 1990), 65; Canter Brown, "Tampa's James McKay and the Frustration of Confederate Cattle-Supply Operations," *Florida Historical Quarterly* 70, no. 4 (Apr. 1992): 424; "Florida Cattle Ranching," *Florida Memory*, State Archives of Florida, http://www.floridamemory.com/photographiccollection/photo_exhibits/ranching/.

5. Joe A. Ackerman Jr., "America's First Cowman," *Forum: Magazine of the Florida Humanities Council*, http://www.flahum.org/Assets/PDFs/Americas_First_Cowman_Winter_2006.pdf; Christen Embry, "Where's the Beef: Florida's Cattle Industry," *Tampa Bay* magazine 12, no. 5 (Sept.–Oct. 1997): 148.

6. *Official Records of the Union and Confederate Armies* (Washington, D.C: Government Printing Office), ser. 1, vol. 30, pt. 4, 551–552.

7. Jerrold Northrop Moore, *Confederate Commissary General* (Shippensburg, PA: White Mane, 1996), 222.

8. *Official Records (Armies)*, ser. 1, vol. 35, pt. 2, 392–395.

9. *Official Records of the Union and Confederate Navies* (Washington, DC: Government Printing Office), ser. 1, vol. 27, 593; James W. Raab, *J. Patton Anderson* (Jefferson, NC: McFarland, 2004), 128; Robert A. Taylor, "A Problem of Supply: Pleasant White and Florida's Cow Cavalry," in *Divided We Fall: Essays on Confederate Nation Building*, ed. John M. Belohlavek and Lewis N. Wynne (St. Leo, FL: St. Leo College Press, 1991), 181; Coles, *Fields of Glory*, 257.

10. *Official Records (Armies)*, ser. 1, vol. 26, pt. 1, 874–875; Rodney E. Dillon, "The Battle of Fort Myers," *Tampa Bay History* 5, no. 2 (Fall/Winter 1983): 28–29, 31–32, 34–35.

11. *Official Records (Armies)*, ser.1, vol. 35, pt. 1, 278.

12. Ibid; *Statutes at Large, Treaties, and Proclamations of the United States of America* (Boston: Little, Brown, 1866), 13:737–739; Samuel Jones, "The Battle of Olustee," in *Battles and Leaders of the Civil War*, ed. Robert Underwood Johnson and Clarence Clough Buel (New York: Thomas Yoseloff, 1956), 4:76; John C. Waugh, *Reelecting Lincoln: The Battle for the 1864 Presidency* (New York: Crown, 1997), 63.

13. *Official Records (Armies)*, ser.1, vol. 35, pt. 1, 279–281.

14. *The Battle of Olustee*, historical documentary video, Olustee Battlefield State Park, Olustee, FL, viewed October 25, 2013.

15. *Official Records (Armies)*, ser.1, vol. 35, pt. 1, 281; Nulty, *Confederate Florida*, 101.

16. William W. Davis, *The Civil War and Reconstruction in Florida* (New York: Columbia University Press, 1913), 284.

17. John E. Johns, *Florida during the Civil War* (Gainesville: University of Florida Press, 1963), 196; Nulty, *Confederate Florida*, 107, 123.

18. US Senate, S. Rep. No. 47, at 7 and 9 (1864), 38th Cong., 1st sess.; Nulty, *Confederate Florida*, 115–116, 127, 131.

19. Historical marker, Olustee Battlefield State Park, Olustee, FL.

20. *Official Records (Armies)*, ser. 1, vol. 35, pt. 1, 298; Coles, *Fields of Glory*, 142; Nulty, *Confederate Florida*, 216–217.

21. *Official Records (Armies)*, ser. 1, vol. 35, pt. 1, 308, 311–312; Coles, *Fields of Glory*, 127–128; Nulty, *Confederate Florida*, 137–145, 154.

22. Nicholas DeGraff (Lieutenant, 115th New York Regiment), *Diary*, February 20, 1864, as quoted in Coles, *Fields of Glory*, 135; Nulty, *Confederate Florida*, 145–158.

23. Jones, "Battle of Olustee," 78; Coles, *Fields of Glory*, 141–142; Nulty, *Confederate Florida*, 167–169, and 205.

24. *Official Records (Armies)*, ser. 1, vol. 35, pt. 1, 298, "Return of Casualties in Engagement Near Olustee, Florida on February 20, 1864"; Johns, *Florida during the Civil War*, 198.

25. *Official Records (Armies)*, ser. 1, vol. 35, pt. 1, 344; "The Repulse in Florida," *New York Times,* March 1, 1864, http://www.nytimes.com/1864/03/01/news/repulse-florida-full-account-late-battle-our-forces-led-into-trap-five-thousand.html; Nulty, *Confederate Florida*, 161, 170, 178, 205.

26. *Official Records (Armies)*, ser. 1. vol. 1, pt. 1, 298, "Return of Casualties in Engagement Near Olustee, Florida on February 20, 1864."

27. David Coles, "'Shooting Niggers, Sir,'" in *Black Flag over Dixie*, ed. Gregory Urwin (Carbondale: Southern Illinois University Press, 2004), 75–76.

28. US Senate, S. Rep. No. 47, at 10.

29. Coles, *Fields of Glory*, 77; Nulty, *Confederate Florida*, 210–213.

30. *Official Records (Armies)*, ser. 1, vol. 1, pt. 1, 618.

31. Robert C. Black III, *Railroads of the Confederacy* (Chapel Hill: University of North Carolina Press, 1951), 200.

32. "The Florida Railroad Story," Florida Railroad Company Inc., http://www.flarr.com/frrstory.htm.

33. "Dickerson Obituary," *New York Times*, December 13, 1889; Robert L. Clarke, "The Florida Railroad Company in the Civil War," *Journal of Southern History* 19, no. 2 (May 1953): 181; Dean C. Allard, "Benjamin Franklin Isherwood: Father of the Modern Steam Navy," in *Captains of the Old Steam Navy*, ed. James C. Bradford (Annapolis: Naval Institute Press, 1986), 310–311; "Roberts Obituary," *New York Times*, September 12, 1880; "Union Ratification," *New York Times*, December 2, 1865.

34. *Official Records (Armies)*, ser. 1, vol. 53, 226; Black, *Railroads*, 213.

35. Clarke, "Florida Railroad Company," 184–186, 186–188, 191.

36. Ibid., 191; "Florida Railroad Story."

37. *Official Records (Armies)*, ser. 1, vol. 35, pt. 1, 485–486; Coles, *Fields of Glory*, 264, 318–319; Dillon, "Battle of Fort Myers," 27–36.

38. Robert A. Taylor, *Rebel Storehouse* (Tuscaloosa: University of Alabama Press, 2003), 118; Taylor, "Problem of Supply," 191.

39. Philip Leigh, "Florida's Cattle Wars," *Opinionator* (blog), *New York Times*, December 19, 2013, http://opinionator.blogs.nytimes.com/2013/12/19/floridas-cattle-wars/?_php=true&_type=blogs&_r=0.

40. *Official Records (Armies)*, ser. 4, vol. 3, 730–731; Bruce Levine, *Confederate Emancipation* (Oxford: Oxford University Press, 2006), 31; Taylor, "Problem of Supply," 195.

41. Leigh, "Florida's Cattle Wars."

42. Johns, *Florida during the Civil War*, 213.

43. Davis, *Civil War and Reconstruction*, 293–294.

44. Brown, "Tampa's James McKay," 426–427, 429–433.

CHAPTER ELEVEN: LINCOLN AND MCCLELLAN

1. George Ticknor Curtis, *McClellan's Last Service to the Republic* (New York: D. Appleton, 1886), 126; Stephen Sears, *George B. McClellan* (New York: Ticknor & Fields, 1988), 390.

2. Robert E. Lee Jr., *Recollections and Letters of General Lee* (New York: Doubleday, Page, 1904), 415–416.

3. John C. Waugh, *Lincoln and McClellan* (New York: Palgrave Macmillan, 2010), 31–33, 38.

4. Ibid., 43, 54–55; Bilby, *Revolution in Arms*, 76–77.

5. Waugh, *Lincoln and McClellan*, 49; Ethan Rafuse, *McClellan's War* (Bloomington: Indiana University Press, 2005), 143.

6. Rafuse, *McClellan's War*, 142; Sears, *George B. McClellan*, 136.

7. Rafuse, *McClellan's War*, 170–171.

8. Ibid.; Waugh, *Lincoln and McClellan*, 61–64.

9. Waugh, *Lincoln and McClellan*, 64–66; Rafuse, *McClellan's War*, 179.

10. Waugh, *Lincoln and McClellan*, 76; Rafuse, *McClellan's War*, 191.

11. Waugh, *Lincoln and McClellan*, 80.

12. Sears, *George B. McClellan*, 170; Waugh, *Lincoln and McClellan*, 82–83, 86.

13. Waugh, *Lincoln and McClellan*, 82, 91, 97.

14. Ibid., 100–101, 110–113.

15. Ibid., 122–123; Sears, *Landscape Turned Red*, 5.

16. Waugh, *Lincoln and McClellan*, 128–130; Sears, *To the Gates of Richmond*, 379–384.

17. Waugh, *Lincoln and McClellan*, 107, 116–117, 191.

18. Bruce Catton, *Terrible Swift Sword* (London: Phoenix Press, 2001), 384.

19. Waugh, *Lincoln and McClellan*, 107.

20. Sears, *George B. McClellan*, 261; George B. McClellan and William Prime, *McClellan's Own Story* (New York: Charles L. Webster, 1887), 543.

21. Sears, *George B. McClellan*, 260; Rafuse, *McClellan's War*, 270.

22. Waugh, *Lincoln and McClellan*, 134–135.

23. Sears, *Landscape Turned Red*, 77–78; Sears, *George B. McClellan*, 348.

24. Waugh, *Lincoln and McClellan*, 147–148, 150–157.

25. Sears, *Landscape Turned Red*, 102.

26. Waugh, *Lincoln and McClellan*, 174, 178; Sears, *George B. McClellan*, 337–338.

27. John J. Hennessy, *Return to Bull Run* (New York: Simon & Schuster, 1993), 26, 30.

28. Waugh, *Lincoln and McClellan*, 183.

29. Lincoln was a proponent of protective tariffs, federal public works spending, and industrial subsidies. Each was outlawed by the Confederate Constitution as inimical to the interests of the South or properly the domain of the states individually. Stampp, *War Came*, 181; David Cohn, *Life and Times of King Cotton* (New York: Oxford University Press, 1956), 149–150.

AFTERWORD

1. William Marvel, *Mr. Lincoln Goes to War* (Boston: Houghton Mifflin, 2006), 155–159.

2. McPherson, *Battle Cry*, 293; Brooksher, *Bloody Hill*, 237–240; Foote, *Civil War*, 1:95.

3. Castel, *General Sterling Price*, 55; Drew Wagenhoffer interview with Larry Wood about his book *Siege of Lexington*, at *Civil War Books and Authors* (blog), http://cwba.blogspot.com/2014/05/author-q-larry-wood-on-siege-of.html.

4. William Shea and Earl Hess, *Pea Ridge: Civil War Campaign in the West* (Chapel Hill: University of North Carolina Press, 1992), 214, 331–339.

5. Catton, *Terrible Swift Sword*, 223.

6. Foote, *Civil War*, 1:278; Thomas Snead, "The First Year of the War In Missouri," in *Battles and Leaders of the Civil War*, ed. Robert Underwood Johnson and Clarence Clough Buel (New York: Thomas Yoseloff, 1956), 1:272.

7. Shea, *Fields of Blood*, 289–292.

8. McPherson, *Battle Cry*, 287.

9. Ibid., 289–290.

10. Seward, *Reminiscences*, 175–178.

11. Marvel, *Mr. Lincoln*, 257–258.

12. Ibid.,72; McPherson, *Battle Cry*, 293.

13. Marvel, *Mr. Lincoln*, 190.

14. McPherson, *Battle Cry*, 293, 296; Hummel, *Emancipating Slaves*, 146.

15. Hummel, *Emancipating Slaves*, 146.

16. Frank Varney, *General Grant and the Rewriting of History* (Eldorado Hills, CA: Savas Beatie, 2013), 260–262.

17. Ludwell Johnson, "Northern Profits and Profiteers: The Cotton Rings of 1864–1865," *Civil War History* 12, no. 2 (June 1996): 114; Craig L. Symonds, *Lincoln and His Admirals* (Oxford: Oxford University Press, 2008), 287.

18. Ward Hill Lamon, *Recollections of Abraham Lincoln* (Cambridge, MA: University Press, 1911), 189.

19. Luraghi, *History of the Confederate Navy*, 70–71.

20. Ibid., 71; Symonds, *Lincoln and His Admirals*, 41.

21. Foreman, *World on Fire*, 822n.

22. Symonds, *Lincoln and His Admirals*, 42–45.

23. Mahin, *One War*, 45–46; Foreman, *World on Fire*, 821–822n.

24. Mahin, *One War*, 48.

25. Hendrick, *Statesmen*, 274–275.

26. Mahin, *One War*, 297.

BIBLIOGRAPHY

MEMOIRS, DIARIES, AND PERSONAL PAPERS

Alexander, E. Porter. *Military Memoirs of a Confederate.* New York: Charles Scribner & Sons, 1907.

Buchanan, James. *Mr. Buchanan's Administration on the Eve of the Rebellion.* New York: D. Appleton, 1866.

Davis, Jefferson. *The Rise and Fall of the Confederate Government.* Vol. 2. New York: D. Appleton, 1881.

Hasty, R. J. *A History of the Seventy-third Regiment of Illinois Infantry Volunteers.* Authority of the Regimental Reunion Association of Survivors of the 73rd Illinois Infantry Volunteers, 1890.

Hood, John B. *Advance and Retreat.* New Orleans: Hood Orphan Memorial Fund, 1880.

Johnston, Joseph E. *Narrative of Military Operations.* New York: D. Appleton, 1874.

Lamon, Ward Hill. *Recollections of Abraham Lincoln.* Cambridge, MA: University Press, 1911.

McClellan, George B. "Letter to D. H. Hill on April 17, 1869." McClellan Papers. Library of Congress.

McClellan, George B., and William Prime. *McClellan's Own Story.* New York: Charles L. Webster, 1887.

Seward, Frederick. *Biography of William Seward.* New York: Derby & Miller, 1891.

———. *Reminiscences of a Wartime Statesman and Diplomat.* Boston: G. Putnam & Sons, 1916.

Sherman, William T. *Memoirs.* 2 vols. New York: D. Appleton, 1876.

Stephens, Alexander. *A Constitutional View of the Late War Between the States.* Vol. 2. Philadelphia: National Publishing, 1870.

Watkins, Sam. *Co. Aytch.* Introduced and annotated by Philip Leigh. Yardley, PA: Westholme, 2013.

Welles, Gideon. *Diary.* Vol. 1. Boston: Houghton Mifflin, 1911.

HISTORICAL DOCUMENTS

Davis, Jefferson. Inaugural address, February 18, 1861. *Avalon Project*, Yale University. http://avalon.law.yale.edu/19th_century/csa _csainau.asp.

Lincoln, Abraham. First inaugural address, March 4, 1861. *Avalon Project*, Yale University. http://avalon.law.yale.edu/19th_century/lincoln1.asp.

Official Records of the Union and Confederate Armies. Ser. 1, vol. 17, pt. 1. Washington, DC: Government Printing Office.

Official Records of the Union and Confederate Navies. Ser. 1, vol. 27, pt. 593. Washington, DC: Government Printing Office.

Sherman, William T. Address to the representatives of the City Council of Atlanta, September 12, 1864. http://gathkinsons.net/sesqui/?p =6819.

Statutes at Large, Treaties, and Proclamations of the United States of America. Vol. 13. Boston: Little, Brown, 1866.

US Department of the Interior. *Agriculture of the United States in 1860: Compiled from the Original Returns of the Eighth Census.* Washington, DC: Government Printing Office, 1864.

US Senate. S. Rep. No. 47 (1864). 38th Cong., 1st sess.

War Department. *United States Strategic Bombing Survey (Europe) Summary Report.* Washington, DC: Government Printing Office, 1945.

BOOKS AND COMPILATIONS

Adams, Charles. *When in the Course of Human Events.* Lanham, MD: Rowman & Littlefield, 2000.

Allard, Dean C. "Benjamin Franklin Isherwood: Father of the Modern Steam Navy." In *Captains of the Old Steam Navy.* Edited by James C. Bradford, 301–322. Annapolis: Naval Institute Press, 1986.

Allen, Thomas. *Intelligence in the Civil War.* Washington, DC: CIA, 2004.

Anders, Curt. *Hearts in Conflict.* New York: Barnes & Noble Books, 1999.

Andreas, Peter. *Smuggler Nation.* Oxford: Oxford University Press, 2013.

Bakeless, John. *Spies of the Confederacy.* Mineola, NY: Dover, 1970.

Belden, Thomas, and Marva Belden. *So Fell the Angels.* Boston: Little, Brown, 1956.

Belohlavek, John M., and Lewis N. Wynne, eds. *Divided We Fall: Essays on Confederate Nation Building.* St. Leo, FL: St. Leo College Press, 1991.

Bilby, Joseph. *A Revolution in Arms.* Yardley, PA: Westholme, 2006.

Black, Robert C., III. *Railroads of the Confederacy.* Chapel Hill: University of North Carolina Press, 1951.

Bobrick, Benson. *Master of War*. New York: Simon & Schuster, 2009.

Bonds, Russell. *War Like a Thunderbolt*. Yardley, PA: Westholme, 2009.

Bostick, Douglas. *The Union Is Dissolved*. Charleston, SC: History Press, 2009.

Brands, H. W. *Greenback Planet*. Austin: University of Texas Press, 2011.

Bridges, Hal. *Lee's Maverick General: Daniel Harvey Hill*. Lincoln, NE: Bison Publishing-University of Nebraska Press, 1991.

Brock, Gerald W. *The Second Information Revolution*. Cambridge: Harvard University Press, 2009.

Brooksher, William. *Bloody Hill*. Washington, DC: Brassey's, 1995.

Bruce, Robert V. *Lincoln and the Tools of War*. Urbana: University of Illinois Press, 1989.

Buell, Thomas. *The Warrior Generals*. New York: Crown, 1997.

Burlingame, Michael. *At Lincoln's Side: John Hay's Civil War Correspondence and Selected Writings*. Carbondale: Southern Illinois University Press, 2000.

Burne, Alfred H. *Lee, Grant and Sherman*. Lawrence: University Press of Kansas, 2000.

Carman, Ezra. *Maryland Campaign of September 1862*. Vol. 1. El Dorado, CA: Savas Beatie, 2010.

Castel, Albert. *Decision in the West*. Lawrence: University Press of Kansas, 1992.

———. *General Sterling Price*. Baton Rouge: Louisiana State University Press, 1968.

———. *Winning and Losing in the Civil War*. Columbia: University of South Carolina Press, 1996.

Catton, Bruce. *The Coming Fury*. Garden City, NY: Doubleday, 1961.

———. *Never Call Retreat*. New York: Random House, 1965.

———. *Terrible Swift Sword*. London: Phoenix Press, 2001.

Chester, James. "Inside Sumter in '61." In *Battles and Leaders of the Civil War*. Vol. 1. Edited by Robert Underwood Johnson and Clarence Clough Buel, 50–74. New York: Thomas Yoseloff, 1956.

Coddington, Edwin. *The Gettysburg Campaign*. New York: Charles Scribner & Sons, 1968.

Coggins, Jack. *Arms and Equipment of the Civil War*. New York: Fairfax Press, 1962.

Coles, David J. "'Shooting Niggers, Sir.'" In *Black Flag over Dixie*. Edited by Gregory Urwin, 65–88. Carbondale: Southern Illinois University Press, 2004.

Colgrove, Silas. "The Finding of Lee's Lost Order." In *Battles and Leaders of the Civil War*. Vol. 2. Edited by Robert Underwood Johnson and Clarence Clough Buel, 603. New York: Thomas Yoseloff, 1956.

Cooper, William J. *We Have the War upon Us*. New York: Alfred Knopf, 2012.

Cooper, William J., and Thomas Terrill. *The American South*. Vol. 2. Lanham, MD: Rowman & Littlefield, 2009.

Cozzens, Peter. *No Better Place to Die*. Urbana: University of Illinois Press, 1991.

———. *The Shipwreck of Their Hopes*. Urbana: University of Illinois Press, 1994.

Curtis, George Ticknor. *McClellan's Last Service to the Republic*. New York: D. Appleton, 1886.

Daniel, Larry. *Shiloh*. New York: Simon & Schuster, 1997.

Dattel, Gene. *Cotton and Race in the Making of America*. Lanham, MD: Ivan R. Dee, 2009.

Davis, Burke. *Sherman's March*. New York: Random House, 1980.

Davis, Stephen. *What the Yankees Did to Us*. Macon, GA: Mercer University Press, 2012.

Davis, William C. *A Government of Their Own*. New York: Free Press, 1998.

Davis, William W. *The Civil War and Reconstruction in Florida*. New York: Columbia University, 1913.

Donald, David. *Lincoln*. London: Jonathan Cape, 1995.

Doubleday, Abner. "From Moultrie to Sumter." In *Battles and Leaders of the Civil War*. Vol. 1. Edited by Robert Underwood Johnson and Clarence Clough Buel, 40–50. New York: Thomas Yoseloff, 1956.

Eicher, David J. *The Longest Night*. New York: Simon & Schuster, 2001.

Eire, Carlos. *Waiting for Snow in Havana*. New York: Free Press, 2003.

Elwell, Craig K. *Brief History of the Gold Standard in the United States*. Washington, DC: Congressional Research Service, 2011.

Fishel, Edwin. *Secret War for the Union*. Boston: Houghton Mifflin, 1996.

Foote, Shelby. *The Civil War: A Narrative*. Vol. 1. New York: Random House, 1958.

———. *The Civil War: A Narrative*. Vol. 2. New York: Random House, 1963.

———. *The Civil War: A Narrative*. Vol. 3. New York: Random House, 1974.

Ford, James. *If You're Lucky, Your Heart Will Break*. Somerville, MA: Wisdom, 2012.

Foreman, Amanda. *A World on Fire*. New York: Random House, 2010.

Freeman, Douglas. *Lee's Lieutenants*. Vol. 2. New York: Scribner's, 1971.

Garrison, Webb. *Friendly Fire in the Civil War*. Nashville: Rutledge, 1999.

Gillum, Jamie. *Twenty Five Hours to Tragedy*. Spring Hill, TN: James Gillum, 2014.

Goodwin, Doris. *Team of Rivals*. New York: Simon & Schuster, 2005.

Groom, Winston. *Shrouds of Glory*. New York: Atlantic Monthly Press, 1995.

Harsh, Joseph L. *Taken at the Flood*. Kent, OH: Kent State University Press, 1999.

Hendrick, Burton. *Statesmen of the Lost Cause*. New York: Literary Guild, 1939.

Hennessy, John J. *Return to Bull Run*. New York: Simon & Schuster, 1993.

Hersh, Seymour. *The Dark Side of Camelot*. Boston: Little, Brown.

Hess, Earl J. *The Rifle Musket in the Civil War*. Lawrence: University Press of Kansas, 2008.

Historical Statistics of the United States: 1789–1945. Washington, DC: Department of Commerce, 1949.

Hoffman, Mark. *My Brave Mechanics*. Detroit: Wayne State University Press, 2007.

Hosch, William. *World War II*. New York: Rosen, 2009.

Hummel, Jeffrey. *Emancipating Slaves, Enslaving Free Men*. Chicago: Open Court, 1996.

Jacobson, Eric, and Richard Rupp. *For Cause and Country*. Franklin, TN: O'More, 2006.

Jermann, Donald. *Antietam: The Lost Order*. Gretna, LA: Pelican, 2006.

Johns, John E. *Florida during the Civil War*. Gainesville: University of Florida Press, 1963.

Johnson, Herbert. *Wingless Eagle*. Chapel Hill: University of North Carolina Press, 2009.

Johnson, Ludwell. *Division and Reunion*. New York: John Wiley & Sons, 1978.

Jones, Samuel. "The Battle of Olustee." In *Battles and Leaders of the Civil War*. Vol. 4. Edited by Robert Underwood Johnson and Clarence Clough Buel, 76–79. New York: Thomas Yoseloff, 1956.

Jones, Terry. *Historical Dictionary of the Civil War*. Lanham, MD: Scarecrow, 2011.

Klein, Maury. *Days of Defiance*. New York: Vintage, 1997.

Lamphier, Peg. *Kate Chase and William Sprague*. Lincoln: University of Nebraska Press, 2003.

Lee, Robert E., Jr. *Recollections and Letters of General Lee*. New York: Doubleday, Page, 1904.

Lee, Willie Rose. *Rehearsal for Reconstruction*. New York: Vintage, 1964.

Leech, Margaret. *Reveille in Washington*. New York: Harper & Brothers, 1941.

Leigh, Philip. *Trading with the Enemy*. Yardley, PA: Westholme, 2014.

Levine, Bruce. *Confederate Emancipation*. Oxford: Oxford University Press, 2006.

Lossing, Benson. *Pictorial History of the Civil War*. Vol. 1. Mansfield, OH: Estill, 1866.

Luraghi, Raimondo. *History of the Confederate Navy*. Annapolis, MD: Naval Institute Press, 1996.

Mahin, Dean B. *One War at a Time*. Washington, DC: Brassey's, 1999.

Marszalek, John. *Sherman*. New York: Free Press, 1993.

Marvel, William. *Mr. Lincoln Goes to War*. Boston: Houghton Mifflin, 2006.

Maslowski, Peter. "Military Intelligence Sources during the American Civil War." In *US Army Military Intelligence History*. Edited by James Finley, 30–51. Fort Huachuca, AZ: US Army Intelligence Center, 1995.

McMurry, Richard. *Atlanta: 1864*. Lincoln: University of Nebraska Press, 2000.

McPherson, James. *Battle Cry of Freedom*. Oxford: Oxford University Press, 1988.

———. *This Mighty Scourge*. Oxford: Oxford University Press, 2007.

Moore, Jerrold Northrop. *Confederate Commissary General*. Shippensburg, PA: White Mane, 1996.

Niven, John. *Salmon P. Chase*. New York: Oxford University Press, 1995.

Nulty, William H. *Confederate Florida: The Road to Olustee*. Tuscaloosa: University of Alabama Press, 1990.

Oberholtzer, Ellis. *Jay Cooke: Financier of the Civil War*. Vol. 1. Philadelphia: George Jacobs, 1907.

Oller, John. *American Queen*. Cambridge, MA: Da Capo, 2014.

Owsley, Frank. *King Cotton Diplomacy*. Chicago: University of Chicago Press, 1931.

Patrick, Rembert. *Jefferson Davis and His Cabinet*. Baton Rouge: Louisiana State University Press, 1944.

Raab, James W. *J. Patton Anderson*. Jefferson, NC: McFarland, 2004.

Rafuse, Ethan. *McClellan's War*. Bloomington: Indiana University Press, 2005.

Rhodes, Richard. *The Making of the Atomic Bomb*. New York: Touchstone, 1988.

Rothbard, Murray N. *A History of Money and Banking in the United States*. Auburn, AL: Ludwig von Mises Institute, 2002.

Rottenberg, Dan. *The Man Who Made Wall Street*. Philadelphia: University of Pennsylvania Press, 2001.

Scruggs, Leonard. *The Uncivil War*. Asheville, NC: Universal Media, 2011.

Sears, Stephen. *Controversies and Commanders*. Boston: Houghton Mifflin, 1999.

———. *George B. McClellan*. New York: Ticknor & Fields, 1988.

———. *Landscape Turned Red*. New York and Boston: Houghton Mifflin, 1983.

———. *To The Gates of Richmond*. New York: Ticknor & Fields, 1992.

Sexton, Jay. *Debtor Diplomacy*. Oxford: Oxford University Press, 2005.

Shea, William. *Fields of Blood*. Chapel Hill: University of North Carolina Press, 2009.

Shea, William, and Earl Hess. *Pea Ridge: Civil War Campaign in the West*. Chapel Hill: University of North Carolina Press, 1992.

Sheinkin, Steven. *Bomb: The Race to Build—and Steal—the World's Most Dangerous Weapon*. New York: Roaring Book, 2012.

Simpson, Brooks. *Ulysses S. Grant*. Boston: Houghton Mifflin, 2000.

Snead, Thomas. "The First Year of the War in Missouri." In *Battles and Leaders of the Civil War*. Vol. 1. Edited by Robert Underwood Johnson and Clarence C. Buel, 262–278. New York: Thomas Yoseloff, 1956.

Stampp, Kenneth. *And the War Came*. Baton Rouge: Louisiana State University Press, 1970.

Studenski, Paul, and Herman Krooss. *Financial History of the United States*. New York: McGraw-Hill, 1952.

Symonds, Craig L. *Lincoln and His Admirals*. Oxford: Oxford University Press, 2008.

———. *Stonewall of the West*. Lawrence: University Press of Kansas, 1997.

Tate, Thomas. *General James Ripley*. Booksurge.com: 2008.

Taylor, Robert A. "A Problem of Supply: Pleasant White and Florida's Cow Cavalry." In *Divided We Fall: Essays on Confederate Nation Building*. Edited by John M. Belohlavek and Lewis N. Wynne, 177–203. St. Leo, FL: St. Leo College Press, 1991.

———. *Rebel Storehouse*. Tuscaloosa: University of Alabama Press, 2003.

Tucker, Glenn. *Chickamauga*. Dayton, OH: Morningside House, 1992.

Tucker, Spencer. *American Civil War*. Vol. 6. Santa Barbara, CA: ABC-CLIO, 2013.

Twain, Mark. *Autobiography*. Vol. 1. Berkeley: University of California Press, 2010.

Upson, Theodore. *With Sherman to the Sea*. Bloomington: Indiana University Press, 1958.

Varney, Frank. *General Grant and the Rewriting of History*. Eldorado Hills, CA: Savas Beatie, 2013.

Walters, John. *Merchant of Terror*. Indianapolis: Bobbs-Merrill, 1973.

Ward, Geoffrey C., with Ric Burns and Ken Burns. *The Civil War: An Illustrated History*. New York: Alfred A. Knopf, 1992.

Watkins, James L. *King Cotton*. New York: J. L. Watkins & Sons, 1908.

Waugh, John C. *Lincoln and McClellan*. New York: Palgrave Macmillan, 2010.

———. *Reelecting Lincoln: The Battle for the 1864 Presidency*. New York: Crown, 1997.

White, Jonathan. *Abraham Lincoln and Treason in the Civil War*. Baton Rouge: Louisiana State University Press, 2011.

Woodworth, Steven. *Davis and Lee at War*. Lawrence: University Press of Kansas, 1995.

———. *Jefferson Davis and His Generals*. Lawrence: University Press of Kansas, 1995.

———. *The Loyal, True, and Brave*. Lantham, MD: Rowman & Littlefield, 2002.

———. *Six Armies in Tennessee*. Lincoln: Nebraska University Press, 1998.

Wortman, Marc. *The Bonfire*. New York: Public Affairs, 2009.

Wyden, Peter. *Day One*. New York: Simon & Schuster, 1984.

ARTICLES

Ackerman, Joe A., Jr. "America's First Cowman." *Forum: Magazine of the Florida Humanities Council*. http://www.flahum.org/Assets/PDFs/Americas_First_Cowman_Winter_2006.pdf.

Bresnan, Andrew. "The Henry Repeating Rifle." RareWinmchesters.com. http://www.rarewinchesters.com/articles/art_hen_01.shtml.

Brown, Canter. "Tampa's James McKay and the Frustration of Confederate Cattle-Supply Operations." *Florida Historical Quarterly* 70, no. 4 (Apr. 1992): 409–433.

"Canonchet, Sprague Home Burned." *New York Times*, October 12, 1909.

Clarke, Robert L. "The Florida Railroad Company in the Civil War." *Journal of Southern History* 19, no. 2 (May 1953): 180–192.

"Dickerson Obituary." *New York Times*, December 13, 1889.

Dillon, Rodney. "The Battle of Fort Myers." *Tampa Bay History* 5, no. 2 (Fall/Winter 1983): 27–36.

Embry, Christen. "Where's the Beef: Florida's Cattle Industry." *Tampa Bay* magazine 12, no. 5 (Sept.-Oct. 1997): 146.

Gains, Frances Elizabeth. "We Begged to Hearts of Stone." Edited by Frances Black. *Northwest Georgia Historical and Genealogical Quarterly* 20, no.1 (Winter 1988): 1–6.

Gugliotta, Guy. "New Estimate Raises Civil War Death Toll." *New York Times*, April 3, 2012.

Janney, Scott. "A Bull Market for Grant, A Bear Market for Lee: History's Judgment of the Two Civil War Generals Is Changing." *New York Times,* September 30, 2000.

Johnson, Ludwell. "Northern Profits and Profiteers: The Cotton Rings of 1864–1865." *Civil War History* 12, no. 2 (June 1996): 101–115.

Leigh, Philip. "The Cotton Bubble." *Opinionator* (blog). *New York Times*, January 30, 2013. http://opinionator.blogs.nytimes.com/2013/01/30/the-cotton-bond-bubble/?_php=true&_type=blogs&_r=0.

———. "Florida's Cattle Wars." *Opinionator* (blog). *New York Times*, December 19, 2013. http://opinionator.blogs.nytimes.com/2013/12/19/floridas-cattle-wars/?_php=true&_type=blogs&_r=0.

———. "Lee's Lost Order." *Opinionator* (blog). *New York Times*, September 12, 2012, http://opinionator.blogs.nytimes.com/2012/09/12/lees-lost-order/?_php=true&_type=blogs&_r=0.

National Tribune, December 11, 1884. http://www.midtneye witnesses.com/eyewitness-book-series/franklin/civilian.

O'Connor, John. "I'm the Guy They Called 'Deep Throat.'" *Vanity Fair*, July 2005.

Remington, J. D. "The Cause of Hood's Failure at Spring Hill." *Confederate Veteran* 21, no. 12 (Dec. 1913): 7–9.

"The Repulse in Florida." *New York Times*, March 1, 1864.

"Roberts Obituary." *New York Times*, September 12, 1880.

"Union Ratification." *New York Times*, December 2, 1865.

White, Theodore. "For President Kennedy: An Epilog." *Life*, December 6, 1963.

"A Yankee Spy Claimed He Saved His Army." *Nashville Tennessean*, December 6, 1964, p. 7-G.

DISSERTATIONS

Coles, David James. "Far from the Fields of Glory: Military Operations in Florida during the Civil War: 1864–1865." PhD diss., Florida State University, 1996.

Futrell, Robert F. "Federal Trade with the Confederate States, 1861–1865." PhD diss., Vanderbilt University, 1950.

MISCELLANEOUS

Anderson County, Tn., Multi-Jurisdictional Hazard Mitigation Plan 2011 Update. http://www.andersontn.org/Emergencymanagement/HMPIMAPFinalOakridge122711.pdf.

Civil War Trust. "Civil War Casualties," http://www.civilwar.org/education/civil-war-casualties.html.

Civil War Trust. "Secession Acts of the Thirteen Confederate States." http:// www.civilwar.org/education/history/primarysources/secession-acts.html.

"Florida Cattle Ranching." *Florida Memory*, Florida State Archives.

http://www.floridamemory.com/photographiccollection/photo_exhibits/ranching/.

"The Florida Railroad Story." Florida Railroad Company Inc. http://www.flarr.com/frrstory.htm.

"Hotels and Other Public Buildings: Willard's Hotel." Mr. Lincoln's White House, Lincoln Institute. http://www.mrlincolnswhitehouse.org/inside.asp?ID=184&subjectID=4.

iPl2. "US Civil War History." http://www.ipl.org/div/pf/entry/48451.

Metro Jacksonville, Old Ortega Historic District. http://www.metrojacksonville.com/article/2010-jun-old-ortega-historic-district#.U_89SU u3ahM.

Myers, General Richard. "Why We Serve." 118th Alf Landon Lecture, April 26, 2000. http://www.k-state.edu/media/newsreleases/landon-lect/myerstext400.html.

National Park Service. *Industry and Economy during the Civil War.* http://www.nps.gov/resources/story.htm?id=251.

Naval Historical Center. *Dictionary of American Naval Fighting Ships.* http://www.history.navy.mil/danfs/p3/pawnee-i.htm.

"Notes." Sprague Project. http://www.sprague-database.org/genealogy/getperson.php?personID=144956&tree=SpragueProject.

"Roscoe Conkling." Oneida County Historical Society. http://www.oneidacountyhistory.org/PublicFigures/Leaders.asp.

slaverebellion.org. "Population of Florida, 1860." *Population Database.* http://slaverebellion.org/population.php?state=Florida&year=1860&submit=view.

Taylor, Brian. "The Confederate Cotton Zombie Bonds." Global Financial Data. https://www.globalfinancialdata.com/gfdblog/?p=2274.

"US and World Population Clock." US Census Bureau. http://www.census.gov/popclock/.

usgovernmentspending.com. "Spending by Decade, 1860s." http://www.usgovernmentspending.com/year1865_0.html.

US House vote no. 81, April 22, 1828. Govtrack.us. https://www.govtrack.us/congress/votes/20-1/h81.

Wood, Larry. Interview by Drew Wagenhoffer about his book *Siege of Lexington. Civil War Books and Authors.* http://cwba.blogspot.com/2014/05/author-q-larry-wood-on-siege-of.html.

INDEX